DRINKING WITH THE VALKYRIES

WRITINGS ON WINE

DRINKING WITH THE VALKYRIES

WRITINGS ON WINE

ANDREW JEFFORD

ACADEMIE DU VIN LIBRARY

Published 2022 by Académie du Vin Library Ltd
academieduvinlibrary.com
Founders: Steven Spurrier and Simon McMurtrie

Publishers: Simon McMurtrie and Hermione Ireland
Editorial Director: Susan Keevil
Art Director: Tim Foster
Index: Hilary Bird

ISBN: 978-1-913141-32-5
Printed and bound in the EU

Articles published with kind permission and
agreement of *Decanter*, *The World of Fine Wine*
and *Noble Rot*. Text © remains with the copyright
holders.

All articles fully edited and revised by the author who
retains copyright on these revisions. The moral right
of the author has been asserted and the intellectual
property remains that of the author.

© 2022 Académie du Vin Library Ltd
All rights reserved. No parts of this publication
may be reproduced, stored in a retrieval system or
transmitted, in any form or by any means, electronic,
mechanical, photocopying, recording or otherwise,
without the prior permission of the publishers.

Contents

Foreword	11
Preface: Why Wine?	15
Chapter One: Origins	17
Homo Imbibens: The Work of Patrick McGovern	18
Chapter Two: Some Soils, Some Skies	31
The Blue Corruptor	32
Earth's Cream, Skimmed	34
Nuance from Disdain	36
Downhill All the Way	38
Time's Engine Room: 2010 Langhorne Creek, Reserve Shiraz, Noon	40
Terroir, Tasting and Tonewood	42
Happy Birthday, Breaky Bottom	45
A Sea Interlude: 2015 Picpoul de Pinet, Cuvée Anniversaire, Beauvignac	47
Angela's Lemon	49
Washed Up on the Shores of Illyria: 2015 Teran, Santa Elisabetta, Benvenuti	52
Dr Mistral	54
Liquid Rags in Your Mouth: 2013 Barbaresco, Produttori del Barbaresco	57
A Honeycomb of Light: 2010 Mas del Serral, Pepe Raventós	59
Touchdown in Wine Central	62

Chapter Three: Taste and Tasting

65

Bags, Butter and Biscuits

66

Through the Mangrove Swamp

69

Taste First, Then Look

71

Tonic Bitterness

73

Tannin and the University of
the Vat

75

Yeast: Call Me Dad

77

Journey into Forbidden Territory

79

Freshness Young and Old

83

Old, Big and Quiet

85

The School of Hard Wines

87

Behind Vinous Eyes

89

Wine Versus Food

91

Palate Fitness

93

Chapter Four: Some Beautiful Wines

97

Jewelled Absence: 2016 Petit Chablis,
Les Crioux, William Fèvre

98

Not Quite the White Queen:
1999 Corton-Charlemagne, Bonneau du Martray

100

Bathing Without Washing: 2005 Châteauneuf
du Pape Blanc, Réservé, Château Rayas

102

Very Like the Cuckoo's Call: 2005 Rioja,
Gran Riserva, La Granja Remelluri

105

Forest Whispers: 2011 Château-Chalon,
Vin Jaune, André and Mireille Tissot

107

The Antidote: 2010 Madiran, Cuvée du Couvent, Domaine Capmartin	110
Some Useless Notes	112
The Two-Pin Dinner	115
A Rosary of Reasons: 1882 Colheita Port, Ne Oublie, Graham's	117

Chapter Five: A Tea Break   121

The Cup that Consoles	122

Chapter Six: Interrogations and Impieties   135

The Illuminati of the Bottle	136
Disarming the Mafia	139
Hot and Bothered	141
Drinking with the Valkyries	143
Of Jellyfish and Guardsmen	145
Wine's Drab Roses	147
Beyond Best	149
Nature in All Her Glory	153
Auction Fever	155
The Party's Over	157
Call in the Plumbers	160
In Praise of Young Wine	162
Wine Is Also a Dream	164

Chapter Seven: Wine Shadows   169

The Crazed Giant	170

Only Endure	172
Burning Vines	174
Wine's Transactional Flaw	176
The Curse of the Vertical	180
Scored Rigid	183
Chapter Eight: Wine In A Life	189
Lucky Us	190
It's a Tough Job	192
Hill Sages	196
An Evening with the Lilac-Berried Mutant: 2008 Gewurztraminer, Herrenweg de Turckheim Vieilles Vignes, Zind-Humbrecht	198
Tears and Threats: 2003 Tokaji Aszú, 6 Puttonyos, Disznókő	201
Knowing and Loving	203
The Ethnologist in the Cellar	206
Up the Steep Hill	209
Mille Fois Morte, Mille Fois Revécue: 2008 Chateau Musar Blanc	211
All Quiet: 2016 Bouzeron, de Villaine	213
Lessons from the Laureate	216
Meanings that Nourish: 2003 Château Meyney, Saint-Estèphe, half-bottle	219
Chapter Nine: Against Wine Worldliness	223
Wine and Astonishment	224

Chapter Ten: Three Last Wines   237

The Startled Hind: 2012 Pouilly-Fumé,   238
    Haute Densité, Château de Tracy

Unsettled: 2014 Cannonau di Sardegna,   240
    Mamuthone, Giuseppe Sedilesu

Restoration: 2018 Saint-Mont, La Madeleine   243
    de Saint-Mont, Producteurs Plaimont

Glossary   247

Chronology   255

Acknowledgements   259

Index   261

10

Foreword

Jay McInerney

In 1996, when I was asked by a close friend who'd just taken over the editorial reins of a venerable Condé Nast title if I would consider writing a wine column, I was reluctant. I told her that while I was passionate about wine, I was not necessarily knowledgeable enough to undertake the task. I wasn't even entirely sure about the meaning of the phrase 'malolactic fermentation'. She urged me on by saying that my skills as a novelist would fill a yawning gap in the field; in her opinion most wine writing of the time was boring and technical, not addressed to readers such as herself who weren't wine geeks, or, for that matter, masochists. And I had to agree. As far as I could see there were the technicians who described Brix and pH levels and there was the fuzzy impressionist school – scent of hawthorn blossom – so cunningly parodied by Evelyn Waugh in *Brideshead Revisited*. And so, not without trepidation, I accepted my friend's offer. If I'd been aware of Andrew Jefford's budding career I might have demurred.

When I did discover Jefford a few years later I was impressed with his writing, his general erudition and his passion as much as I was with his wine knowledge. He had all the skills that had seemed to me to be in short supply in the field of wine criticism. As he has said himself in an interview: 'What Roland Barthes called "the pleasure of the text" doesn't often emerge in wine writing, yet that pleasure is an essential requirement if a text is to endure.' I have been enjoying his work for the last two decades. Like many other wine lovers, I was deeply impressed and edified by his landmark book, *The New France*, published in 2002, at a time when the French wine industry was undergoing a bit of an identity crisis while Spain and Italy were reinventing themselves – and many drinkers were turning their attention to the latest danceable hits from the New World. Jefford's book reminded us that France remains the motherland of fine wine, and that many of its 14 major regions besides Bordeaux and Burgundy were blossoming with a new generation of talent. And it was, like all of his work, a pleasure to read.

This book showcases Jefford's shorter essays for magazines such as *Decanter* and *The World of Fine Wine* over the last 20 years. And because they all demonstrate 'the pleasure of the text', their myriad satisfactions have endured. I can't think of any other writer who would elucidate the concept of terroir in wine with an exploration of the idea of 'tonewoods' in the production of violins. 'For at least six centuries, European luthiers have considered spruce grown in cold Alpine conditions the best, thanks to its fine growth rings and even grain. In Italy's Parco Naturale Paneveggio Pale di San Martino in Trento, you'll find *la foresta dei violini* – the violin forest – so called because its spruce tonewood is of unequalled density, hence musical quality. It is cut during a waning moon between October and November, to minimize the quantity of sap it contains. Even musical sound, thus, has a terroir dimension.' (Echoes of *biodynamie*.)

For all the honours he has received, and all the admiration of his fellow scribes and critics, Jefford remains a bit of an iconoclast in the world of wine writing. He calls into question some of the standard practices of his peers; although he praises Robert Parker's contributions to the field – a bit of iconoclasm in itself at this point – he is deeply sceptical of the 100-point scale system that Parker popularized. And he is sceptical, ultimately of the idea of hierarchy, which numerical ratings promote, railing against the search for the 'best'. Jefford calls for a horizontal rather than a vertical appreciation of wine; that is, he believes in the ideal of diversity and difference among wines – an appreciation of the way different wines express their places of origin and the winemaker's signature – more than he does in a quest for the best. 'No other alcoholic drink matches wine's multitudes,' he writes in 'The Curse of the Vertical' (page 180). 'It's a kind of sensual barometer for difference itself, reflecting the ever-changing places and climates in which vines are grown, and the variety of cultures and talents of the craftswomen and craftsmen who vinify it. If I taste wine, I taste difference.'

He's dubious about the virtues of blind tastings and about the conditions in which professional critics generally assess wine – en masse, sans food and out of context. In 'Wine Is Also a Dream' (page 164), he references a visit to Philippe Guigal in Côte Rôtie. Jefford's party barraged him with technical questions about pH and acidification, which Guigal smilingly parried. 'And then he said this: "Wine is also a dream."' Jefford seizes on this idea of the dream in a bottle of wine, the dream of the maker and of the drinker. 'Wine drunk under true blind-test conditions, or wine reduced to its existential, dream-stripped residuum, couldn't be enjoyed. We need (and have paid for) the dream, too. The dream is always part of the pleasure. It may, indeed, be most of the pleasure.'

Jefford likewise has reservations about tasting notes, about the reduction of a wine to a list of alleged flavour and scent components, although in fact he is certainly more than capable of (or guilty of) virtuoso riffs in this vein, as in this description of an 1882 Symington Colheita: 'The wine was salty, deep, profoundly aromatic, sweet and acidic, too. Despite prodigious wealth of flavour, it was seamlessly harmonious, thick yet almost silky, its spirit smoothed into the wine to the point of invisibility. Apples and cinders, burnt raisins, thyme and pomegranate, creosote and apricot skins, liquorice and treacle, chocolate and toasted almond: off it went again, ceaselessly murmuring its rosary of sensual reasons as to why staying alive might be a good idea. It was almost as if the wine had been out and about for all this time, wandering the hills and the plains and the entrepôts, gathering sackfuls of scent and flavour as it travelled.' The description of the wine, the catalogue of flavours and scents, is certainly dazzling as an example of wine writing. But the last sentence is pure Jefford. It's not wine writing. It's writing.

Andrew Jefford

Andrew Jefford was born in Gloucestershire, but grew up beneath the wide skies of Norfolk. Having discovered the pleasures of wine in his early teens, he learned more about it by making it – from carrots, apples, nettles, elderflowers ... and grape-juice concentrate. The quiet plop-plop-plop of fermenting wine in air-locked demi-johns tissued the night silence of the family home, while the finished wines (swallowed with a grimace) contributed to mealtime merriment.

After study at the Universities of Reading and East Anglia, Andrew Jefford worked first in publishing as an editor and then, from 1988, as a wine writer, taster, educator, tour guide and occasional radio presenter (on BBC Radio 4). He has written for many British newspapers, notably *The Evening Standard* and *The Financial Times*, and continues to contribute columns to *Decanter* and *The World of Fine Wine*; he also acts a co-chair for the Decanter World Wine Awards and as academic advisor to The Wine Scholar Guild.

His books include *The New France* (2002), *Andrew Jefford's Wine Course* (2008, revised and updated edition 2016) and *Whisky Island* (2019; first published as *Peat Smoke and Spirit* in 2004), a book about the Hebridean island of Islay. He has also published poems in *The Spectator* and *The Independent*.

Andrew Jefford and his family moved to Australia in 2009 and to France in 2010, where they still live. He enjoys music and walking, but no longer makes his own wine.

Preface

Why Wine?

I was once asked to give a five-hour masterclass and tasting in Spain. Marriages have been contracted and ceasefires brokered more swiftly than that, so I decided – having been offered the fullness of time – to begin with a little perspective and context. Imagine being asked on your deathbed (those attending looked alarmed) why you pursued your chosen profession. Some, for example, are born to wine, and simply choose not to opt out; I chose to opt in. Why pick wine for a half-century of labour? Is wine good enough?

There might be reasons for considering wine a poor choice of the only working life you'll ever have. It's an alcoholic drink, after all: addictive for some; damaging for all if mis-used; necessary for none. Wine brings pleasure, but you can't call it art; wine softens life's edges, but it's not first aid, nor does it constitute primary care. You don't make the world a better place, nor society more just, with wine; it cannot replace the force of arms in overcoming tyranny. Harvest dates are an excellent way to measure climate change, but wine itself – much travelled, heavy, and bottled in cumbersome, absurdly shaped containers made of melted sand – contributes more to the problem than the solution. 'Well then,' I could see the Reaper grimly concluding, as he scythed through my 50 years of efforts, 'what was the point in all this?'

My starting point for a career in wine was wonder at the world, in all its diversity. This topic is beyond full comprehension, but many working lifetimes – from the tight focus of research science to the struggles of poet or painter – constitute a kind of investigation into the world's intricacy and beauty, both inanimate and animate. For all we know, ours may be the sole living world in our galaxy: 100 billion stars, surrounded by a detritus of planets, and all of them a dead mixture of toxic gases, rock and dust, burning or freezing at vast distances one from another. To have taken part in the adventure of earthly life is astonishing, a chance of inconceivable rarity.

How do we communicate that astonishment, and use it to foster the reverence and respect which might sustain biodiversity for the future? We can't all be wildlife camera operators, climate scientists or astrophysicists. Wine, I quickly felt as I first began to explore it, was a unique way to apprehend the world's variousness. Every bottle of wine was a bottle of somewhere or other; the difference between wines was, at least in part, the difference between those places. Drinking wine was a kind of surrogate journeying: Italy's Valtellina Inferno one night, South Africa's Darling Hills the next. On your kitchen table.

Moreover, this was a difference that you didn't just read about in a magazine or watch on television. You smelled and tasted wine; you then took it into your body. Wine was a most intimate way to know the world. This sensual engagement with place and with difference was a supplementary astonishment, a doubling of wonder, and it was one to which wine's perfectly calibrated alcohol content lent emotional force. The engagement with place through wine was, thus, not only educational and inspiring, but consoling, too. If, of course, used wisely.

This, perhaps, was a message worth spreading, which was all (I shall tell the Reaper) I felt able to do. But would it not be better to make wine, and thereby bring a place into sensual being for those who may find themselves thousands of miles away? That, I think, must be uniquely exciting: a bond with place which it is possible to have in no other way, as well as the best route to understanding wine itself. But there is much chance in life. I didn't have the chance to make it but to write about it; you might have the chance to sell it, to see it safely across the oceans, or simply to drink it and appreciate it after your own day's work is done. What matters, in the end, is that we value wine as one of the most beautiful of human artifacts, and one whose being reflects, with shocking fidelity, the unconformities and irregularities of our earthly home.

Andrew Jefford
March 2022

CHAPTER ONE

ORIGINS

Homo Imbibens:

The Work of Patrick McGovern

A glass of wine poured at the end of the day, quietly surrendering its scents and stories: we know no moment quite like this. Daylight is going or gone, and with it the obligation to work, to act and to analyse; that glass guides us towards ease, imagination and emotion, all of them proper to darkness, and a fitting prelude to sleep. The wine nuances our lived experience, bringing both perspective and chiaroscuro. At times, indeed, it can seem to furnish a kind of spiritual nourishment. Our involvement with it triggers a cascade of sensual delight, and sometimes more than that, too. Chosen with care, stored for some years, a bottle may come both laden with memories and pregnant with expectation; those expectations will then be dashed, matched or exceeded by its performance in nose and mouth. This sensual delight, in other words, is richly invested. No moment like it, but no substance like it, either.

Our enjoyment of that glass of wine, though, is also the individual successor to countless acts of drinking. We no longer fashion arrowheads, using them to kill our dinner; we no longer dry the skin and fur our dinner was ripped from, and use it to stitch clothes and craft shoes. Our ancestors, by contrast, never spent the day online, sat in traffic jams, or felt existentially superfluous. The consumption of an alcoholic beverage by candlelight or firelight is one of the few intimate daily acts we share with those who have gone before us; it may be the most culturally rich of these. But how far before? Shakespeare's Falstaff, alone in the forest, hymning sack; the Chinese T'ang poet Li Bai, watching snowflakes melt into his wine; Homer's Odysseus and his sailors, fortifying themselves with the 'plentiful supply of meat, and sparkling ruddy wine' provided by Circe before braving Scylla and Charybdis: literature provides us with a few delicious fragments... but then we lose the trace.

Traces have furnished a life's work for Patrick McGovern, scientific director of the Biomolecular Archaeology Laboratory for Cuisine, Fermented Beverages, and Health at the University of Pennsylvania Museum; his project is to piece together the 'before'. 'What do you do?' I asked him (in October 2017). 'I am a combination chemist and archaeologist,' he replied. 'The general idea is to recover the ancient organics that were contained within certain vessels, and find out what they were.' But as his books (notably *Uncorking The Past: The quest for wine, beer, and other alcoholic beverages* (2009) hereafter *UP*, and *Ancient Wine: The Search for the Origins of Viniculture* (2019)) make clear, in synthesizing both his own work and that of others, he suggests something more startling: that man is *Homo imbibens*, driven by biological, social and religious imperatives to consume alcohol, and that this relationship with alcohol is a key to 'understanding the development of our species and its cultures'.

From murex to mead

A talented pianist who considered a career in music, McGovern opted to study undergraduate chemistry at Cornell, taking a minor in English literature, and soon after became fascinated by ancient history: you can see the rangy mind. He switched to Near Eastern archaeology and history for his doctoral research, and began work studying pottery and glass fragments before specializing in the 'royal purple' of the Canaanites and the Phoenicians (extracted from the Mediterranean murex mollusc, and once the most expensive dye in the world). This in turn led him to specialize more generally in ancient organic materials, and in particular the residues left inside the pottery fragments of jars and other vessel forms.

It seems hard to believe today, but standard archaeological practice in the past was to clean away these residues with acid to remove carbonates, the better to see and understand the pottery itself. 'We were always curious as to what was inside these vessels,' he points out. 'If you could identify the organic components, you could actually say something about the contents. Then you could say more about what it meant to humans – who are organic creatures.' The great breakthrough came with liquid and gas chromatography, and in particular mass spectrometry. By looking for specific chemical markers of natural products (biomarkers, or fingerprint compounds), you could then say what the jar or other vessel was likely to have contained.

Alcohol is entirely unrecoverable: it simply evaporates. But McGovern and his collegues developed a series of tests for the other constituents of different alcoholic beverages. For Middle Eastern and European wines, for example, they test for tartaric acid, found in large quantity only in the Eurasian grape, together with other organic acids (lactic, citric and succinic acid) common to this grape; background amounts produced by microorganisms are also checked. Grape pips and other remains, if they are preserved and recovered, help confirm the analysis. For mead, the analysts search for beeswax compounds, which are difficult to filter out, especially using ancient techniques. Beer is a more complex challenge, since few biomarkers exist for the different cereals (principally barley, wheat, rice, millet, sorghum and maize). The fermentation of beer from barley, though, produces calcium oxalate – traditionally known as 'beerstone' – so that is what the team searches for in residues. Other archaeological criteria must be applied for substantiation, because this compound is widespread in nature (it is, for example, the most common constituent of human kidney stones).

Setting the clock

Humans are one of four extant hominid genera (*Pongo, Gorilla, Pan* and *Homo*). The most recent common ancestor of all four lived around 14 million years ago, so we might choose to set our ancestral clock at that point. Alcohol (ethanol) itself is much older: 'sugar fermentation (or glycolysis) is thought to be the earliest form of energy production used by life on Earth,' writes McGovern (*UP*, p2), suggesting a date of about four billion years ago for microbial transformation of sugar to ethanol and carbon dioxide on planet earth. Clouds of ethanol and other alcohols billions of kilometres across, by the way, exist in star-forming regions elsewhere at the centre of our galaxy, the Milky Way, and throughout the much larger universe.

Homo erectus appeared about two million years ago in Africa, from where the species migrated to Eurasia; it became extinct about 70,000 years ago. By then, however, *Homo sapiens sapiens* had evolved (around 200,000 years ago), again in Africa, from which this new species migrated 100,000–60,000 years ago. It is now the only surviving member of the genus *Homo*, other archaic humans (such as *Homo neanderthalensis*) having become extinct around 40,000 years ago. Most of us carry the genetic signatures of interbreeding between these species.

Humans began making pottery in China some 18,000 years ago. The oldest attested alcoholic beverage so far identified by McGovern's laboratory, working with colleagues from China, Germany and the USA, is that of Jiahu in Central China's Henan Province: it's 9,000 years old. Authenticated human consumption of alcohol thus begins at this point, though the relative sophistication of the site strongly suggests that it was itself an heir to earlier traditions. Teams are working on residues found in natural or artificial landscape features that might pre-date the creation of pottery, especially in Anatolia, but no earlier dates have yet been established, so we can only speculate on the use of alcohol by hominids prior to that point.

And not merely hominids. Fruits naturally ferment, producing 'wild' alcohol, and fruit-eating animals (notably primates) gorge on this fermented fruit, becoming inebriated as a consequence. Primate lineage goes back some 65 million years, and the genetic equipment to deal effectively with the toxic by-products of ethanol digestion (notably acetaldehyde) dates from around 10 million years ago; this is the ALDH gene. 'We're really set up,' summarizes McGovern, 'to to drink an alcoholic beverage. And we have the right apparatus to pick up all the sensory aromatics.' When, I asked McGovern, might intentionality in this process have begun? 'I see it as being way back into the higher primate era,' he replied, contending that our intimacy with alcohol is not only as old as we as a species are, but was a trait acquired, with varying degrees of organization, by our primate ancestors.

Flute music at dusk

Let's return to China. Jiahu was a substantial (5.5-hectare) Neolithic settlement surrounded by a moat and settled by between 250 and 800 people between 9,000 and 7,700 years ago, when it was destroyed in a flood. So far,

45 residences have been excavated and nine pottery kilns found; analysis of the skeletal remains reveals that Jiahu inhabitants experienced improving health and longevity over the life of the settlement. They farmed millet and rice; they raised pigs, dogs, poultry and cattle; they gathered and foraged wild pears, apricots, chestnuts, broad beans and soya beans; they fished for carp, and hunted wild boar, deer and rabbits. And, come day's end, they drank alcohol.

Made from what, and in what form? One of the insights of McGovern's work is that the pure forms of alcoholic beverages with which we are familiar today were rare in the distant past. Analyses of the Jiahu residues revealed mixtures that included tartaric acid (derived from a native wild grape and/or hawthorn tree in China; the only seeds recovered at this site were of these fruits), fingerprint compounds of beeswax, and ferulate phytosterol esters pointing to rice. They drank, in other words, a mixed beverage made from wine produced from either native wild grapes or hawthorne fruit (probably both) mingled with mead and rice beer. The beverage was likely to have been drunk from a communal vessel of some sort using straws to avoid floating debris, or so later traditions suggest. This drink, at least for the time being, is the first ancestor of Romanée-Conti and Montrachet, of Haut-Brion and Pétrus.

That's not all, though. Jiahu has its own symbols – possibly pictograms, since their similarity to later Chinese characters is striking; in that case they are a form of proto-writing. Nine were found on tortoise shells (used, in later Chinese culture, for divination) and two on bone. Even more movingly, Jiahu is celebrated for its 33 flutes (20 of them intact), all of them made from the wing-bones of the red-crowned crane, a presently endangered species celebrated for its beautiful mating dance, and a Taoist symbol of longevity and immortality. Facsmiles of these flutes are playable by musicians today. Wine, music, poetry and dance: we cannot see the scene clearly through the mist of 80 or 90 centuries, but perhaps they came together, as they have so often since, in the firelight of Jiahu.

22   ORIGINS

Six jars in the kitchen

Jiahu is just one of a number of Chinese Neolithic sites currently being excavated; McGovern has even examined and analysed a liquid sample from Yinxu ('the ruins of Yin') or Anyang, a Shang-dynasty capital city also in Henan Province, dating back 3,000 years. The liquid had evaporated to around a quarter of its original volume, and the bronze vessel was eventually totally sealed by corrosion. 'It had the characteristic fragrance of fine rice or millet wine made the traditional way,' recalled McGovern, 'slightly oxidized like sherry, with a perfumed bouquet' (*UP*, p47). A second Shang-dynasty site in Henan (Changzikou) surrendered no fewer than 52 liquid samples inside bronze vessels; the analysis of one of these revealed a rice beverage with added China fir sap, chrysanthemum and/or a member of the Artemisia (wormwood) family. Given China's 10,000-year pottery headstart on the Middle East, we might expect further discoveries and insights into Neolithic drinking habits from the Middle Kingdom in the years ahead.

Another key area of interest for McGovern is whether excavation in China will reveal more about the domestication of the wild vine there. 'China has more wild species than anywhere else in the world, and some of those species have a very high sugar content, up to 20%, but so far as we know these wild vines were never domesticated. Maybe archaeological investigation will show that the Chinese did domesticate at a much earlier date than previously determined. They are technologically advanced in so many areas.' Prior to the Chinese discoveries, though, it was excavations in the Near East, Anatolia, the Caucusus and the Fertile Crescent that provided much of the excitement felt by McGovern and his colleagues, expecially once sensitive and precise chemical techniques had opened up their field.

One of the oldest of these sites is Hajji Firuz Tepe, in present-day northernwestern Iran (West Azerbaijan Province), excavated by the University of Pennsylvania Museum of Archaeology and Anthropology team between 1958 and 1968; the remains date back 7,400–7,000 years. The Neolithic inhabitants of this high-sited (1,300-metre) village in the Zagros Mountains 'appear to have enjoyed a very comfortable life. Animal and plant resources were abundant. Their well-made mudbrick homes ... are nearly identical to those still seen in the area today and could have accommodated an extended family then as now' (*UP*, p74). In one 'kitchen', six jars of nine litres each had been set into the clay floor and lined up against one wall. The team initially concluded they were used for some sort of dairy product, but analysis eventually revealed not only that they contained wine flavoured with a tree resin, but that they had probably also had clay stoppers to conserve their liquid contents. McGovern and his colleagues were surprised by their discovery. 'If the six jars in the kitchen of one ordinary house are any measure, drinking in the village was not a privilege of only the rich and famous. ... If the other households at the site (which has not been excavated fully) followed the same pattern of usage, we are talking about a lot of wine, roughly 5,000 litres for 100 houses. The availability of such a large quantity of wine implies that the Eurasian grapevine had already come under cultivation at Hajji Firuz' (*UP*, p76).

The cradle

This in turn leads us to one of the most vexed questions of all in McGovern's field, and one on which he is constantly called to pronounce: which country in this region can lay claim to being to being 'the cradle of wine' or 'the birthplace of wine'? Even if it is eventually proved that China was cultivating one or some of its own wild vines at an earlier stage of the Neolithic, it seems likely that the vine that wine lovers continue to treasure today, *Vitis vinifera ssp vinifera* (the Eurasian grape), was first domesticated in this part of the world.

It is, in a way, an absurd question, since the rival states trying to wrestle the archaeological crown from each other were unknown to the first tribal Caucasian or Anatolian vine tenders, setting about their work on rampant forest climbers. But for a plant with the vine's cultural significance, the claim matters – which was why the findings released in a paper called 'Early Neolithic wine of Georgia in the South Caucasus' published by the *Proceedings of the National Academy of Sciences of the United States of America* on November 17th 2017 under an 18-author byline were greeted with such elation in Georgia.

This study focused on two small Neolithic villages in the Georgian region of Lower Kartli, Shulaveris Gora and Gadachrili Gora (these sites, by the way, lie only 500 kilometres north of Hajji Firuz). Nineteen different jar samples were analysed, of which eight tested positively for both tartaric acid and other organic acids (including malic, succinic and citric acid). These pottery samples have been dated back 8,000 to 7,800 years, making this 'the earliest biomolecular archaeological evidence for grape vine and viticulture from the Near East'. No less significantly, the Georgian finds do not contain resin or other flavourings, nor are they a mixed beverage, both of which are highly unusual for the ancient residues that McGovern has spent much of his career analysing. This, believes McGovern, might be a kind of evidence for domestication in this zone. 'The fact that there isn't any tree resin in it and that it is from grape alone is very interesting. It suggests that they really appreciated the pure grape, and that they could preserve their wines, which suggests a higher alcohol level and therefore higher sugar levels. Initially the wild vine would have been more acidic than it is today, when it was a climber growing up trees and producing berries to attract birds. It wasn't necessarily something that humans would have gravitated to.' Once, though, cultivation rendered the berries sweeter and juicier, 'then you have a perfect resource for making a wine quite easily. It has the yeast nutrient you need on the skins, the fermentation starts naturally, and it produces 1,000 aromatic compounds by itself: it's the perfect medium for fermentation.' It's also perhaps worth noting that, even today, vines are trained up trees by a practice known as *maglari* in the Western Georgian regions of Ajara, Guria and Samegrelo: the transitional stage between wild-vine domestication and today's lower-level cultivation systems.

Toasting Midas

Other residues analysed by McGovern and colleagues from the Caucasus, Anatolia and the Near East include those from the significant sites of Godin Tepe (in the central Zagros Mountains of western Iran, south of Hajji Firuz Tepe) and Gordion (on the central Anatolian plateau close to present-day Ankara), though these are more recent than the Georgian Neolithic villages and Hajji Firuz Tepe itself.

Godin Tepe was a military or trading base dating back 5,500 to 5,100 years (the Late Uruk period), and the site contains different types of residues: one reddish, which analysis showed to be grape wine, and another yellowish, suggesting barley beer. 'This period was the beginning of urbanism and the rise of the cities, of the first "civilization", you could say; it was characterized by a lot of specialized activities, in lower Mesopotamia, down in the Tigris-Euphrates Valley. That was where they could produce a lot of grain, which was very important for beer, but if they wanted wine, that would have to take place up in the hill country, where the grapevine thrives, up in the Zagros Mountains.' One feature of Godin Tepe was the way that the wine jars had been laid on their sides so as to keep their clay stoppers moist inside narrow mouths and so prevent the contents from acetification, suggesting a process of maturation that might have lasted several years; the jars containing beer, by contrast, were wide-mouthed, suggesting more rapid consumption using straws: a scene often duplicated in pictorial form on Mesopotamian cylinder seals.

Gordion or Gordium (modern Yassıhüyük) was the capital of the Phrygians, a Western Anatolian people who formed a dominant kingdom in Asia Minor some 3,200 to 2,700 years ago; according to the *Iliad*, the Phrygians fought alongside the Trojans against the Achaeans. The excavation of the Gordion tumulus, or 'Midas mound', was carried out by the Penn Museum in 1957, and that of the adjacent city mound has continued for over 50 years. The tomb itself was opened and the riches within revealed in a moment of excitement reminiscent of Howard Carter's 1922 opening of Tutankhamun's burial chamber. The 'left-over' residues of a funerary feast for the king – whether Midas himself or his father, Gordias – suggested a wake. 'When excavators broke through the wall of the tomb in 1957, they came face to face with ... the body of a 60- to 65-year-old male, laid out on a thick pile of blue and purple textiles, the colours of regal splendour. In the background gleamed the largest Iron Age drinking set ever found: 157 bronze vessels, including vats, jugs and drinking bowls, which were used in a dinner bidding farewell to the tomb's occupant,' (*UP*, p131). When McGovern and his team analysed the yellowish residues found inside the *situlae* and the bowls that the tomb contained, they found that, as at

26   ORIGINS

Jiahu, it was a mixed beverage, in this instance containing Eurasian grape wine, barley (rather than rice) beer and honey mead.

A final fascinating analysis of pottery vessel residues undertaken by McGovern and his colleagues is that of the tomb of the early Egyptian king Scorpion I, who died around 5,000 years ago, half a millennium before the building of the first Egyptian pyramid. Three rooms in Scorpion's tomb at Abydos, downstream from Luxor, were stacked with wine jars – some 700 altogether, around 4,500 litres of wine, underlining the high status of what was certainly an imported beverage at the time. Vines did not naturally grow in the Nile Valley, and were not transplanted to the Nile Delta until several centuries after Scorpion's death; the style of the jars, confirmed by chemical analysis of their clays, indicated that the vast quantity of wine that they contained had been imported from the area of the present-day Gaza, the Jordan Valley and the adjacent hill country to the east (Transjordan) and west (the West Bank). A small number of the jars, indeed, seem to have originated in Petra.

Analysis of the residues inside Scorpion's jars showed that all were, as so often in the ancient world, resinated; anyone who'd like to replicate the wine-drinking experience of our earliest ancestors should always begin with a bottle of Greek retsina. Some jars, moreover, contained whole preserved raisins and carefully sliced figs – perhaps to enhance the wines' flavour, or perhaps as a fermentation aid. But a wide range of other flavourings were also chemically identified by McGovern and his colleagues, including savory, balm, senna, coriander, germander, mint, sage and thyme: a pharaonic vermouth.

The 'original universal medicine'

In addition to his work with residues, McGovern also provides (notably in *Uncorking the Past*) a comprehensive overview of the astonishingly creative ways in which humans in different global locations and cultures have been able to produce alcoholic beverages. This account of raw materials, ways and means, via the archaeological record, goes some way to substantiate his theory that *Homo sapiens sapiens* might also be considered *Homo imbibens*. His overall suggestion is that alcoholic beverages became, from the earliest years of human cultural development, emotionally, religiously and intellectually necessary to human mental health in the same way that food staples were necessary to physical health; moreover, alcoholic beverages occupied, until relatively recently, a privileged place both as a medicine and as a means for preserving and ingesting medical plants, herbs and roots.

'Which came first, bread or beer?' he asks. 'You need food to exist. But if you want to have a good time, if you want to have something safer than water to drink, if you want to have something safe to take medicine in and so live longer, if you want social lubrication, if you want to up your sexual relations and so produce more children, then alcoholic beverages help. Then you get into the mind-altering effect, more or less having a mystery of sorts in that there seems to be some supernatural force at work both in fermentation and in your brain. You can relate that to some meaning in the universe, and that's why alcoholic beverages are usually incorporated right at the centre of all religions.'

The challenge for those producing alcoholic beverages was sourcing suitable levels of fermentable sugars; the fact that *Vitis vinifera* does this so admirably, McGovern believes, may be the key to the wine grape's pre-eminence. 'The Eurasian grape, once a juice has been expressed, is the perfect nutritional medium for native yeast to become active and produce a high-alcoholic beverage, a constant goal of humankind. Moreover, the Eurasian grape has been cloned and transplanted by humans to produce an enormous number of varieties (estimates vary from 8,000 to 10,000) with a seemingly infinite range of flavours and aromas, unlike any other plant. Its higher alcohol compared to beer assures its better preservation, and wine can be aged, thus adding to its mysterious allure and flavour and aroma profile.'

The cereal grains used for beer production, by contrast, do not – as harvested – contain fermentable sugars. They contain starch that requires conversion to sugar. The classic means of doing this is by sprouting and malting, which releases the diastase enzyme, which converts starch to maltose and then to glucose. This, though, is a process of some sophistication, and may not have been the earliest technique used to render cereal grains fermentable. McGovern considers it most likely that the rice component of the Jiahu mixed beverage, for example, was prepared by mastication. When the rice grains are chewed, an enzyme called ptyalin (or salivary amylase) breaks starch down into maltose and dextrin. Further processing yields glucose, a simple sugar, ripe for yeast fermentation. 'In remote areas of Japan and Taiwan,' he writes, 'you can still find women sitting around a large bowl, masticating and spitting rice juice into the vessel as they prepare the rice wine for a marriage ceremony. In fact, this method of making an alcoholic beverage from a grain spans the globe, from the corn beers or *chichas* of the Americas to the sorghum and millet beers of Africa' (*UP*, pp38–39).

Another obvious source of fermentable sugar, particularly in high-latitude climates that did not produce sugar-rich fruits, was honey – but honey in its raw state is too sweet to be readily fermentable; it needs dilution with between five and six parts of water to two to three parts honey to produce an ideal medium for fermentation, yielding a mead of between 8 and 13% alcohol by volume (abv). Given the fact that modern humans originated in sub-Saharan Africa, spreading from the Great Rift Valley northwards from around 100,000 years ago, it is noteworthy that even today Ethiopia's national beverage, *tej*, is a mead (flavoured with *Rhamnus prinoides*, shiny-leaf buckthorn or *gesho*). 'Many African peoples,' McGovern points out, 'have been drinking some variation of a fermented honey beverage for a very long time throughout the continent,' (*UP*, p234).

He also notes that chimpanzees (our closest ancestor, and a primate with whom we share 96 percent of our genome) are ingenious honey-hunters and beehive-raiders, improvising natural tools of all kinds to pry open the hive (such as a chisel-like branch) and swish out (with a willow-like branch) the honey within; 10,000-year-old rock paintings in the Matopo hills of Zimbabwe show human hunters smoking out beehives. 'Perhaps, in Palaeolithic times, the hunters brought back not only honey but also on occasion an animal skin or gourd full of mead. Rainwater might have filled the nest of a fallen tree and fermented the honey ... Eventually, an enterprising human might have thought of making mead in a more controlled fashion in a leather bag, gourd or bark container' (*UP*, p237). Bags, gourds and bark containers rot away in time, though, so no residues remain; thus the notion that our earliest forebears brought a mead-fermenting and mead-drinking culture with them when they came out of Africa must, like so much else, remain conjectural.

McGovern's account of the many plants used for the preparation of alcoholic beverages in *Uncorking the Past* is comprehensive. He is in particular awe of the Mesoamerican domestication of maize from teosinte, thereby turning 'a minuscule mountain grass into the world's most prolific source of alcohol' (*UP*, p226). Other major sources of alcohol for different societies in the past have included cacao/chocolate, *Schinus molle* (the Peruvian pepper tree), manioc, cassava, sorghum, millet, date palm and countless other local fruits and berries.

Might, though, the *Homo imbibens* hypothesis be pushing evidence too far? Is McGovern according too prominent a role to alcohol consumption, which is never nutritionally necessary, and to the creation of alcoholic beverages in ancient societies? 'Amazingly, that pushback hasn't come up too much. Of course it's true that other technologies have had a great influence, but I think in general that the importance of alcoholic beverages has been if anything rather overlooked. Ten percent of the enzymes in the human liver are devoted to processing alcohol, after all. We have enzymes in our mouths to convert starch to sugar. As I said earlier, we're set up to consume an alcoholic beverage. It's an important part of human biology, social relations, religions, economy. It has very far-flung dimensions to it which aren't as widely appreciated as they could be.'

Are the efforts that are poured into encouraging and enforcing absention, whether by doctors or clerics, doomed in the long run? 'I think so. Ultimately, humans will always come back to it. They have an urge to drink alcohol. Though I would also say that moderate consumption is what we are adapted to, and that also probably goes back to the Palaeolithic period. Alcohol is so readily available now that people overdo it. But that doesn't mean you have to ignore its positive effects. Before you had synthetic medicine, what was the medicine that was used to prevent disease? In China, India, Greece, Rome, Egypt ... it was an alcoholic medium which dissolves herbs, but the alcohol itself has a multiple number of health benefits. We know it is anti-cholesterol, anti-cancer, an analgesic that numbs pain; it would have been the original universal medicine. That's the way I see it.'

CHAPTER TWO

SOME SOILS, SOME SKIES

The Blue Corruptor

We've probably all imagined the scene. That unexpected letter, one Thursday, from a provincial solicitor. The curious, dry phrasing, outlining the 'bequest' from the 'deceased', whose name means nothing to you. You read the letter several times. The sum looks improbably large: it must be a hoax. Nonetheless you phone; the details are politely and impassively confirmed, and arrangements put in hand for a bank transfer. It takes a week to sink in, and another week to hand in your notice. And then you begin to look for a vineyard.

It hasn't happened to me yet, and I don't suppose it ever will. But this may be your future. Where would you choose to buy?

Bandol, I have often thought, has a lot going for it. Wherever you are in this Provençal appellation, you're never more than 15 kilometres from the Mediterranean; you can see the glitter of the waves in many vineyards as you prune. You're within an easy drive of the sunniest city in France, Marseille; nearer still to a tidier naval town with fewer gangland killings, Toulon. Tourists flock to the pretty little seaside port that gives this appellation its name, and there's an *oenothèque* there near the seafront to help sell your wine. Every serious restaurant wine list between Arles and Menton, of course, needs to feature a range of Bandol, while no French three-star restaurant can ignore you, either. The walled terraces of this stony amphitheatre may constitute the greatest site in the world for the Mourvèdre grape variety. Why bother being an also-ran in Bordeaux, a nobody in Languedoc or a beggarly outsider in the Hautes Côtes de Beaune? Buy in Bandol.

'The problem of Bandol,' Freddy Estienne of Domaine de la Laidière told me, 'is that it's too near to the sea.' What? I thought that was its gift. It was only when I spent a couple of days tasting and touring in the AOC that I came to realize that sometimes, in the wine world as in life more generally, what seems at first like a blessing can in fact be a curse.

The Mourvèdre grape variety makes difficult, rewarding red wines. It's not the only one grown in this 1,500-hectare appellation: the rules stipulate that the wines must be between 50 percent and 95 percent Mourvèdre, with the balance coming from Grenache, Cinsault, Carignan and Syrah. 'Pure Mourvèdre is beautiful,' says Reynald Delille of Domaine de Terrebrune, 'but it's always better with a little bit of something else' – and most growers seem to agree. Perhaps they're right, but the greatest Bandols nonetheless strike me as being the richest in Mourvèdre, and Mourvèdre here acquires a completeness, a harmony and an equilibrium that seems to elude it elsewhere. These dense, allusive, textured reds turn magnificently savoury as the years pass. Bandol is one of the great red wines of France.

It's disconcerting, therefore, to discover that only just over 30 percent of the wine produced in this relatively small AOC is in fact red. There's a little white, but most Bandol is rosé – because that's what the holidaymakers want. And then… there are all those little houses, where elderly Parisians potter through retirement with a poodle or two. When I mentioned this, a communal wail went up. 'It's the biggest worry we have,' said Patricia Ferrero, who directs the local growers' grouping. 'We are eight little communes, and whenever anyone wants to build anything, it is always in the vines.' The appellation is an amphitheatre, and villages like Le Castellet and La Cadière d'Azur have an almost Tuscan beauty; the whole place could easily become a gigantic rest home. I began to look at the beautiful Mediterranean rather differently – as the blue corruptor, determined to usurp the land for its own ends.

Things haven't quite gone critical yet; perhaps the quality of the best Bandol will one day be more widely recognized than at present. Nonetheless the fact remains that what may well be the greatest site in the world for an important red grape variety, one capable of producing great, cellar-seeking red wines, turns most of it into rosé. The customer isn't always right.

Earth's Cream, Skimmed

As anyone taking California's Highway 29 north as it leads into Napa will know, the wine thereabouts is, ahem, 'bottled poetry'. The famous sign ('WELCOME to this world famous wine growing region') is garnished with a bunch of purple grapes and what looks like the end of a large oval tun on which Robert Louis Stevenson's now-celebrated words are inscribed. So far, so corny.

Trace the words back to their original source, by contrast, and you will learn much. Stevenson loved wine. Indeed his last living act was to bring a bottle of 'old burgundy' up from his Samoan cellar in December 1894 (this was a man who, in seeking to express the depth of his devotion to sailing ships, wrote that he loved them 'as a man loves burgundy or daybreak'). A few minutes later, the old burgundy untouched, he was dead, aged 44. The 'bottled poetry' quotation comes from *The Silverado Squatters*, a series of Californian sketches based on the 1880 honeymoon spell that RLS and his American wife, Fanny, spent in an abandoned mining camp on Mount Saint Helena. 'I am interested in all wines,' he confessed at the beginning of the sketch called 'Napa wine', 'and have been all my life, from the raisin wine that a school-fellow kept secreted in his play-box up to my last discovery, those notable Valtellines, that once shone upon the board of Caesar.' (He was living in Switzerland by the time he made the final drafts, so the Nebbioli of Valtellina would have been local.)

Note, though, the date of his Napa sojourn. Stevenson wrote about the nascent wines of California, including those of 'Mr Schram' and 'Mr M'Eckron' (sic), with more than usual feeling. Why? 'Some of us, kind old Pagans, watch with dread the shadows falling on the age: how the unconquerable worm invades the sunny terraces of France, and Bordeaux is no more, and the Rhône a mere Arabia Petraea. Château Neuf is dead, and I have never tasted it; Hermitage – a hermitage indeed from all life's sorrows

– lies expiring by the river.' It's hard to imagine now, but when Stevenson wrote, the phylloxera-induced eclipse of Europe's classics was near-total. 'And at the same time,' he continued, 'we look timidly forward, with a spark of hope, to where the new lands, already weary of producing gold, begin to green with vineyards. A nice point in human history falls to be decided by Californian and Australian wines.' Napa and Geelong, in sum, were set to take over from collapsing France.

The paragraph that follows makes it clear that Stevenson understood the principles of terroir; indeed his 'bottled poetry' had nothing to do with Napa but was, rather, the ideal of a great terroir wine. 'The beginning of vine-planting is like the beginning of mining for the precious metals: the wine-grower also "prospects". One corner of land is tried with one kind of grape after another. This is a failure; that is better; a third best. So, bit by bit, they grope about for their Clos Vougeot and Lafite. Those lodes are pockets of earth, more precious than the precious ores, that yield inimitable fragrance and soft fire; those virtuous Bonanzas, where the soil has sublimated under sun and stars to something finer, and the wine is bottled poetry: these still lie undiscovered; chaparral conceals, thicket embowers them; the miner chips the rock and wanders further, and the grizzly muses undisturbed. But there they bide their hour, awaiting their Columbus; and nature nurses and prepares them.' If anyone has ever written a more lyrical yet more succinct account of the great adventure of wine creation outside Europe, I have yet to read it.

Not only that, but he understood, too, the nuances of site selection. Napa's interest lay in the fact that the vineyard 'did not here begin, as it does too often, in the low valley lands along the river, but took at once to the rough foothills, where alone it can be expected to prosper. A basking inclination, and stones, to be a reservoir of the day's heat, seem necessary to the soil for wine; the grossness of the earth must be evaporated, its marrow daily melted and refined for ages; until at length these clods that break below our footing, and to the eye appear but common earth, are truly and to the perceiving mind, a masterpiece of nature.'

Napa, of course, wasn't quite there yet. 'Meanwhile the wine is merely a good wine' was the Stevensonian assessment. Its style, moreover, was evidently lighter back then than today: 'The best that I have tasted better than a Beaujolais, and not unlike.' Stevenson was again ahead of his time in castigating the fact that it was sold under borrowed European names. The resolution is not yet complete.

He also perfectly summarized the joy of drinking terroir wines far from their place of origin. Most of Mr Schram's wine was London-bound. 'Here, also, earth's cream was being skimmed and garnered; and the London customers can taste, such as it is, the tang of the earth in this green valley.' We still can. Indeed, since 'the worm' has been conquered, we're luckier still; we can taste the 'blood and sun' of an entire world via a few clicks of the mouse. RLS would have loved it.

Nuance from Disdain

A pleasure postponed can be a pleasure intensified. I finally reached Japan in April 2019, after dreaming of the place for decades. The cherry trees were in flower. Their clouds of white, exploding like magician's handkerchiefs, lit spotless Tokyo by day and night alike. A notice in the island park near where I stayed (Hama-rikyu Gardens) implored visitors who had come to see the blossoms 'NOT to party or make noise in the garden. Let's be considerate to others.' I held my breath in wonder. In Yamanashi Prefecture, the wild cherries punctuated the leafless woods on the mountain edges: pink clouds in sombre dusk sky.

Understanding the intricacy of Japanese culture is not for those in a hurry, and a mere two days spent researching Koshu in Yamanashi underscored the problem. Nothing is simple here; everything is deeply embedded in time and practice. Why does Koshu taste as it does? Even answering that question proved rewardingly difficult.

First, though, let me tell you what it is, since I'm aware that Koshu remains a rare bird, even on the world's most eclectic wine-shop shelves. This white wine is made from the most widely grown winemaking grape variety in Japan's leading wine-producing region, Yamanashi. It's clean, fresh and understated, with relatively low alcohol – an Asian cousin, perhaps, to Muscadet, Vinho Verde, Albariño and Txakoli. You might assume that this character derives from Japanese intent, and relates to Japanese cuisine. Indeed – but that's far from the whole story.

Japan's fruit-growing culture is one of extraordinary sophistication, not only in terms of the number of its unique specialities, but also by origin (like cheese in France), and eventual retail price. A bunch of 30 grapes selling for just under £250 sounds like a joke. In Japan, when the first immaculately packaged seasonal fruits arrive, it isn't. Koshu was originally a table-grape variety, and it is now generally a secondary crop in Yamanashi. The principal money-earners for most farmers (who rarely own more than a single hectare of land) are cosseted, hand-gardened table grapes like Shine Muscat, growing under individually fashioned paper umbrellas. Yes, Japanese sommeliers are some of the best trained in the world; yes, Tokyo's Michelin stars outnumber and outwink those of Paris. For all that, wine only accounts for four percent of Japan's alcohol consumption – and most wine sold in Japan is imported (including bulk wine, and wine fermented locally from imported concentrates).

Summer is often awful: rain, humidity, heat, typhoons. Yamanashi's Köppen climate classification is 'monsoon-influenced humid subtropical', and a major reason for growing Koshu at all is that its thick skins resist Japan's implacable skies. Astonishingly enough for a hot climate whose August daily mean temperature is 26.6°C (compare Bordeaux: just 21.4°C), Koshu's natural alcohol levels – when picked in early October – are often no more than 14 or 15 Brix (meaning a potential alcohol of 7.6 to 8.2%). Colossal yields (100 hectolitres per hectare (hl/ha) is not unusual) on these pergola-grown vines have much to do with this; so too does altitude. Yamanashi is 80 percent mountain; many vineyards lie at 500 metres or more. Chaptalization is routine for most; concentration and acidification are also sometimes necessary.

Taking all this into account, I came to see Koshu, in all its nuance, its graceful slenderness and its restraint of allusion, as a triumph of the Japanese spirit of optimization, of ceaseless effort, of unwearying attention to detail. Wines made from grapes like these should be poor, thin little runts. In Europe, they would be. The Japanese salvage beauty from nature's disdain.

At times, Koshu suggests the apple and pear orchard, sap rising in spring, or a salty tang on a sea breeze; its vivacity is always tender, never raw. A little lees contact fills its dimples with cream. It does indeed partner sushi and tempura exquisitely, or fish and shellfish more generally, but I'm not sure it isn't at its best when sipped on its own. By a tree, under moonlight, after a long-deferred journey. Or something very like.

Downhill All the Way

Limestone and marl (limey clay) tend to be regarded with warm affection by wine lovers; as soil types, they bring us some of the world's finest wines, from Montrachet to Barolo. On a wet winter's night almost 770 years ago in France's Savoie, though, the combination proved a deadly one, bringing about what is thought the biggest landslide in recorded European history.

Here's the geologists' reconstruction. Mont Granier, a 1,933-metre peak at the northern end of the Massif de Chartreuse, is a limestone summit surrounded by extensive marl deposits. Thanks to its limestone, the mountain is riddled with water-eaten caverns, channels and faults: there are 341 sink-holes and caves in it today, and 66 kilometres of galleries.

November 1248 had been a month of intense rain. During the night of the 24th to the 25th of November, vast slabs, blocks and sections of limestone high up on the mountain gave way, thundering down onto the sodden marls below. In rockslides, water (which has no strength) gets trapped between rock particles, rendering the entire mass of material ultra-weak (this liquefaction is also common during earthquakes). A tsunami of rock and clay then surged for seven kilometres out into the valley, burying five villages without trace, including their 1,000 or more inhabitants and 'innumerable livestock'. The collapse left a cliff face almost 900 metres high, and entirely remodelled the valley lands beneath. For decades, little grew there.

The mountain was already known, back then, as Apremont, 'bitter mountain'; no doubt there had been previous incidents of this sort. Indeed it is still quietly haemorrhaging today: there were three small landslides in January, April and May 2016, and its fissures are constantly surveyed. After the 1248 tragedy, the 'bitter mountain' was rebaptized with the name of one of its lost villages, Granier, but the original lives on as one of the two white-wine appellations sited on the debris. Abymes, no less descriptive, is the other.

I looked about these vineyards in January 2018. Even 770 years later, the landscape is chaotically rumpled; giant blocks of limestone sprawl here and there, and the vineyards are stitched onto the marl like a quilt made of left-over scraps of cloth, broken by woods in the tougher spots, and by ponds and marshes in the dips. What would that night have been like? A deafening roar, a sudden awakening in terror for the victims, perhaps some attempt at flight, then likely nothing more.

Mountain wine regions are complex for a reason: their topographical challenges have meant, through most of history, that they were a series of little kingdoms and fiefdoms, clinging on to traditions that reflect, with some fidelity, precise and highly contrastive local conditions. Savoie is no exception; its wines Abymes and Apremont, made from the Jacquère variety, constitute just one of its many specialities.

Few take Jacquère very seriously, at least from a critical perspective. This early-budding, generously yielding variety, one of the many Gouais progeny, occupies half of the 2,077 hectares of the region, so is by far the most widely planted of Savoie's 23 grape varieties. There has, though, been a history of commercial insouciance with it, making white wines of '*petit degré*' (11% or even less) which are bundled off up to the ski stations to be tossed back with mouthfuls of gluey cheese. Wine fans may rhapsodize about Altesse, Bergeron (Roussanne) or the rare Persan, but they tend to skim over Jacquère.

Why so? Its moving history aside, a great Abymes or Apremont can represent the essence of the mountain wine ideal more memorably than any other in Savoie, and perhaps in Europe more generally. It is indeed always light in alcohol. Even when produced from older vines and October-harvested, it rarely exceeds 11.5%; its natural state, if you like, is aerial. Its flavours are sculpted by fresh, sappy acidity, but at the same time it is not burdened by excessive or overt fruit flavours. It whispers stone rather than singing fruit. Lees contact can add a little discreet creaminess of texture – though a spritz, contrariwise, can give it even more lift and pungency. You'll find both styles.

Above all, it's mouth-watering; its natural balance tends to and trends towards that. You may not ski (I don't), but we can all shut our eyes and dream about what it must be like to blitz downhill in a crisp, twisting swirl of brilliance and powder and chill. Imagine your tongue doing that, and you'll have some idea about how a good glass of Jacquère tastes. No Roussanne or Altesse can match it for sheer downhill glee. It grows on an ancient necropolis. The best Jacquère of Apremont and Abymes, though, seethes with life.

Time's Engine Room:

2010 Langhorne Creek, Reserve Shiraz, Noon

One sniff, and I was back. Deep, luscious fruits, tar, creosote; there was a throaty fullness, too. Call it an anti-Riesling: warm, languid, savoury and salty, in place of all that orchard freshness. If Riesling is dawn, this Shiraz was day's end.

There was a smell of warm belt leather, and the leaf litter under a eucalyptus tree. Even though the wine was a young one, the aromas were harmonious and serene, un-thrusting and un-showy. You sat down beside it, and it chatted to you, companionably; a magpie carolled in the distance. It smelled of Australia: warm, dry, ancient. If time itself had an engine room, idling out the millennia, it would surely smell something like this.

I remember the place well. You drove out of Adelaide, and straight up into the hills, past the high lands where they grew pristine Chardonnay, strong lettuces and celery as thick as your leg. Then you followed the hill line south, as the elevation dropped gradually away: Mount Barker, Macclesfield.

By Strathalbyn, you're off those private, intricate, braided hills, where every farm commands a little world of its own, and you'd turned your shoulder, too, on the Gulf of St Vincent. There was no sense of a loitering open sea any more; instead, delta country beckoned. You could feel the light gathering like gold in a bank vault ahead of you. And eventually, there it would be, glimmering on the other side of wide mudflats: Lake Alexandrina, or what was left of it. (Not much when I was in Australia in 2009, towards the end of an El Niño cycle.) If South Australia has an equivalent of France's Camargue, here it is. We used to come down here regularly; some friends had a shack at an easy-going, camper-friendly place on the lake called Clayton. The frogs would croak us all to sleep under a shower of bright stars.

Before you got to the lake, though, you'd drive through Langhorne Creek. It was a sudden explosion of vines, clustering around the little roads that knotted themselves just here: around 6,000 hectares altogether, making the place bigger than Châteauneuf-du-Pape. The oldest vines owed their existence to the seasonal river that flows through the town, the Bremer; it rises east of Mount Lofty, the highest spot in the Adelaide Hills, and then drops south like a plumb line, down into the lake. One of South Australia's pioneer settlers, Frank Potts, initially cleared the land hereabouts and diverted the river to provide flood irrigation when it was in spate. That was in 1850, using muscle power. The vineyards that produced this wine are still flood-irrigated 160 years later. They had a deep drink in the winter that preceded the 2010 harvest.

The soils are free-draining sandy clay loams: exactly what all of Australia's 19th-century pioneer wine-growers looked for. The flood fills them with the winter water that splashes out of the sky on dark nights in the Adelaide Hills. Water almost up to the bottom trellis wire will be gone from the surface in 24 hours, but it hides deep in the soils, gradually drying over summer. These soils need no other irrigation.

Most of Langhorne Creek's vines, by contrast, lie up off the floodplain, in land that Potts and his mates never considered cultivable. They're drip-irrigated with Alexandrina water, and run for quantity: 'Riverland in a cooler climate,' as one grower put it. The quality of Langhorne Creek fruit is always beguiling (it was Wolf Blass's secret fuel in his ascent to acclaim), but viticulture like that can never deliver the density and profundity that packs cartilage around this wine's spine.

The fruit comes from the Borrett family's '20 Rows' vineyard; George Borrett hand-harvests it, and personally drives it up to Drew Noon's farm a little further north, in McLaren Vale. It's fermented with natural yeast, and no acid additions; no additions of any sort, indeed, other than a little sulphur. This, in other words, is the essence: what Langhorne Creek Shiraz tastes like, if left to its own devices.

It is peaceable – yet astonishing: massive beyond ordinary measure. We sipped it over three days, during which it changed little. It was rich, deliciously rank, its tarry fruit flavours pressed into complexity by mint, resin, cineole. Properly tannic, too: it hadn't been hurried into finishing its fermentation in barrel, but had loitered in Drew Noon's vats with its skins. There was ironstone dust in there somewhere, and a saline edge: the sea breach down the road. You couldn't, though, deny its freshness, either, ready to carry it into the storm of years ahead. Its 14.7% of alcohol was necessary – but its strength lay elsewhere: in its great wave-like heave of flavour, in its résumé of an unimaginably old land.

Terroir, Tasting and Tonewood

The wines of the neighbouring Médoc communes of Pauillac, Saint Julien and Margaux possess contrasting personalities, French wine culture insists. (Few drinkers demur.) Why? In part because of inherent singularities in the physical environment in which their grapes came into being. That's terroir.

Terroir goes further, underwriting the unique character of other single-origin foods and drinks – like Darjeeling tea, Beaufort cheese, Espelette peppers. It may go further still. Wherever the search for quality is imperative and a crafted product is fashioned with natural materials, terroir might play a role. Here's an intriguing example.

It involves an intoxicating experience – without wine. You're listening to a violin concerto (Bruch's first, say, or that by Brahms) played by a violinist such as Anne-Sophie Mutter or Maxim Vengerov. Most of your pleasure, of course, will derive from the music and the playing – but the quality of the instrument counts, too. The belly of a fine violin is generally made from spruce and its back from figured maple, with ebony for the fingerboard and pegs. Of the three, it's the spruce that has most to do with the quality of the sound – such woods are known as tonewoods.

For at least six centuries, European luthiers have considered spruce grown in cold Alpine conditions the best, thanks to its fine growth rings and even grain. In Italy's Parco Naturale Paneveggio Pale di San Martino in Trento, you'll find *la foresta dei violini* – the violin forest – so called because its spruce tonewood is of unequalled density, hence musical quality. It is cut during a waning moon between October and November, to minimize the quantity of sap it contains. Even musical sound, thus, has a terroir dimension.

Both Mutter and Vengerov play Stradivari instruments, and Stradivari himself is (legendarily, at least) said to have made the 250-kilometre journey from Cremona to the violin forest to choose trees and wood. Moreover, Stradivari's life (1644–1737) overlapped with the Maunder Minimum (1645–1715), a period of reduced sunspot activity which is thought to have been a cause of the period of intense cold that began at around 1650. This cold gave rise to spruce of even slower growth and greater density than usual, confirmed by analysis of the growth rings in Stradivari instruments. In winemaking terms, it would seem as if Stradivari was lucky enough to be working during a period of great vintages. Present-day luthiers even distinguish between trees grown at different precise altitudes, and between wedges grown on the north- or south-facing sides of an individual tree.

Before we get carried away with all of this, though, here's a couple more details. Stradivari treated his wood chemically. According to a scientific study by biochemistry professor Joseph Nagyvary (the results were published in *Nature* in 2006) analysis of minute wood samples obtained from those restoring Stradivari instruments revealed the presence of borax, fluorides, chromium and iron salts, probably used as preservative against the woodworm infestations that were common at the time. Why shouldn't great winemakers use a little sulphur?

And those of us with less than perfect blind-tasting abilities might be comforted to know that in a 1977 programme on BBC Radio Three, violin virtuosi Isaac Stern and Pinchas Zukerman together with the violin expert Charles Beare were 'blind tested' by hearing four instruments played behind a screen: three great historical violins (including one Stradivari) and a contemporary British violin. Despite having been allowed to play the instruments beforehand, the two violinists identified only two of the four; one thought the British violin was the Stradivari. Another (double-blind) test run at the 2010 International Violin Competition of Indianapolis suggested that both competitors and judges actually preferred modern instruments to two Strads and a Guarneri, based on sound quality alone.

Non-European wines, of course, have famously beaten their classical European counterparts under blind-tasting conditions (such as the celebrated 'Judgement of Paris' organized by Steven Spurrier in 1976); even skilled tasters, confronted by a plain wine in a plain glass, can utterly lose their bearings in attempting to hunt down both origin and quality. Conceptualizing terroir is simple. Its clear identification in practice is complex, and its trace (in a wine's taste, in a violin's resonance) the faintest watermark.

For all that, we taste and we listen, year after year, in our tens and hundreds of thousands. 'The market' is not stupid: it's us. Reputation is incessantly sifted by this algorithmic mass of the world's drinkers and listeners. We do find differences, sublimities, in both tastes and sounds, secreted there by nature and all the more precious for being so. Land prices are the proof.

Happy Birthday, Breaky Bottom

Breaky Bottom is the only vineyard I know intimately. It was in 1974 that a young livestock farmer called Peter Hall decided, in a moment of life-changing temerity, to wave his piglets goodbye and plant 1.6 hectares of vines on the tiny Sussex farm he tenanted, and which he and his second wife Christina now own. This place is called Breaky Bottom.

There were 150 hectares in production in the UK in 1975; by 2014 the total exceeded 1,500; by 2020 it had reached 3,800 hectares. Only the quixotic chanced it back in the '70s; now vines are lavishly buttered over south-facing hillsides by former London hedge-fund managers and retired investment bankers, on the soundest advice.

There are bigger vineyards than Breaky Bottom; others are more influential, have better international distribution, garner more publicity, make more money, flaunt more swank. But this I can guarantee: those who make their way along the lonely, chassis-scraping mud track that unthreads its way up and over the brow of the Sussex Downs and spools into the green fold below (and they are many) never forget their visit. In the minds of most, Breaky Bottom has a habit of becoming England's emblematic vineyard, and its engaging, combative and articulate worker-proprietor their English wine grower of reference.

I first made my way over that track a quarter-century ago, and I've often been back since. Peter is an old friend. When I met him on October 1st 1989, he was on the verge of bankruptcy – after two catastrophic vintages in which he had fermented only 1,000 bottles in total. The '89 was a generous vintage in both quantity and quality but Peter didn't have the money to buy bottles, labels or boxes. The bank refused to increase his existing loans by a penny; indeed it muttered about 'calling them in'. A benefactor kept the leaky little ship afloat.

Over the years, setback has followed setback. The vineyard and farmhouse were flooded and muddied 31 times between autumn 2000 and spring 2001, perhaps the worst pass; Peter and Christina had to spend the following two years living in a caravan. Peter has since fought adversity on two fronts: repeated mass invasion from grape-greedy farmed pheasants at harvest time, and vineyard difficulties caused by the supply of diseased young vines. I said he was combative. Just as well: legal redress for the negligence of neighbours and suppliers has been as important as professional resilience in supporting Breaky Bottom. It requires nerve to seek justice through recourse to law.

None of this, though, matters when it comes to what we might call the achievement of Breaky Bottom, and the reason why Peter is regarded as an inspiring model by the talented younger generation of English winemakers.

What counts is that Peter (in part thanks to his French mother) grew up drinking good wine. What tells is that (in part thanks to his literary father) he loves poetry, art, conversation and music. In the early years opera was performed in Breaky Bottom's flint barn, and anyone who wanders along the hilltop paths early one morning when Peter is out pruning or trimming may well hear the valley echo quietly to Bruckner, Brahms or Brubeck, emanating from a battered radio taped to his waist. A sense of aesthetic rightness pervades everything at Breaky Bottom. It is a place of much-assailed perfection. Sheep still fulfil the hillside's downland vocation, and Peter has his hands bloodied at lambing every spring; owls haunt its nights. The winery name on label and box is in lettering designed by the great English wood engraver and typographer Reynolds Stone. There is a vision here. Music and wine draw on the same vein of inspiration. We taste the music of place.

This is not the only way to make great wine, but it is most definitely one way. In the early years, Peter produced resolutely dry, vinous white wines that aged superbly from a tight-buttoned youth to an ampler, more expressive middle age, at a time when most English growers were floundering in a lake of lame medium-dry wine based on exotic, cold-hardy German crosses. Like most English growers, he came to realize that the land really wanted to produce fine sparkling wine; unlike most English growers, he had chalk soils with which to do that. He's now planted the Champagne varietal troika – but firmly believes that his beloved Seyval Blanc can, just here, match them for nobility. There is no 'Brut NV'; every cuvée in every vintage is differently fashioned, and named after a person of some significance. This is fine, pure English sparkling wine from Sussex chalklands, made without concessions or shortcuts. Since 2014, indeed, recognition has come, and the tide of fortune has begun to flow. In an astonishing reversal, the wine grower whose car (in 1989) had grass growing from its back seats now finds himself rubbing elbows, on the Corney & Barrow wine list, with Salon and Domaine de la Romanée-Conti.

The 40-year mark is where the next generation normally begins to take over; for the time being, though, Peter's four children are otherwise employed. This secret valley doesn't have to be a vineyard, of course; but I can't be alone in finding it impossible to imagine those familiar soft contours unquartered by vines. Happy Birthday, Breaky Bottom, and may there be many more decades ahead.

A Sea Interlude:

2015 Picpoul de Pinet, Cuvée Anniversaire, Beauvignac

Revisionism – the calling into question of orthodox views about a subject – is one of the duties imposed on a historian; indeed it should form part of all intellectual effort. We never understand; all we do is strive to understand. Asking questions provides the motor force in that striving. This, after all, is how the scientific method works (though orthodoxy has no place in science).

If revisionism has a bad reputation, it is because it has been claimed by negationists who wish to deny proven facts on feeble evidence, often for populist political effect; by irredentists and revanchists obsessed with lost cartographic orthodoxies, as an incitement to violent action; or as a screen for extremism. That which is wise, after all, can (and should) be put to revisionist test. Only thus will we be able to distinguish between the soundly orthodox and the superannuated: infirm, inappropriate or inaccurate orthodoxies.

What the heck, you may reasonably be wondering, has all that to do with Picpoul de Pinet? It's a machine-harvested white wine, dominated by co-operative producers, whose ex-cellars price lies south of 10 euros. Therefore (orthodoxy would hold) it can't be 'fine wine'. A case for revisionism?

Yes, for three reasons. First, a sizeable percentage of what we think of as 'fine wine' is not fine (meaning exquisite) at all, but simply good wine that is lucky enough to go to market under names that evoke great expectations. Were the 75 centilitres of Picpoul de Pinet in front of me to be filled into bottles labelled with a fair Côte de Beaune Premier Cru or Chablis Premier Cru label, it would meet (or exceed) the expectations of most restaurant customers and most occasional retail customers. In this sense, the orthodoxies surrounding which wines are 'fine' and which are not are indeed inaccurate (if not necessarily infirm).

The second reason is that, when we come to define fine wine, we tend to equate noise (volume of sound) with music. This prejudices the chances of quiet wines. A noisy wine is one that is emphatically characterful in one way or another, one that advances towards you offering a variety of handles and triggers. It will probably be 'intense' and 'concentrated' (though the impression of intensity and concentration is easy to achieve by artificial means, especially the use of oak and acidification). A quiet wine will do none of these things. It may barely allude at all, nor will it seem either intense or concentrated – but it will have an inner shapeliness, grace, logic and purity of its own, and it will compel and reward attention via its drinking qualities. That is wine's music. Picpoul de Pinet is a quiet wine of this sort: limpid, sappy, fresh, like unaccompanied flute variations, or a classical guitar fandanguillo, coming and going on the wind.

And the third reason? What is truly fine in wine is not that which is expensive (an effect of market forces, sustained within a culture over a long historical period, and thus not immune to orthodoxies of its own) but that which is both beautiful and unique, in the sense of being true to a particular place and impossible to duplicate elsewhere. Picpoul in this sense is one of Languedoc's most interesting wines, grown on 1,400 hectares that slope down to the most significant of all the coastal lagoons dominating the Mediterranean coast between the Camargue and Catalonia: the Etang de Thau. The grape was once one of the triad, along with Clairette and Terret, that dominated local vermouth production. This production continues today, albeit in much reduced volume, via Noilly Prat's elaborate recipe, produced at Marseillan on the Etang de Thau.

The grape seems to be indigenous to this part of the coast and produces balanced, fresh whites without the compromise of early picking over the long, sunny Mediterranean summer. Those wines partner the 13,000 tonnes of oysters that are harvested from the Etang de Thau each year (90 percent of France's Mediterranean oyster production) winningly. There are no other Picpoul appellations (though it could be used, on its own if wished, for white Châteauneuf), and no IGP Pays d'Oc Picpoul wines, either; almost none is planted outside France. This is it. And if you do search around for allusions, you might find a lemony cascade, a saline edge, a sappy sweetness behind its slaking poise. A sweet shell around a salty oyster, with lemon squeezed on top: there's the meal, and there's the wine, too.

I have one final piece of revisionism, though for someone who writes about wine for a living it's almost heresy: it doesn't matter too much which producer's Picpoul you buy. I'm drinking the Beauvignac old-vine version, but I've tasted or drunk almost two dozen this year, and in the main they're all good, within a point or two of each other (should you be point-addicted) on any unhysterical scoring scale. The four co-operatives that produce over 80 percent of Picpoul are all careful vinifiers: cool temperatures, lees contact, a blocked malo. After that it's the place that comes tumbling out: sunlight, fresh white, quiet music, a sea interlude. All fine.

Angela's Lemon

I have the significant lemon in front of me. What, though, should I do with it? I'm not sure. Here's its story.

Ever since I first saw photographs of the acid-soiled Ligurian vineyards of the Cinque Terre, I've wanted to go there. There are many astonishing terraced vineyards in the world (like those of the Rhine and the Mosel, of the Valais, of the Douro, of Banyuls) but these trump the lot and are closest to oblivion: a stairway from sea to sky, a green sandwich in wild blue bread. I doubt Babylon's hanging gardens defied gravity with greater fecundity. They yo-yo up and down from improbable, sea-nibbled villages whose pale houses are stacked as casually as dominoes on a table's edge. Tough farmers made them between 900 and 1,000 years ago; was the temerity of their creation driven by optimism or desperation? Until a railway masterpiece was threaded into the skirt of the hillsides in the 1870s, the only way in or out of the five villages was by boat or boot. Road transport only reached the Cinque Terre in the 1960s.

That road, according to Matteo Bonanini, the director of the Cinque Terre's wine co-operative, has been a disaster. 'The road caused the abandonment of the vineyards, because it has brought tourists here, which meant a much easier living than working the terraces.' There are around 1,400 hectares of terraces in the whole 3,860-hectare zone (which is both a National Park and a World Heritage Site); 500 hectares of these were cultivated by 200 growers prior to the arrival of the roads, in the 1950s. Now there are just 80 hectares of vineyard left, shared by around 120 growers, 100 of whom bring their fruit to the co-operative. 'Many of the owners are in their 80s,' continued Matteo, who was taking time off to meet us from his main job in the naval shipyards of La Spezia; there are no full-time wine-growers here. 'Every time someone dies, it means another 300 square metres are abandoned. Those who die love their parcels; the next generation doesn't love them but knows where they are; and the third generation doesn't even know where they are.'

Given the difficulties of production and the fact that imposing quality requirements on growers who harvest only a few crates of grapes each isn't viable, it's remarkable how good the wines of the Cantina Cinque Terre are: delicate, poised, refreshing and seemingly saline. Whether or not this is due to the sea breezes against which the vines have to be protected, traditionally by tree heather (*Erica arborea*) windbreaks but latterly by adapting the vines to *pergola bassa* training systems, is hard to say. Alcohol levels, unusually, have sunk here from 13.5% to 12.5% in recent decades – as the higher yielding green grapes grown under *pergola bassa* slowly replace the golden grapes that used to be the result of each vine being trained to a separate vertical stake.

In addition to the dry whites made by blending the indigenous Bosco with Albarola (on the lower plots) or Vermentino (on the higher plots), there is also a fine if necessarily expensive passito called Sciacchetrà, which is reductively made in stainless steel but fermented with its skins, giving it gently tannic complexities.

And so to the vineyards. Co-operative worker Sauro Bordoni gave each of us a folded cardboard box to sit on, and we clambered aboard one of the little *trenini* (funicular monorails) used to get equipment up and baskets of grapes down. It lurched off into the sky. We tumbled out on to a footpath 100 metres later, marvelled at the views, and started walking. And then, by chance, we met Angela Capellini: the embodiment of everything we had just been discussing back at the co-operative.

It was the smoke I saw first, then a slight figure dressed in lilac with pink trousers, a russet scarf and a striped pink hat moving about nearby. She was quietly tidying her tiny vineyard in readiness for spring, and raking a little grass debris into a companionable bonfire. Her husband had died; she had two children, both of whom worked in offices. She was 82, though she looked younger. Her legs were fine, we learned in reply to our enquiry. They'd need to be: her home was a great many stone steps beneath us. There was a lemon tree in the vineyard, and she offered us each a lemon – so good, she said, that she sometimes just peeled one and ate it.

It was hard not be elated in that extraordinary environment, talking to one of Europe's oldest wine growers 300 metres above the fishes, surrounded by wild oregano, wild asparagus and sweet-scented tree heather, and with the sappy freshness of the 2014 Cinque Terre Costa da' Posa perfuming our breath; hard, too, not to reach facile conclusions about health, long life and the indomitability of the wine-growing act. Yet, a week later, I remembered what Matteo Bonanini's words were in reply to our first questions: '*Tanti problemi.*' Perhaps Angela deserved a rest; perhaps her children deserved their office jobs; and perhaps the future of the Cinque Terre lies in hiking and honeymoons rather than haunting white wines. Perhaps, too, I'll try eating Angela's lemon, to find out if there can be any sweetness in that which is intrinsically sour.

Washed Up on the Shores of Illyria:

2015 Teran, Santa Elisabetta, Benvenuti

It's humbling, surely. Yet strangely reassuring.

You travel the world's wine roads for 30 years, stay curious at every turn, fill a shelf full of notebooks, bring back tidings from afar, seem to have surveyed the boundaries of the known world. Then comes a day of novelty when, as if shipwrecked, you find yourself on a new shore, served affronting wine, strangely named, by kind and hospitable strangers. You turn the wine in the glass, try to gauge its measure. You assay others of its kind. You listen to its music, and begin to disentangle those chords and progressions that seemed at first so jangling. There is a sense there; perhaps a beauty too. Enthusiasm kindles. Before you know it, a fire is crackling, and you're warming your hands in its glow.

So with this fine wine, made from a grape about which until very recently I knew nothing. Like Viola and Sebastian in Shakespeare's *Twelfth Night*, I found myself washed up on the shores of Illyria – or, to be accurate, driven from Zagreb to the Istrian peninsula, so named after the Histri, the Illyrian tribe whose land it was prior to Roman conquest. Croatia's Istria lies towards the southern end of Teran's range: the variety spreads north and then south into Italy, as Terrano, down as far as Emilia-Romagna. It seems to be at its best in Istria itself, though, as well as in Slovenia's Kras and Italy's Carso: the original karstlands, gurgling and intestinal beneath their white surfaces.

Nikola Benvenuti showed me his Teran vines, growing in the Santa Elisabetta vineyard, close to the inland hilltop town of Motovun. What strange bunches: long, loose and open, the grapes themselves so widely spaced that the bunch seemed half-formed. But prolific in number: a green harvest is essential. 'You can make good Malvazija at seven or eight tonnes per hectare. Six is absolute tops for Teran, and four is better.' The harvest

52 SOME SOILS, SOME SKIES

comes late, usually in the second week of October, maybe a month after the Merlot has been gathered in. Encouraging: we will need late ripeners for our hot tomorrows.

I tasted 24 wines made from Teran. The first few seemed unpleasant: tart, almost rancid; livid and raw; austere; tough; bitter; caustic. Affronting, indeed: a shock to delicate, claret-softened palates. It was like stumbling back into the Middle Ages, where surgeons were sawbones, where the mad roamed unconfined, where the contents of chamber pots came showering from oriel windows.

As the tasting unfolded, though, the wines grew older; older wines implied higher levels of ambition; ambition unearthed an inner warmth, brocaded complexities, pristine fruits. The shock of Teran never completely abandons its wines, and you should at all times be ready for 'a terrible oath, with a swaggering accent sharply twanged off'. There are countryside smells; the acidity is always insistent; the fruits themselves are the taut, tight, harsh kind (sloe, elder, damson) you might forage after shipwreck. As I tasted one wine, I wondered if my tongue might dissolve, leaving me with a stump and a void in its place. It didn't happen. The longer such wines spend in the mouth, the more you see their ripeness and saturation. They grow and billow; there's even an aching bitter chocolate sweetness – 'This is the air, that is the glorious sun' – to be found somewhere. You detect a kindness and generosity behind its rapscallion character. 'In nature ... None can be call'd deform'd but the unkind.'

This wine was the best of the younger set. In scent there was nothing affronting about it at all. There were soft, moist, pruney fruits, and fine leather; there was countryside resource. It was possible to imagine the truffles that secretly stud the woods hereabouts figured in the wine. On the palate, too, all the asperities had been gathered up and subsumed into something dense, weighty, graceful, deep and tender. The wine was grandly dark, brooding, rich, earthy, sooty with black chocolate. The acidity was still prominent, but not at all caustic, so tightly was it bonded to the dark wildwood fruits. The tannins were lush. Not quite velvety but not far off.

Older wines still showed how the progress continues, though the colours remain sombre at all times. The 2009 Teran from Benvenuti (which contained fruit from Santa Elisabetta, not made separately at the time) amplified the leather and vellum still further, though the chocolate and truffle were no longer visible. This was intense, a wine of extreme vigour, almost rapacious yet seductive. The 2003 Gran Teran from another fine producer, Coronica, was more evolved but still vital: allusion-packed, with lemon, tobacco and oak leaf as well as the woodland plums and cocoa dust. 'And thus the whirligig of time brings in his revenges.'

Proof, at any rate, of the underrated Teran's quality comes when you match it to food: the needed foil to its profusion of character. You might imagine two minor Illyrian noblemen, projected 450 years forward, sitting down with relish to a venison ragout partnered by dark, challenging, timeless wine of this sort. 'Does not,' asks the more portly of the two, 'our life consist of the four elements?' 'Faith,' his slender companion replies, 'so they say, but I rather think it consists of eating and drinking.' 'Th'art a scholar,' retorts the first: 'Let us therefore eat and drink. Marian, I say! a stoup of wine!'

Dr Mistral

It was grey and overcast when I climbed aboard the train for Avignon, and barely brighter when I got off. When I reached Châteauneuf-du-Pape, though, the horizon to the north was clearing; the brooding silhouette of Mont Ventoux began to loom. Mid-morning came; the cypress tops swayed.

By lunchtime, the sky was brilliant blue, and the spring sunlight glittered as if filled with tiny ice particles. The air grew brisk, agitated, lively, alert; there was drama in the scene. Every stone in the vineyards took on shape, form and detail, as far as fallible eyes could reach. Light filled every tree, too; each leaf was in movement. It was a storm of light.

I'd been thinking about the possible influence of wind on terroir, and had noted how often the Mistral was written about as a major hazard of viticulture in the Southern Rhône. This, I felt, just had to be wrong.

The glory of Châteauneuf as a wine – its amplitude and breadth, its concentration, its extravagance of flavour – owes much to the extraordinary combination of sunlight and wind you find on the stony plateau around the town. I took a day in Châteauneuf to talk to growers and understand the effects of this wind a little better. The Mistral chose to charge in and clear the midday sky while I was there, in deft illustration.

First, though, a brief description of what the Mistral is, and why it happens. When high pressure in the Bay of Biscay coincides with low pressure in the Gulf of Genoa, a current of cold air is drawn from the north of France southwards to the Mediterranean. This air is funnelled down the Rhône Valley, running high above the vines in the Northern Rhône, but swooping down to bush-vine level through Châteauneuf and the Southern Rhône. The near-hurricane-force record was logged at 116 kilometres per hour on April 6th 2003 (a hurricane is categorized as 118 km/hour or more, according to the Beaufort scale).

'For me,' said Catherine Armenier at Domaine du Marcoux, 'it's Dr Mistral. It has a hundred times more advantages than disadvantages. It's truly a part of the terroir here, and Châteauneuf just wouldn't be Châteauneuf without the Mistral.' Consultant Philippe Cambie pointed out that it makes organic cultivation relatively straightforward, and 'gives you savings of at least 50 percent of treatments' compared to other regions without the Mistral. 'It's a privilege for us,' said Jean-Pierre Usseglio, 'even though it's difficult for us to put up with sometimes.'

Human discomfort may account for much of the wind's sometimes villainous reputation. Animal perception of the Mistral, after all, is very different from plant perception. We feel a drop of 1°C for every 10 kilometres per hour of wind, so a winter day of –3°C can feel like –11°C or more in a strong Mistral. 'In some years,' says Catherine Armenier, 'we don't go out for 15 days. Even in August, if there is a celebration or something in the evening, we're all wearing thick jumpers and the tourists are freezing.' 'You can handle one or two days,' says Harry Karis, author of *The Châteauneuf-du-Pape Wine Book*: 'After three to six days you get a bit sad, and after that you get depressed. You hear the cracking of the ceiling, the whole building is moving... not just outsiders like me, but the locals, too. You can see it in their faces.'

There are, of course, some genuine viticultural drawbacks to the Mistral. The worst risk is when the new vine shoots are about six to nine centimetres long (and April is historically the most Mistral-vulnerable month), as the wind can then snap the shoots, provoking harvest losses. You can use attaching wires above the bush vines to hold the shoots in place, and in any case shoots will usably re-grow, provided you are prepared to harvest their fruit later than the rest. But Catherine Armenier is philosophical about the losses. 'I think if you have broken branches in spring it's a little like making a sacrifice, in order to have something better later on.'

Other disadvantages? There don't seem to be any, other than those maddened humans. A high wind at flowering doesn't necessarily mean crop-setting problems. Grenache (the main grape variety in Châteauneuf) is *coulure*-prone, it's true, but this tends to be for mysterious reasons, and can happen in calm periods as well as windy ones. High wind at the very end of the season will mean a loss of juice, as water begins to evaporate through the berry skins – but that may be a factor behind the ravishing, palate-seducing concentration you find in great Châteauneuf, and thus a positive terroir trait. The Mistral is especially good for drying the vineyards after the heavy downpours to which the region is prone – '50 to 60 mm of rain,' according to Philippe Cambie, 'will dry in three to four days if there is a Mistral afterwards'.

Not only is the Mistral very good at keeping fungal diseases at bay, it is also good at repelling insect pests (especially grape moths) – since they don't like being hurled around in the wind any more than humans do. Jean-Pierre Usseglio says he has always noticed that there are fewer insects in plateau vineyards (those most exposed to the wind) than in vineyards on slopes.

In the winter, the Mistral will keep frosts at bay, and Usseglio also says that he prefers to work the soils when there is a Mistral, since the wind 'lightens and opens up the soil'. Once the goblet vines have a canopy, the leaf movement provoked by the wind provides ideal intermittent sunlight exposure as well as prophylactic ventilation. The Mistral evidently mitigates summer temperature extremes, and dramatically so. All of the growers confirmed, too, that the wind (and the consequent drop in air humidity – it fell to an astonishing 13 percent in 2003, according to Harry Karis) encourages the vine

56   SOME SOILS, SOME SKIES

to send down deeper roots in search of the moisture that they are losing in transpiration. Deep roots are a hallmark of most great vineyards.

Châteauneuf, finally, has few rivals in France in terms of its old-vine patrimony: it's a viticultural 'blue zone'. Many vines here have 100 years of Mistral in their memory bank. If they weren't happy with the health benefits provided by that tearing wind – no matter what the humans think – they'd have upped and died decades ago.

Liquid Rags in Your Mouth:

2013 Barbaresco, Produttori del Barbaresco

You remember Italy? If so, you probably remember ancient towers. Most weren't built to look beautiful; it's only the passage of centuries that has given them a patina of charm. Tuscany's San Gimignano bristles with 14, but once there were 72: an insanity of towers, a forest of clannish fingers stabbing the sky, their elevation very nearly as mysterious a project as the sculpting of Easter Island's moai.

Barbaresco has just one 12th-century siege tower. It's there, on the label of this wine. Ugly: jagged windows, nibbled crenellations and a strange white square half-way up its side, though perfectly positioned at the prow of the village, commanding both the vineyards, which spread out immaculately on three sides, and the wooded slope that drops like an apron down towards the River Tànaro. It certainly belongs on the label of this wine, because if ever a wine gathered a place into itself – not just the topographical place, but the historical place, too – it's this one.

Barbaresco, so far as anyone knows, was one of the sources of 'Barolo' in the days before precision of origin was considered significant. What would have mattered during those undocumented centuries in the Langhe was the ability of a vineyard to ripen Nebbiolo rather than the other varieties of the place (Barbera, Dolcetto, Moscato). The dipping, unfurling vineyards around Barbaresco village had the warmth to do this. Did Barbaresco's wines, though, have a character of their own? One late 19th-century author (Lorenzo Fantini, in his 1879 *Monografia*, published in 1895) identified a point of difference between the Nebbiolo of Barbaresco and that of Barolo: a refinement of bouquet. If we know more today, and are able to enjoy this wine as a Barbaresco benchmark, it is in part due to a contemporary of Fantini's called Domizio Cavazza.

Cavazza witnessed catastrophe and salvation. A bright young Milanese agriculture student, he won a scholarship to study in France. After a year of fruit and horticulture at Versailles, he went south to phylloxera-devastated Montpellier in 1879, where he worked under the great viticulturist Pierre Viala and saw Planchon's work with grafted vines. He returned to Italy (as yet unaffected by phylloxera) in 1880. Though only a young man of 26, he was nominated to lead Alba's newly founded oenological school the following year. He chose to live in Barbaresco, where he bought a property in 1886. In order to help create a separate reputation and identity for the village, he corralled nine growers to found a pioneering co-operative, the Cantina Sociale di Barbaresco, in 1894. It lasted just 30 years. Cavazza died young, at just 57, in 1913; World War I drained the region of manpower; phylloxera struck; and when Mussolini came to power in 1922, he told grape growers to switch to grain production. Its memory, though, lived on, and when a new crisis of depopulation again threatened the village in the 1950s (the lure of Fiat), its priest, Fiorino Marengo, encouraged 19 local growers to form the 'Produttori'. Three vintages were made in the church basement.

There are now 54 growers, bringing all of their Nebbiolo (and nothing else) from a total of 105 hectares to the co-operative. The great village sites are in here somewhere (only five percent of the Produttori's intake comes from outside the village), and any wine that is not judged worthy of this cuvée, which accounts for half of total production, is declassified to Nebbiolo delle Langhe. In good years, around 30 percent of total production is made as individual cru wines (including Asili, Pajè, Rabajà and Montefico). There are other village benchmarks, notably the wine of Gaja (made in smaller quantities from 13 different sites) and Giacosa, but the wine of the Produttori competes very fairly for its price – a fraction of theirs.

It's not easy to say where Barbaresco's refinement come from, since its general altitude is lower, not higher, than Barolo, and it tends to harvest earlier. You might, thus, expect a louder beat, not a softer one. The soil definitions on geological maps are the same (Sant'Agata fossil marls, interbedded with sandy conglomerates; and the Lequio Formation – silty marls), but locals suggest that these 'identical' soils in fact carry a higher percentage of sand in Barbaresco, and that Barbaresco has fewer south-facing slopes and more west-facing slopes than Barolo. It's also an airier location, thanks to the river, and less given to the stacked, menacingly humid heat of thundery afternoons than Barolo.

Tasted four years later, the 2013 is pale, clear and translucent, betraying a long, slow fermentation and maceration, and cellar years passed in big wood, not small. An opening strawberry sweetness grows more expansive with air but there is no sense of autumn, mushroom or underbrush yet, implying that the wine might linger longer with some profit.

The flavour shocks after those sweet scents. Strawberries are forgotten; cranberries loom. And then you ditch fruit altogether, for the great Nebbiolo wines of the Langhe are really an essay in structure and energy. This is no exception, though the tannins are finely milled; you taste drama, dust and bitterness as the wine turns to liquid rags in your mouth, and sails off with an angry asperity you never dreamed about on first approach. This is all, somehow, as it should be. The wine's glow grows; the tower on the label glares.

A Honeycomb of Light:

2010 Mas del Serral, Pepe Raventós

The wine's bright. A pale gold, though true gold for all that: gold you might imagine finding among shadows. Something precious, old, hidden. Warmth and wealth, carefully laid aside for later.

There's a steady stream of fine bubbles: seams of life now unwrapped, liberated, murmuring in the glass. My bottle (number 132 out of 2,047) needed air to clear a little. That's fine: it's the wine of a farm, and you need to meet the farm first. You need to walk out of the city and on to the farm. You need to leave ducting and communal upholstery and cleanser behind you. Then, adjusted, naturalized, you will find the treasures of the farm laid out before you, as precisely as in the painting itself. Which painting? More of that later. Enjoy, first, the smells of straw, of almonds, of shelled beans, of thyme, of the hive. The wine is busy with scent, as the farm is with life.

We can see a shape forming already: round, arched, brick-thick, fat-stoned, Romanesque. This is Romanesque wine in a genre dominated, for too long, by Gothic ideals. Forget Reims cathedral, its beaky angel and its soaring, icy interior. This sparkling wine is the cloister of Santo Domingo de Silos: a honeycomb of light, chased about by the dragons, centaurs and mermaids imagined by lost stone carvers.

The wine is pure in the mouth; it's larger and richer than you may have expected. The bubbles swarm the tongue like bees, pollen tumbling from their legs. The wine's acidity is more like a sea swell, carrying the inner contours of flavour: all lemon, no apple. Tannin, too, sensed as much as felt: an abiding austerity inside the richness, rendering it limpid and uncloying. Earth, bitter plants, lemons, straw, dry hillside grasses, herbs, stone, dust – and the sun on all, the sun that bakes the earth of the farm brown, the sun that sets the cloisters aglow. Spotless, elemental, taut and shocking: that is what illumination does. Yet tender, too. Like the farm.

The farm is Miró's *La masía*: nine months' work between 1920 and 1921: 'minute realism,' the artist said, 'as far as I could take it'. The painting teems with life, light, warmth – but no chaos; the scene is as intricately constructed as a watch. Like most watches, and like most Romanesque churches, too, it is round; the painting is structured horizontally as well as vertically. All the parts of life fit together here in a complementarity of purpose, a community of being neither happy nor sad; there is no yearning for Gothic escape.

In September 1925 in Paris, Ernest Hemingway bought this painting for 5,000 francs as a birthday present for his first wife, Hadley. She kept it after their divorce – though Hemingway subsequently 'borrowed' it. For the rest of his life. 'It contained,' he wrote, 'all that you feel about Spain when

you are there, and all that you feel when you are away and cannot go there.'
It was squabbled over after his suicide, and eventually left by his fourth wife
and widow, Mary, to the National Gallery of Art in Washington.

Pepe Raventós saw *La masía* when loaned to the Tate Modern in
London for 'Miró – The Ladder of Escape' in 2011. He was, he says, 'far
from home' at the time: 'relaxed, sensitive and open to learning'. The
painting was an epiphany. It stirred memories of the remote Pyrenean
farmhouse at Feitús his own family had restored at weekends when he was
younger, just as Miró was painting (in Paris) from his recollections of the
family farm at Mont-roig del Camp near Tarragona, where he had gone
to recover from typhus. Joan Miró had leaves and flowers sent to him in
envelopes from Mont-roig to Paris as he struggled to finish it, surrounded
by grey skies, the smell of sewers, pandemic chaos. Goats, rabbits, hens, a
barking dog, a tethered donkey patiently circling a millstone, a woman bent
over a washing trough; bottles, buckets, baskets. The walls of the farmhouse
crack and stain like a shoreline, while stones rise from the ground in
strangely encrusted perfection.

'I saw the light, I visualized this farm.' The winemaker in 2011 echoed
the painter in 1921. 'That's where I belong, it's where I'm from. It's my
origins. That's what we have in the Mediterranean. That's our climate, those
are our animals … our plants. That is what we can offer.'

This wine already existed, but *La masía* crystallized his views about
what Mas del Sarral should be: 'a pathway with a single destination: the
origin. Maximum potential of the plot. Xarel-lo; austerity. Minerality,
salinity.' Since then, Pepe has been trying 'to restore the farm organism' and
thereby discover 'how the past and the future meet'. He has gathered animals
about him; he's gone back to the old ways.

No less importantly – and perhaps this is where others lose their
way – he has tried to lend the act of wine creation the sincerity of artistic
endeavour. This he does not claim, but it's what I see. I don't mean that
2010 Mas del Sarral is 'a work of art'; no wine is a work of art. But it's Pepe's
way of telling the truth about a place, his place, and that truth is something
beautiful that we can take with us on our own journeys. Mas del Sarral, he
says, is: 'A *camí* – a path. It will reach where it has to go.'

Touchdown in Wine Central

Empty bottles lined the windows, greening the grey Tbilisi afternoon; I sat next to Metropolitan Davit of Alaverdi in the gathering gloom. We stared together at a deeply coloured white wine in our glasses. It had been made at his monastery.

That wine seemed, strangely, to gather and amplify the remaining light. I asked the bishop (a former architect) what words he might use to describe it. 'Golden wine,' he said, after a pause. 'Gold is a thing of great value. When the painters were choosing colours, gold would give the most depth of impression. The wine has spring aromas, but at the same time those of golden autumn, because it has passed through those periods. You can even feel a bit of winter freeze in it, a coolness experience. If gold could have an aroma and a flavour, this would be it.' And then his iPhone rang.

The following day, I was tasting in the cellar of Alaverdi Monastery in Kakheti with one of the bishop's fellow monks, Father Ioseb. The sky darkened as we arrived at the scattered buildings, parts of which have seen 1,000 years of winemaking, and the rain began to spatter. Thunder followed; rain became hail; then the lights went out, sinking us in darkness. Someone brought candles; the golden wine became more golden still, while the red wine blackened. 'We were waiting for this storm,' murmured Ioseb, a little later. 'When the first thunderstorm of spring comes, it's a sign that the first *qvevri* should be opened.' (A *qvevri* is a buried clay fermentation jar.)

Even a cursory study of the history of wine underlines the influence of religion (especially Zoroastrianism, Judaism and Christianity) on its development. For many wine lovers today, of course, the link is anecdotal; wine has become a wholly secular pleasure. Not, though, in Georgia. Nowhere on earth does wine's history infuse its present more comprehensively than here. When I finally landed in Tbilisi, I felt like a Jew making aliyah. Historically and culturally speaking, this is Wine Central: 8,000 years of unbroken tradition (*see* page 25).

The practical intricacies of Georgian wine – its 500 indigenous varieties, wines fermented in buried clay jars – of course fascinate, and have been much described. What I hadn't foreseen was the intimate interweaving of viticulture with national identity: Georgia considers itself far more of a 'wine nation' than does France. The national saint (and bringer of Christianity to Georgia) is St Nino, whose distinctive droop-sided cross is so shaped because it was made from vine wood and bound with her own hair. Visitors will be told that Georgian fighters traditionally carried vines in their armour. If they fell, a vine would grow; travellers would then know a Georgian had died there. 'A man without a vineyard is a pauper,' declared Georgia's 18th-century polymath monarch Vakhtang VI in his Book of Laws, 'no matter how many estates he may have'. Geography means that the country has been much invaded; viticulture and winemaking have been an act both of defiance and of endurance. 'The country turned into the Lord's vineyard,' claimed Bishop Davit in a 2011 sermon.

Half of the population, he told me, either work in vineyards or make their own wine in some way. He grew up in Tbilisi itself, yet he remembers his parents used to buy grapes in the countryside and made wine in barrels on the balcony of their flat. 'Many do this without realizing why they are doing this.' Was it, I wondered, because Georgia had been a frontier between the Christian world and the Islamic world?

He rejected that idea, pointing out that Georgian vine-tending pre-dated the Islamic proscription of wine not just by centuries, but by millennia. 'In origin, it was always a road to God. Growing grapes and making wine without praising God doesn't make any sense. For many Georgians, wine is a connection to God, a thanksgiving to God, a road back to God.' Even *qvevri*, he claimed, were a part of this process. 'God created man from clay; *qvevri* are made from clay and lie up to their necks in the earth; they give birth to wine like a mother to a child, from within, and from within the earth. Then the wines age, like a child grows. The whole process is like a prayer.' Were wines made in *qvevri* 'more spiritual' than conventionally made wines? 'I fully agree, but it would be a bit pretentious to say it loudly. Perhaps we can say that wines which have lost their stems and their skins very early are motherless.'

Of course you don't have to be a believer to enjoy the strange beauty of Georgian wines; hedonic magnetism is enough. This spiritual tradition, though, gives Georgian winemakers a unique sense of purpose. 'Hence we love earth,' continues Bishop Davit in that 2011 sermon. '[It is] our homeland not only because our ancestors' bones, sinews and gristle, turned into dust, lie in it … [but because it is also] a thread of memory tied in the sky. It is a bitter nerve of our fall. It is a key to the covenant given to us – humble labour. It is the root of the vine – the Lord's blood.' You don't hear this sort of thing much in Bordeaux, Adelaide or Napa. Alone at dusk in a Georgian vineyard, though, the long echo may console.

CHAPTER THREE

TASTE AND TASTING

Bags, Butter and Biscuits

'Bags of fruit.' I remember having trouble with that one. Which fruit, first of all, were the famous bags filled with? Fresh raspberries? Mouth-puckering blackcurrants? Squishy peaches? Hard green apples? Dried figs? All different, every one. And none of them tasted much like a glass of wine.

'Buttery' was another problem. How could wine be like butter? Butter is fat; wine is carbohydrate. Butter melts and drips and dribbles and turns toasted crumpets from chunks of sofa upholstery into something delicious. Whereas all wine is acidic, with a pH of less than 4. They're almost opposites.

Champagne is still more piercing than most wines, yet I remember reading that it was 'biscuity'. What can a glass of austere fizz have in common with a McVitie's Digestive? And 'nutty', if anything, was worse. Nuts were dry and crunchy, and got richer as you went on chewing with what proved to be highly distinctive, fatty tastes… and you're telling me that's what a glass of Amontillado sherry does?

Nuts to that. You're all nutty, you wine nuts.

Wait a minute… Why should we say 'nuts' to something we are about to reject or show contempt for? What, exactly, do nuts have to do with a temporary loss of rationality? And why is an enthusiast a nut? The answer in each case is that it's slangily conventional to say so. Senseless but memorable and economical – hence the convention. Which has little to do with nuts themselves.

Isn't wine-tasting language the same? It begins with some sort of metaphorical insight – the glimpse of something in a wine's scent or flavour that reminds the taster of blackcurrant or butter – but then quickly moves to a conventional level. Any easy, friendly young red wine necessarily becomes 'fruity'; any oaked Chardonnay ends up 'buttery'.

This is the language of wine used at its most mechanical. You could call it jargon; it's also hype. Every wine, even the most mediocre, will be described at some point in routinely flattering terms – on its back label, in a wine list, by a pliant critic or journalist. The standard descriptors are wheeled out, most of which are usually based on some sort of metaphor or allusion. Whereas truthful descriptions for most wines would involve terms like thin, hollow, simple, crass, awkward or confected.

Language is how we make sense of the world and everything in it. Each subject, therefore, needs the nourishing humus of its own language – otherwise we can't learn or understand anything about that subject. Expanding the limits of your language will expand the horizons of your world, as Wittgenstein famously observed. Wine is no different in this respect from physics or philosophy. Those who say that all discussion of wine should be in 'plain English' are plain wrong. The results would be plain boring. We must do better than that.

Wine's problem is that humans have always been lazy about finding unique, specific words for what we smell and taste. If dogs could talk, no doubt they would have thousands of doggy words for smells of different sorts, just as we have a multitude of verbal options to describe what we see, via colours and shapes and sizes. As it is, nose-feeble humans relate particular smells and flavours to things that they remind us of. Wine made from the Cabernet Sauvignon grape variety to blackcurrants, for example; Sauvignon Blanc wines to grass or asparagus. Oaked Chardonnay to butter.

There's nothing wrong with this, provided it is sensitive, nuanced, accurate and innovative where necessary, and provided that these analogies are not allowed to take over the entire description, or dominate the wine lexicon. Too often, though, this is exactly what happens. Poor little wines get so laden down with descriptors that they can barely move, and totter off into the world like donkeys with wardrobes strapped onto their backs.

The use of specific flavour analogies is not the only way to talk about wines, and often these analogies are not even interesting or communicative. I did eventually learn to recognize fruitiness or butteriness or nuttiness in a wine, but for a year or two, those terms left me foxed. If I'm told a white wine has 'a compelling nose of enoki, toasted buckwheat, tangerine, guava and yuzu' with a flavour 'of lemon oil and pounded hazel, zest of lime with cherry kernel and apple core' I'm still bemused. It's more interesting to hear about the particular way in which a wine is a wine, about its energy, its personality, its structure, its context.

There are no rules for perfect communication about wines and, as in every field, skilled practitioners are rare. But everyone should be able to communicate something about a wine. Here are a few tips for happy and safe home wine-description.

Talk about specific aroma and flavour analogies if you like, but don't overdo them, and don't make them up out of desperation – or mischief. If none come to mind, don't stress. Some wines just taste of wine. (If this is the case, take a look at 'Behind Vinous Eyes' on page 89.)

Remember the wine, like you, has a body and a structure: how does it feel in your mouth when you first sip? When you hold it there for a while? What kind of texture can you find? How does the wine slide down your throat? Balance means the way the component parts (including acidity, flavour, texture and alcohol) mesh together, and the best wines are usually also the best balanced wines; take time to analyse that and describe that.

Finally, open your mind to the wider possibilities the wine suggests: not simply flavour analogies, but any telling metaphor drawn from your own experience. Wines could be like a landscape, like a building, like a piece of music, like a particular room in a house. Wines are as various as the people we know, and we have little difficulty describing our friends. Don't be afraid of being called pretentious: that's just a term humourless philistines use to compensate for their own imaginative inadequacies. Unleash your own mental resources. Respond. React. Be honest. The result will be a deeper understanding of wine – and still more fun as you drink it.

Through the Mangrove Swamp

What's the best way to taste wine? It's a simple question – but the answer is as tangled as the root system in a mangrove swamp.

Most tastings are sighted: you know a wine's origins as you assess it. With blind tasting, by contrast, those origins are concealed.

Or are they? Blind tastings are generally conducted by bracketing together some kind of peer group, so in part the wine's origin is known or intuited. (There are, in fact, many levels of half-sightedness in what is casually called 'blind' wine tasting. Scientific experimental standards for single-blind trials, let alone double-blind, are never met in the wine world.)

Most professional wine tastings involve assessment of 20 to 50 wines at a sitting, and sometimes more. Panels for *Decanter* magazine's World Wine Awards competition are given around 80 wines to assess every day. You sniff, you taste, you spit. No one drinks.

Alas. This is a necessary flaw in wine tasting. It means that every tasting note is a hypothesis. Drinking is the proof. Hypotheses aren't always correct.

No wine is ever fully and satisfactorily assessed until it has passed through the back of the mouth, down the oesophagus, and into the digestive system. Digestibility is as much a hallmark of fine wine as are beauty, intricacy and harmony. In the 'real' world, everyone drinks. No one tastes and spits.

Thirty years of reading wine assessments, as well as providing assessments of my own, have convinced me that tasting without drinking is a monstrous flaw in all wine criticism. I'd like to see critics append an asterisk to any numeric score or tasting note for a wine that has been drunk rather than merely assessed by tasting. Any critic who claims that they have never had to adjust, after drinking, an initial assessment based on tasting alone is lying.

If tasting alone is necessary, though, which is better: blind tasting or sighted tasting?

In theory, blind tasting is best. The less you know, the less your judgement will be clouded, and the freer you will be to speak your mind. You can concentrate on the naked wine itself. It's common for wine enthusiasts to serve their friends anonymous wines at dinner; discussions and guesses follow. It's often humiliating, but always instructive – though often the wrong lesson is drawn (this taster is inadequate) rather than the right one (why is this wine communicating its personality in this way?).

The problem with blind tasting is that even panels of skilled tasters don't always come up with the 'right' results. Wines whose showy charms prove ephemeral regularly triumph, in blind tastings, over quieter wines of enduring greatness.

Tasters are subjective; they are also fallible; there is never enough time. Not every tasting is run in an exemplary manner. Committee verdicts conflate the findings of the most cultured or experienced tasters in a panel with those of less seasoned peers. The amply experienced, by contrast, may find raw percipience blunted by the years. An extravagant scorer can swing a verdict against half a dozen cautious scorers. And it's still only tasting, not drinking.

I admire the frankness sanctioned by blind tasting, but sighted tasting has its merits, too. Yes, tasters can be influenced by label and reputation – yet reputation, after all, is the communal verdict of thousands of drinkers through history. Reputation, too, is always founded on drinking.

A courageous critic should call against reputation if he or she feels that renown is not justified by the evidence in the glass, but in a sighted tasting, the taster is aware of the implications of that decision. If you back a rank outsider with the highest score in the tasting, it's done knowingly: statement intended. You live with the consequences. In a blind tasting, the call is made unknowingly; that's different.

In truth, we need both sorts of tasting: they correct each other. Blind tasting scythes inflated reputations; sighted tasting furnishes benchmarks and builds cultural insight. Since assessment is always made after drinking, beyond the narrow confines of the wine profession, the wine market itself can be regarded as a kind of super-taster, winnowing the good from the better, and the best from the worse. Irrational exuberance on the part of critics or cults will, sooner or later, be found out. Overpriced wines don't sell.

Taste First, Then Look

No one seems quite sure when former Polish president Lech Wałęsa first said it, but this phrase later became one of his stock answers to difficult political questions: 'I am for, and even against' ('*Jestem za, a nawet przeciw*'). When I look at the alcohol level displayed on wine labels, I know exactly what he meant.

Consumers should be informed about what's in the bottle of wine they are about to drink. The alcohol level is obviously a useful piece of information, and vital for assessing personal intake accurately for practical reasons, and for its health implications.

From an aesthetic perspective, though, I regret the free availability of this information, the prominence with which it appears on front labels, and its growing ubiquity alongside all tasting notes. Why? Because it unduly influences tasting judgements. On occasion, indeed, it can damage tasting ability by kicking away sensual objectivity.

Worse still, the idea that a wine with an alcohol level of 14.5% or 15% might be intrinsically 'unbalanced' is now unthinkingly accepted by many. Producer neuroses about alcohol levels lead to a fetish for early harvesting. In some cases, this means that wines are robbed of the aromatic and flavour resonance, the flesh and the texture that they would otherwise possess had they been harvested at perfect maturity. That in turn steals the potential pleasure drinkers might otherwise have taken in a well-vinified wine. Knowing the alcohol level of a wine, in sum, leads to cognitive bias.

A cognitive bias is a deviation from rationality in judgement. These biases are manifold. It's hard to exclude all cognitive biases from any judgement, but that's not a reason to abandon the effort. Knowing that a particular wine contains 14.5% or 15% alcohol may exert a disproportionate effect on the way in which you taste that wine. The figure itself may prompt you to find such a wine 'over-alcoholic'. Given the option, I always ask not to be given this information as I taste. If it's there, I do my best to ignore it until I have reached a verdict on the wine.

Tasters, remember, are surrogate drinkers; they are looking to find and to assess drinking pleasure. What matters is what is tasted, not what is known. If knowing a particular fact will vitiate your tasting pleasure (and we are now getting to the stage where sight of '15%' on a label will do just that for many), then it is better not to know. If you don't know, you'll taste the wine more justly.

I realize that this will seem incendiary to some, so let me quickly list some of the things I am not suggesting.

I'm not suggesting that all information about wines has a negative effect on tasting ability. On the contrary, knowledge about origin is vital, since there is no single aesthetic ideal for wine. Beauty in wine is predicated on origin. (It is not predicated on alcohol.)

I'm not suggesting that balance in wine is an irrelevant or over-rated virtue. It is both desirable in its own right, and the basis of drinkability: a defining quality of both good wine and fine wine. I'm simply suggesting that alcohol is a less prominent element in balance than it is modishly made out to be.

I'm not suggesting that 'unbalanced' wines do not exist. They do indeed exist, for a multitude of reasons. Early picked, under-ripe wines can also be unbalanced; so, too, can over-oaked or over-ripe wines. But you can't tell that a wine is over-ripe by looking at its alcohol level. You can only tell if a wine is over-ripe by tasting it and drinking it, and that is best done by first removing the potential for cognitive bias.

I'm not suggesting that 'early picking' is always an error. The perfect picking date is always a question of judgement, of winemaking aesthetics; it cannot be decided by the figures alone. Fashion swings to and fro, and it's true that the 21st century opened with a fashion for ultra-ripe wines that has now abated. To race for the opposite extreme amid rapidly warming global temperatures, though, is to court disaster: hard, rigid, inarticulate wines whose only appeal is intellectual, not sensual.

The grossest error is to assume or assert that wines cannot be balanced at 15%, 15.5% or 16% – or at whatever strength the yeasts finally abandon their fermentative quest and die. Balance is a function of the sum of

72   TASTE AND TASTING

constituents in a wine and the manner in which they are disposed within that wine. Together, they form a complex equation; to focus on alcohol alone is reductive. Wines deserve better of their drinkers.

Tonic Bitterness

Unpleasantly sour and bitter: that's how debutant drinkers find their first glass of red wine. Since most of us come to wine via soft drinks and fruit juices, we're used to acidity: the strangeness of red wine is that it's delivered without any balancing sweetness. Semi-sweet wines provide an access route, and it's not long before we come to appreciate 'dry' acidity, especially with food.

Bitterness is more intriguing. In evolutionary terms, we have only recently ceased being hunter-gathering omnivores, and bitter flavours were a warning signal that plants or animal parts might contain toxins. A sensitivity to the bitterness of the anti-thyroid drug propylthiouracil or PROP was identified (by psychologist Linda Bartoshuk in 1991) as the key test for distinguishing so-called 'supertasters' from the rest of the population; such individuals are also said to find the taste of cabbage or broccoli unpleasantly bitter. They would struggle to like red wine. But, out in the primeval forests, they might have survived long enough to reproduce.

The science of taste sensitivity has moved on since 1991, and differing sensitivities to other substances including salt, citric acid, quinine and sucrose suggest that 'supertasting' is a complex picture. It's not necessarily a wine-tasting advantage, by the way, since it may simply result in extreme pickiness.

What interests me, though, is the ability to override such sensitivities. PROP does taste bitter to me, given the standard test – yet I was a strange child who, when asked by indulgent strangers what my favourite food was, used to reply 'Savoy cabbage' (it helped that my mother never overcooked it). I drink copious quantities of black and green tea daily; I adore intensely hopped bitter ales and 'peppery' olive oil. A *ristretto*, in Italy, is a treat.

Tastes can be acquired. Indeed the ubiquity with which coffee, beer and bitter–sweet aperitifs and cocktails (think of Campari – or gin and tonic) are enjoyed around the world suggests that modern humans relish 'dangerous' bitter flavours. It's a kind of cultural appurtenance.

Those flavours might also, paradoxically, do us good. 'Tonic' water (note the name) contains quinine, an anti-malarial, and at least some of the bitterness of tea and of wine derives from the tannins present in the leaves and stalks of *Camellia sinensis* and the fruit skins and stems of *Vitis vinifera*. Plants produce tannins to dissuade predators from destroying them, so they are meant to taste unpleasant. But studies have shown that tannins can be anti-carcinogenic and are a useful antioxidant, as well as having the ability to accelerate blood clotting, reduce blood pressure and reduce serum lipid levels. They also have preservative, anti-microbial properties – which might be why they found their way into grape skins. (Nature intended grapes to be eaten by birds, who don't taste much anyway: parrots have just 400 tastebuds, whereas humans have 9,000 or more.)

My contention, then, is that wine-drinkers come to understand that bitter flavours in wine are in some sense tonic, since they are associated with some of the health-bringing substances that wine, and particularly red wine, contains.

'Bitter', though, is a wildly unsatisfying term in wine-tasting terminology (as is 'acid'): it is descriptive only in the most primitive sense. Any kind of extraneous or 'chemical' bitterness in wine is indeed repellent. This, though, has nothing to do with the rich, affirmative bitterness that is such a feature not merely of tannic red wines such as Barolo and Barbaresco, Bordeaux, Madiran, Bandol, Napa Cabernet, Lebanese Beka'a Valley red wines and others, but also of less tannic red wines whose distinctive flavour profile includes a bitter component – such as most red wines from the Veneto, and red wines from the Languedoc, too (that herbal '*garrigue*' note, careful tasters will note, is a distinctively nuanced bitterness). What matters is that the bitter flavours themselves should be saturated with and informed by other flavours – not naked and uncovered. The same thing applies to acidity in wine, which is why additions are usually a mistake. Richness is all.

Tannin and the University of the Vat

All wines, until you open them and begin to drink, are enigmatic: perhaps that's a part of their attraction. This is even true of wines you know well, purchased in case quantities. The next bottle will be a little different from the last bottle, and not just because of a subtle modulation in its maturity; weather conditions, the turning seasons, even your own mood and health at the time of drinking can affect the way a wine takes you. As time goes by, moreover, your own tastes evolve. I am not the same drinker I once was – or will be.

One quality in red wine that I value more than ever before is tannin – though I appreciate that this bald statement may mislead. So let me put it differently. When I drink red wines, I tend to look for a sense of gravity, of density, of ballast. When I find it, I think of the wine in question as a 'serious red' – and the best serious reds can be profound. They travel a little way beyond straightforward expectations, in other words; they seem to suggest some greater emotional truth about the world and our perception of its beauty in an argument that begins not with words or ideas, but with flavours and textures. They catch, linger and loiter in mouth and mind. Memory, imagination, empathy: the ripples spread.

Tannin is a key element of this gravity, this ballast, this profundity. The scientifically minded should probably look away at this point, but I've often thought that the personality and 'intellect' of almost all red grape varieties lies in their skins and their pips. Parting a new red wine from its skins and pips too soon is like forcing a child to leave the education system prematurely. The wine may be intact – but it could have learned so much more via an unhurried exchange with those tutorial skins (the grape's interface with the world) and those inspirational pips (nursing their reproductive message). That leaching, exchanging and soaking process in the university of the vat seems to bring culture and depth to a red wine. This is as true of transparent reds like burgundy and Barolo as it is of darker, more obviously 'extractive' wines like Bordeaux or Brunello di Montalcino.

I'm astonished, too, at how much progress winemakers have made over my career in terms of tannin expression. I can still remember a little of what the Bordeaux 1975s were like in their youth. Brutal and stalky – but that was the paradigm for most palpable tannin presences back then, even from regions like Rioja or the Southern Rhône. The sumptuous iridescence of tannin structures in contemporary Bordeaux wasn't even a distant dream; it was inconceivable.

What's changed? Carefully grown, fully ripened, minutely sorted grapes mean near-perfect skins and pips to begin with. The grapes can enjoy a cold soak, are on the receiving end of a kind of extended massage rather than any violence of extraction, and are given as much time as they need to macerate before gravity parts liquid from solid. Then comes further rest and recuperation in contact with the lees, and without manic racking. The result is wonderfully, alluringly corporeal. Tannins, extracted in this way, cascade and caress rather than seeming dry or Velcro-like, and have finely accommodated astringency and bitterness, perhaps because their bond with the fruit is so intimate. They are, in themselves, fleshy – and flavoury. Their flavour spectrum (mineral–vegetal) makes them a perfect foil to the fruit.

Quickly extracted, water-soluble skin tannins, according to Dr Paul Smith of the Australian Wine Research Institute, are very different from slowly extracted, alcohol-soluble seed tannins. Smith also points out that wine tannin itself is a different thing from the grape tannins extracted from skins and pips. What happens is an orgy of rearrangement and recombination of these chemically highly unstable compounds once they have been extracted, and as they 'head off down a merry path of polymerization'. Most wine tannin, in other words, is not grape extract, but a new product altogether. Smith also points out that the fibre in grape residues has a kind of fining effect on tannins – which is why very long macerations may in fact result in wines with a less palpable (or softer) tannic presences than those with medium-length macerations. Longer extraction, too, draws out polysaccharides, which may also soften the perception of astringency.

One question, though, continues to trouble me: why do the world's most significantly and palpably tannic red wines tend to be European? Napa is an exception – but Napa's prodigious tannins are soft, and all but disappear into the valley's succulently amiable fruit. Argentina's Mendoza can occasionally be an exception too: beef served rare solicits textured wine as a partner. Those regions aside, though, it is hard to find a wealth of palpable, fleshy, structuring, skin-and-pip tannin in non-European red wines (though these Southern Hemisphere or North American wines often exhibit 'powdery' oak tannins or added tannins).

Is this nature's doing? Is there something about European high latitudes, often cloudy climates and preponderantly limey soils that more readily generates tannin formation of this sort? Or is it cultural: a dislike, mistrust or fear of the taste and texture of ample tannic presences in local wine markets outside Europe, and an acceptance of them in Europe? Will it always be so, or will it change? I don't know.

Yeast: Call Me Dad

I've always been a moral relativist. As time goes by, I seem to be becoming a vinous relativist, too. There are some wine questions that just don't have a wrong or right answer. Such as those we ask about yeast, for example.

It's impossible, when you sniff and taste a wine, to separate out those aromas and flavours that are derived in some way from yeast strains and fermentation from those that relate to variety, season and site. They are, in other words, much more than merely 'yeasty', but colour, shape and mould the entire sensual presence of the wine. This (though no one ever mentions it) is the biggest of all obstacles to the clear identification of terroir presence in wine.

Yeast's invisibility to the naked eye seems regrettable, since it makes us wildly underestimate the significance of these microorganisms. Harvested grapes mother wine – but yeast is wine's father. Wine only comes into being when the two (metaphorically speaking) copulate with one another. Grape juice from any vineyard at all is a preposterously simpler drink than the wine that results from fermentation. We cannot take yeast seriously enough.

Most of us know that *Saccharomyces cerevisiae* is the principal wine yeast – and beer yeast and bread yeast. Few micro-organisms are more benignly significant to humankind. Its DNA has been found in 5,000-year-old wine jars.

For wine, though, *Saccharomyces cerevisiae* is only a small part of the story. It's not airborne, for a start, nor is it present in more than tiny quantities on grape skins; it is rarely important in initiating fermentation. Once active, though, it behaves like a kind of cuckoo, outgrowing and evicting rival yeast strains. These tumble haplessly from the nest as the alcohol level rises.

One of the standard questions wine journalists like to ask wine producers is whether or not they allow 'wild' or 'indigenous' yeasts to accomplish fermentation as opposed to adding a cultured yeast strain. For the past two decades, I've assumed that the right answer is 'yes'. Why? Because yeasts are everywhere: in the air, on fruits, on flowers, on objects, in the soil, in your guts, between your toes. Yeast populations in different locations, though, are never identical. Indigenous yeast, therefore, has the potential to underscore the terroir character of a wine. If it's part of the place, indeed, it might properly be construed as an intrinsic element of any wine terroir, given that yeast is wine's father.

Cynics often counter that indigenous yeast is principally cultured yeast that has 'gone native'. Not so. In an influential 2009 paper, the New Zealand-based researcher Matthew Goddard and colleagues showed that the strains of *Saccharomyces cerevisiae* in spontaneous ferments in nine locations in New Zealand had been vectored by local insects, as well as by isolates from imported French barrels. Research by the Burgundy-based researcher Raphaëlle Tourdot-Maréchal showed that commercial yeast strains can be discerned in cellars in the year following a vintage in only one in 12 cases. Most of the time, the yeast population begins anew each year. That population may even shape vintage character.

The biggest argument against the use of indigenous yeast is that it can be tardy or ineffective. This fermentative languor then allows strains like Brettanomyces/Dekkera free rein (*see* 'Journey Into Forbidden Territory' below).

78   TASTE AND TASTING

Indigenous fermentations certainly need a beady supervisory eye; they entail more risk than cultured yeast fermentations. It seems, too, to be harder to use indigenous yeast away from established wine regions, or in isolated locations.

The aesthetic profile of some varieties, moreover, solicits indigenous fermentation more readily than others. Most ambitious Australian Chardonnays are indigenously fermented today, complexity being their desideratum. Most Australian Riesling, by contrast, is still fermented using cultured yeast, in the name of fruit purity. If you want varietal character in a Sauvignon Blanc wine, use selected yeasts; if you want to mute that character in a Sauvignon Blanc wine, use indigenous yeasts.

Or not – since there have also been huge advances in the range and artfulness of cultured yeasts, of which there are well over 250 on the market. Many now use a number of different yeast strains in addition to *Saccharomyces cerevisiae*, mimicking the complex 'crowd fermentation' of an indigenous yeast population. Painstaking wine producers (such as Brian Croser of Tapanappa) have for many years created their own yeast selections. All cultured yeasts, in any case, begin life as 'indigenous', just as every clone was once plucked from a massal selection.

Perhaps we invent these dichotomies to amuse ourselves. Remember what matters: yeast is Dad.

Journey into Forbidden Territory

In 2015, I took part in a blind tasting of some leading Napa and Australian Cabernets. One of the wines to which I (and the two other tasters) gave a lowly rather than an outstanding score to was the 2008 Cain Five. I'd regularly been in touch over the past few years with Chris Howell, who makes this wine. He's a deep wine thinker, as well as being someone who understands the terroir of the valley as few do. I thought my score might upset Chris, so I dropped him a line to warn him in advance.

'Not to worry,' he wrote cheerfully back. All three tasters had queried the wine's aromas, and one felt that the wine might be reduced. 'Cain wines run reduced (by intention) and fermentation by *Brettanomyces* yeasts is not only tolerated but encouraged in the Cain Five. These two factors alone would set any tasting panel off. Should you sometime wish to explore how someone you've known could venture into what is for modern winemaking "forbidden territory", or if you just want to know my reflections on wine tasting, I am here for you.'

This was an invitation I wasn't going to decline, so over late summer 2015 we corresponded. He mentioned some of the wines that had most influenced him, such as the 1964 Clos des Lambrays (red burgundy) and the 1978 Château Rayas (Châteauneuf-du-Pape). 'What they all seem to have in common is complexity, nuance, intrigue and of course a balanced and flowing palate with a lengthy finish. What they also have in common is that they don't play by the rules of modern oenology. Is this negative attribute – the failure to conform – the cause of the attributes that interest me?' This was the question that had led him to try to weigh up the role of 'wine flaws' for himself. 'Some, such as TCA, are intolerable and simply cannot be debated. But others, such as volatile acidity, might be subject of discussion and enquiry. It may not be a matter of degree, but of character and how it inflects the wine. Also a matter of context – and of wine culture. So it is with oxidation, reduction and mercaptans. Also certain lactic aromas, such as diacetyl.'

And brett? 'Brett in itself is not the flaw – rather it is the experience of the aromas of certain molecules that can be produced by brett that we do not like. Brett is an agent, not the outcome. And the agent should not be confused with the outcome, of which many are possible.' Wines with some brett needn't invoke horse blankets and sticking plasters, according to Howell; you might find roses and jasmine, toasted hazelnuts and truffles.

Craft brewers would support the Howell thesis. Brett is a vital component of certain indigenous Belgian beer styles (such as Lambic and Gueuze), just as sulphury notes are sought-after in pale ales based on the Burton-upon-Trent ideal (where it could be said to be a terroir note, since the town's brewing water filters up through gypsum beds that leave it sulphur-rich). Dimethyl sulphide is welcome in much-enjoyed British lager styles. If these notes are loved in beer, why should they be loathed in wine?

The correspondence left me wanting to give the 2008 Cain Five a second chance, but a second chance under different circumstances from the first. Well away, in other words, from the sensitivities and neuroses of the wine community, and away from the artificiality of the tasting bench.

The best palates among all my non-wine friends belong, without question, to a British couple called Stuart Tunstall and Zo Pacuła; I've known them for 35 years. I love dining with them, in part since Zo cooks so well, but in part since we can discuss the wines I bring along in a manner entirely free from all vinous political correctness. They don't know the debates, the fashions, the postures, the trends, the label and vintage reputations; they just like to eat and drink, and then talk frankly about what we've just eaten and drunk. So when staying with them back in September, I served the 2008 Cain Five in an unmarked decanter alongside another decanter containing Christian Moueix's 2009 Napanook. I chose the latter wine as a point of comparison since I know that Christian Moueix values 'complexity, nuance, intrigue and of course a balanced and flowing palate with a lengthy finish' as much as Chris Howell does. I told Stuart and Zo that these were two California reds. Nothing more.

The results were striking. They both immediately warmed to the Cain Five. 'It reminds me of claret,' said Stuart. 'It's a quality wine that is structured and elegant, and dry in the mouth. It's holding itself together very well. It's not overvoluptuous. It's not allowing the sweetness to take control. It's really fine-tuned, and not a formula. It's got the kind of complexity you find in the great French wines. What else can you ask for? I normally avoid American wines as I hate vanilla and find a lot of them infantile, but this is very subtle and understated.' Zo loved the nose: 'It's refreshing. I want to get into it.' She liked its faint bitterness, and found it herby, 'like Languedoc wines'. The Napanook (a cheaper wine, it should be said, than the Cain Five) they liked less because it was indeed sweeter; they said it had fewer notes, was probably younger, lacked the bitterness they sought despite having a little more tannin, and was 'less austere'. 'It didn't have the adjectives,' summarized Stuart. It was, nonetheless, liked, and lost some of its sweetness, as well as acquiring more structure, as it nuzzled up comfortably to Gower Peninsula salt-marsh lamb from Wales.

The notion that the Cain Five might be 'faulty' in any way never crossed any of our minds, mine included, and I could find no notes in it that resembled anything I associate with brett. To me on this occasion it smelled of blood (the scent of blood as it leaches from raw beef or game) and clay (a slabby, low-humus, wettish earthiness). Nor was the palate in any way forceful, but rather subtle, complex, quiet and undemonstrative. There was some fruit here, hovering in the background; the wine was settled, soft and un-throbbing.

Yet I'd given this secondary and satisfying food wine a dusty note and score in the original blind tasting. I could see how this had happened – surrounded by wines whose high-quality assets were flamboyant and showy. Asking the Cain Five to come through under those circumstances is rather like asking a marathon runner to win a wrestling bout. The standard objection to blind tasting is that certain wines work in such a different manner to the majority of their peers that the drinker needs the cultural signature of the label to appreciate them at all. It's a strong objection. Blind tastings also prejudice wines (like this) that perform better at table than in isolation on the tasting bench.

A quick skim through some of the critical scores for this wine threw up a couple of 88s and a 15.5. When I outlined the various scoring systems to Stuart and Zo, they were both emphatic that this much-enjoyed wine deserved over 90 points, though they found the scoring concept faintly risible.

Lessons? Get out of the wine ghetto. Taste for drinkers, not tasters. Cherish those who walk a lonely path.

Freshness Young and Old

There's no equivocating over freshness. Everyone loves the bustling, sparkling, well-washed qualities implied by the word; we're all seduced by the youth and novelty it implies, and its association with the year's first season. What, though, might it mean when applied to wine?

You could argue that a 'fresh' wine is the positive antonym of an oxidized one, since oxidation implies flatness and tiredness. You might also argue that freshness is synonymous with youthfulness in wine, though here the ground is a little shakier. Young wines should be fresh, but they don't have a monopoly on freshness. It's perfectly possible, and indeed desirable, that an old wine might retain some freshness. That's what stops it tumbling into the tomb.

Nonetheless if you want to go looking for 'freshness' in wine, it's best to start with something young. Germany would be one source: a new-minted Kabinett from the cool, sharp-angled vineyards of the Saar or the Ruwer. Another would be Muscadet, no sooner dragged off its yeast into bottle than unbottled, and pitched up against an oyster or two. Further uncomplicated classics serve the same purpose: Picpoul du Pinet, Sancerre, Chablis, dry Minho or Galician whites, the latest Verdicchio or Fiano. Australian Rieslings and New Zealand Sauvignons jostle in the same frame. When it comes to red wines, a Beaujolais Cru wine from the most recently bottled vintage, seething with fruited vivacity, should be freshness incarnate.

Acidity, you might assume from the above list, is a key to freshness. Indeed; though I would qualify the noun with the adjective 'juicy'. Freshness in wine really comes into its own when youthful acidity is intimately bonded with primary fruit, hence juicy; the acid-fruit bond is the key to freshness, not acidity alone.

What happens as the wine ages? Nothing stands still, though at first there is simply a settling of all the elements, as the wine finds its early harmony and equilibrium. That's desirable – but you might say that it comes at the expense of a little freshness (the hurly-burly of extreme youthfulness). As more time passes, the fruit flavours begin their long journey towards quietness and understatement, towards presence without overt contour. In good or great wines, that gentle metamorphosis of fruit will draw the acids seamlessly along with it, and it is during this process that your sensory apparatus will tell you how many different forms, shapes and personalities of acidity lie hidden within the fruit. In less successful wines, the fruit will simply begin to fade, and the acidity part company with the fruit: adieu freshness.

What I've learned from the most subtle and undogmatic palates is that to assume that freshness depends on acidity alone is a grave mistake. It's better seen as a tension in wine, a tension that is scattered through the wine most disarmingly in youth, when it is most juicily fruit-clad, but which can endure in wine thanks to a number of factors and incarnations beyond acidity alone.

Notes from the bitter spectrum of flavours are what bring that sort of tension to olive oil, for example – a product where quality is associated with low acidity, not high. Bitterness can freshen wines, too. Skin tannins bring freshness to red wines; and the single reason advanced time and time again by winemakers who have chosen to use a percentage of stems in their red-winemaking is, once again, 'freshness'. I remember being shocked at first, and later enlightened, to see how freshness in Condrieu is more closely associated with what local growers call 'mineral' flavours (non-fruity, faintly textured) than with its often low acid levels. I've also noticed repeatedly how the very gentle acid balances in the rosé wines of Provence contrive to suggest freshness and delicacy better than rosé wines made elsewhere, in places where it's wrongly assumed that freshness depends on a more prominent acid balance. Acid rosé, indeed, is hard and unfresh, since there is rarely enough juicy fruit to match it in a wine style whose very ideal is built on discretion and understatement.

Freshness is lovely. Like everything else in wine, it's complex, too.

84   TASTE AND TASTING

Old, Big and Quiet

Oak, particularly new French oak, is the most expensive container you can choose in which to age your new wines. We've all damned wines for being over-oaked. 'This wine needs more oak,' by contrast, is a comment I've never heard from anyone. The imbalance is striking. Is all that money being wasted?

Not necessarily. Successful oaking, most of us would agree, is when oak fills out, supports and amplifies a wine to seamless and impalpable effect. Since oak (and especially new oak) carries an overt and easily recognizable sensorial print, pointing your finger – or your tongue – at any perceived excess is a straightforward matter. Indeed, together with spotting TCA in a 'corked' wine, it might even be the easiest comment of all to make about a wine. Tastes vary in this respect, though; my over-oaked wine may taste just right to you (or vice versa).

Working out that a wine is 'under-oaked', by contrast, is no easy matter. If I feel dissatisfied with such a wine, I will probably complain about something else altogether. An aggressive flavour profile, perhaps; the stinkiness of reduction; or an overall lack of harmony and equilibrium. It's an impressive feat to imagine such a wine with another eight months in oak, or with 70 percent rather than 20 percent new oak, or with 10 months in second-use oak rather than in concrete tanks. Extra time in oak, remember, may actually lessen rather than intensify the perceived 'oakiness' of a wine, just as extra post-fermentation maceration can soften tannic grip. The degree of toasting of the staves is another variable with huge sensorial significance; and the number of rackings is a third important decision.

'Oak', in fact, is about much more than 'oakiness'. What the Riojans call 'noble oxidation' is at least as important as any kind of flavour enhancement, and there is no other container that can readily duplicate the oxidative effects of barrels and three-monthly rackings for young, dense, vital red wine. (Wood is porous, and barrels are a kind of three-dimensional jigsaw puzzle.) The nourishing, fattening relationship between wines – even red wines – and their maternal lees, too, has never been more important than it is today, and small oak barrels permit a much higher contact ratio with lees than alternative containers. If we say wines are 'over-oaked', of course, we are normally referring to the flavour print rather than any oxidative fatigue, or some misjudgement concerning lees contact.

All of that said, there is no doubt that new oak is less widely used in the fine wine world today than at the turn of the century. Peter Sisseck's journey with Pingus from '200% new oak' for some parcels to no new oak at all for his 2008 vintage was a typical early 21st-century journey for the fine-wine avant-garde; the story has grown more common since.

Every Bordeaux château uses less oak than it once did. Malolactic fermentation in barrique is no longer the dogma of the day. You'll barely see a new cask during a visit to Chablis, while any overt oakiness is almost a badge of shame for the avant-garde in Australia's Victoria (though less so in South Australia and New Zealand). Châteauneuf-du-Pape and Bandol both flirted with small oak and new oak in the face of tradition a decade ago, but both have backed briskly away since. Much the same is true of Tuscany and Piedmont; this switch is overdue in Languedoc. The makers of large or very large oak vessels (*botte* in Italian and *foudres* in French), by contrast, have bulging order-books. Concrete eggs and earthenware jars and amphorae are increasingly common.

Honestly, I'm thrilled. Subtlety, savouriness, textural grace and a widening of the general allusive range are all benefits of reduced new-oak or reduced high-toast usage, and the crushing totalitarianism of new oak as it stomped all over wines to which it was never innately suited (notably reds based on Grenache, Mourvèdre, Nebbiolo or Sangiovese) is now rare.

That doesn't mean, of course, that wood has no role; we just need to conceive that role differently. 'Noble oxidation' may in fact be the most important contribution any container can make to a developing, ripening wine. Wooden vessels accomplish this well – if old, big and quiet.

The School of Hard Wines

How about this for an axiom: 'There are no great hard wines.' Can you disprove it?

Mature wines, for example, are loved by many; a great mature bottle often serves as inspiration and model for a lifetime's drinking and collecting. What is successful maturity in a fine wine other than a softening and mellowing of the gathered forces of youth? This may come at the cost of some allusive detail; but the loveliness of that harmony more than compensates. A time-softened wine swims, gently and resonantly, over the tongue and melts into the throat, the stomach, the body. Unsuccessful maturation, by contrast, often reveals not softness but hardness, notably as the wine's acid components assume a disproportionate significance within the overall structure of the wine.

Acidity is one of the three main sources of hardness in wines. Aggressive oak is another, in both textural and flavour terms; and the third is dry, biting tannins, especially common if those tannins have been added or result from excessive oak, or if the crop has been handled brutally. Alcohol, since its intrinsic flavour seems to us slightly sweet and its texture glycerous, might be considered a softening element in wine. Even alcohol, though, can seem 'hot' and hard – if anything jolts it away from the wine's other elements, as both acidification and aggressive oaking can do.

A prime cause of hardness is coarse fruit handling or misjudged red wine extraction during fermentation. Both oxidation and its reduction can be sources of hardness, too, as well as endangering freshness and disfiguring wines with unattractive aromas: these are mishaps of vinification, ageing and bottling. Other causes of hardness include chemical adjustments of all sorts and the use of unripe grapes. Some grape varieties seem to flirt with hardness of flavour more than others (Savagnin, Carignan). An unexpected hardness, though, may suggest that a grape variety has been planted in the wrong place.

Structural wealth and density of flavour, though, need not (indeed should not) equate with hardness, even in youth. Great examples of those mellow, mature wines I referred to above would include the best red Bordeaux and the best Vintage port. Both begin life with extraordinary density of flavour and structure; both finish, 30 or 40 years later, in beguiling silkiness. The fruit is the fulcrum through which all the other elements must pass: if both acidity and tannins are rounded, succulent and fruit-bonded, such wines will not even be hard in youth – though they may be so energetic and forceful as to be indigestible at that stage. The fruit, too, must have the upper hand over both oak and alcohol, not vice versa: a fulcrum once again.

What about crisp white wines like young Chablis, for example, pungent Sauvignon Blanc, or crunchy young dry Riesling? Great examples of even these wines will never be hard or unyielding. Crispness and crunchiness generally mean youthful, mouth-watering and exuberant acidity working in combination once again with fruit flavours, and sometimes, too, with the non-fruit flavours we call 'mineral'. Hardness would mean there wasn't enough fruit density to support that acidity – or that the acidity came from unripeness... or as an addition.

All this came to mind after a month spent judging wines. The more you judge, the more sensitive you become to hardness – and it's a particular shame when excessive oaking is the cause, since it would be so easy (and economical) to avoid. Yet I can't say 'the softer, the better' either. Some categories are naturally super-soft and in these cases a lack of vitality is the pitfall to avoid; well-judged grape-skin tannins and juicy, natural acidity can be great allies. As always in the wine world, the overall aroma and flavour ensemble is what counts.

Behind Vinous Eyes

I used the word 'vinosity' in a text about white Châteauneuf-du-Pape. One of *Decanter*'s Chinese translators, Sylvia Wu, queried the word with me. She'd looked it up, and it seemed to mean 'wine-like'. Was I saying that a wine was wine-like? If so, was it worth saying?

I set off into the dictionaries, including my micrographic edition of the complete *Oxford English Dictionary*. Sylvia was right. Usage reveals some delicious metaphorical resonances – like Thackeray's '*Winking at his cousin with a pair of vinous eyes*' or Meredith's '*He determined to overbear his cousin vinously*'. The word's plain meaning, however, goes no further than 'Of the nature of wine; having the qualities of wine; tasting or smelling like wine; made of, or prepared with, wine' (though I note this entry in the *OED* hasn't been updated since 1917).

To me, however, 'vinous' is a precious tasting term, and a distinctive quality of certain wines only. I'll attempt to describe what I mean by it below. First, though, I decided to ask two of my friends (educator and author of *Essential Winetasting*, Michael Schuster, and collector and connoisseur Frank Ward) for their thoughts on this sometimes vexing term.

Frank Ward cited Alexis Lichine, who said that vinosity was 'The essential quality or heart of a wine'. Ward defined a vinous wine as one that contains 'noticeable alcohol … giving energy, flow, warmth'. Michael Schuster, too, suggested alcohol was important in this 'positive, complimentary character': 'A mouth-filling quality from a certain weight of alcohol, but supported by a distinct richness and tenacity of flavour. Powerful, without necessarily being strong or forceful. Indeed any "fierce" characteristics detract from the sensuous pleasure of vinosity.'

Both pointed out that great, delicate Rieslings (at 7% or 8% abv) seem to have no vinosity, but that vinosity also goes missing in the case of what

Frank Ward called 'potent, inebriating, spirity' wines of 15% or more. 'A vinous wine,' he summarized, 'is so constituted that its bouquet and flavour, with concentrated fruit at the core, are very much to the fore while the alcohol (like the bloodstream in humans) is present implicitly rather than explicitly, its role being to provide unifying energy and flow, a sense of warmth without hotness.'

Where have we got to? The 'wine-like' definition is beginning to look inadequate, since alcoholically light or over-burdened wines do not possess vinosity; could it be defined, therefore, as a seamless alcoholic equilibrium in a wine of middling strength?

It's important not to lose sight of the fact that 'vinous' is definitely a fermentative character; no fruit juice, for example, is ever vinous, and it is this fermentative character that the standard 'wine-like' definition alludes to. It's a kind of flavour development, a complexity in place of simplicity, which we have no other term for. Yet many wines, even in the middle range of alcoholic strengths, do not seem noticeably vinous to me. In other words, they seem to lack what I would call sinew or sap, pull and drive, line and length: all 'vinous' qualities.

A wealth of primary fruit, notably, seems to obscure any sense of vinosity in a wine. Intensely fruity wines are not vinous. Nor is it the first word that would come to mind in the case of an extravagantly sweet wine; an oaky wine; or a tannic, extractive wine. Vinosity is likewise missing in wines made from prematurely picked fruit; indeed part of the definition of 'perfect ripeness', I'd suggest, would be to deliver a sense of vinosity to the finished wine.

'Vinous' is a term I'd use more often about a white wine than a red; more often about a light or medium-bodied red wine than about a deep red wine; and more often about a mature red wine than a young red wine (though young white wines can certainly be vinous). In other words, any kind of flavoury loudness or 'noise' in a wine – what Schuster called fierce characteristics – will obscure such vinosity as that wine might possess.

The term is of value not least because vinous wines seem to me to be eminently gastronomic and digestible. Michael Schuster felt it was 'best exemplified by fine Grand Cru burgundy, white or red,' and to me it's a quality particularly associated with successful white burgundy, and with good red burgundy at maturity. It's a quality, in other words, that any global producer of Chardonnay or Pinot should give a little thought to trying to achieve or express – though it's also a quality potentially open to almost any serious, well-constituted wine from almost any variety at some stage of its life. (I don't feel there is necessarily an upper alcohol limit for a vinous wine, though a very fruity wine in which alcohol was not palpable would not be vinous.)

My finishing definition, then, is that vinosity is 'a quality of seamless alcoholic warmth and palpable fermentative complexity in a wine of harmonious, balanced character'. This definition, though, still seems a little cumbersome. If you can do better, I'd love to hear from you.

Wine Versus Food

Is there some fundamental difference between the flavours of wine and those of food? This question has long nagged me. If there isn't, why does wine have such a hold over us? Why do fine wines sell at the prices they do? Why are there wine auctions, wine libraries, wine tastings and wine cellars? Why, indeed, do wine magazines exist? There's no equivalent for fish, meat or vegetables, though these items are no less diverse and are still more widely consumed than wine.

Alcohol is an answer. Other alcoholic beverages, though, don't command equivalent attention, even if whisky comes close. We return to flavour (and remember that this also means aroma: a continuum, perceived in different ways).

Food flavours are often simple: think of celery, cucumber or lettuce. Foods, though, have an overwhelming textural presence that is absent from wine. Those textures distract – and gratify in themselves, since ingesting mass and substance is a vital part of sustenance. If you eat a bowl of pasta with tomato sauce after a long day's walking, as much of your pleasure will derive from chewing and swallowing this familiar and trusted food as it will from the taste of the dish itself. The joy of a buttered crumpet, a freshly baked croissant or a slice of pavlova is at least in part textural.

We're particularly fond of fatty foods and sweet foods – but not because of their flavours as such. It's because our bodies recognize that they are calorifically dense. A little of each would, in the prehistoric past, have got us a long way across the savannah, and much further than another handful of tough roots.

There are a number of reasons why we cook food. Safety is one of them, and digestibility another: the heat involved in cooking both kills bacteria and breaks down the indigestible tissues of many raw food items. Just as important to modern humans, though, is that in assembling and transforming raw ingredients, we can create flavours of greater complexity than those which the ingredients possessed on their own. Eating different foods together achieves the same end. Hence the popularity of 'recipes'. They're routes to complexity of flavour: that which satisfies as well as gratifies.

Good or fine wine has the hold it does over us, I'd suggest, because it offers the most complex single-item flavour package we can put into our mouths, rivalled only (if at all) by a great chef's work on a sauce or a composed dish. Wine's complexity replicates and even exceeds that delivered by cooked foods... and it brings us the mood enhancement of alcohol as it does so. This is why great wine may be best partnered by simple food – to avoid a 'clash of complexities'.

Where do these layers of flavour come from? Grapes, oddly enough, seem to be less complex in flavour than other fresh fruits like peaches or nectarines; indeed the sugar–acid balance in grape juice makes it seem almost insipid by comparison with orange juice or grapefruit juice. It's the transformation of grape juice into wine via fermentation, and the maceration of its skins, pips and sometimes stems in red winemaking, that increases its complexity to an unparalleled degree.

This is partly because it re-arranges the balance in grape juice: since sugars are converted to alcohol, acidity suddenly swings into prominence when grape juice becomes wine. But it's also because of the complex of flavours that emerge from the action of yeast itself, both as it is active in must and after it dies and sinks to the bottom of a fermentation vessel, together with the extraction of elements hidden in grape skins for red (and amber) wine. The way in which wines are made, and the vessels in which they are calmed and matured after fermentation, adds further layers of complexity, as does bottle ageing itself. The result, as all wine lovers know, is that a single sip of wine can speak to us, even sing to us. Wine truly seems to be more complex than almost everything else we eat and drink.

Palate Fitness

How fit is your palate? And how do you maintain and train it? In 30 years of wine labour, no one has ever asked me these questions. So I try to pose them to myself from time to time.

A few definitions, first of all. I'm not thinking about palate acuity, which obviously varies from individual to individual, and which certainly declines with age (though few care to admit it).

Maximum acuity comes at around 11 years old, but since most of us have had zero experience of wine at that point, these sensitivities only serve to make the choice between strawberry, pistachio and chocolate-chip ice-cream worth weeping over. Acuity needs to be correlated to experience; acquiring wine experience can't be hurried. Palate fitness means making the most of the innate acuity that you once had and have managed to retain.

Those who have accumulated most tasting experience don't necessarily have the fittest palates. It's uncommon now, but I remember a couple of decades back that colossal consumption on all fronts was considered the ideal, and expertise was naturally accorded to those of enormous girth, foul breath, dyspeptic eructations and drifting gaze, simply because they spent almost all their waking hours staggering between tastings and restaurant tables. The evident bodily cost constituted a set of campaign medals, and was borne with pride.

Experience in wine tasting is vital, since most of wine's interest is predicated on difference, but it is not acquired mathematically, by gross accumulation. It is, rather, the use you make of your experiences that counts. No one can taste every wine or even every wine style; there aren't enough hours in a lifetime, and in any case the wine universe never stops expanding. It's how your tasting faculties are wired to your brain that makes experience valuable – what you notice and remember, in other words, about what you taste. I've come to think that tasting wine with your experiences in the background rather than the foreground – 'innocent', expansive or appreciative tasting – is actually more useful than tasting against a wall of previous experiences, since that can often lead to reductive, exclusive or dismissive responses. Once again, palate fitness can help you make the most of your experience.

So how do you acquire and maintain a fit palate? I may not be a model but, for what it's worth, my informal and improvised palate-fitness programme has five strands:

Physical fitness. A human body is a whole; it's hard to have a fit palate in an unfit body. Cardiovascular fitness in particular seems to help palate fitness, and you can acquire that no matter what bodily type you have, by any sensible means that appeals to you – walking, running, cycling, swimming. Try to remedy environmental issues if you can. I suffered chest infections and nasal congestion when I lived in a cold, damp house in a cool, damp place. It was a hard fix, but my apparatus is now in better shape in a modern house in dryer air. Avoid blow-outs, of course; the palate is directly linked to the stomach, and both need to be happy and working well for peak synergy.

Dental health. It's sometimes painful and expensive, but there's no escaping this one: the dentist is the wine taster's friend (though dentists often fiercely disapprove of wine tasting). Don't go anywhere without sugar-free gum and toothpicks, and tooth-brushing gear for each day's beginning and end. Wine tasting happens in the mouth, so the cleaner and healthier the oral environment, the better the result. Healthy gums, too, make wine-tasting comfortable rather than painful.

Look after your tastebuds. A tongue scraper is a disconcerting utensil, and I find you can replicate its effect by dragging the tongue firmly over your own incisors and molars, but this activity is worthwhile – the tongue is a rough surface that hosts cities of bacteria, and clean is much better than filmy for wine tasting. Try to let very hot food or drinks cool a little, too, before allowing them to cauterize your ever-diminishing supply of buds.

Palate downtime. Solutions of ethanol, acid and sometimes tannin and sugar are aggressive; the palate needs a break. I've reluctantly come to recognize that my wine-tasting palate often seems to work better after a day or two away from wine (and other palate-aggressive substances). No one tastes well 'the morning after'. If you've been tasting wine all day, end it with the soothing rehydration of tea – or water.

Constant recalibration. Don't just taste wine; taste everything in exactly the same sort of way in which you taste wine. Smell the air, the flowers, the washing, your children's hair. Taste different teas, coffees, sauces or soups as if they were wine. Take a break from wine, but never switch your palate off; exercise slows the loss of every faculty. Wine is a part of the broader sensual world, and is best seen, described, enjoyed, understood and celebrated in that way.

96   TASTE AND TASTING

CHAPTER FOUR

SOME BEAUTIFUL WINES

Jewelled Absence:

2016 Petit Chablis, Les Crioux, William Fèvre

Here's a shock, in a glass. A step out on deck in a winter gale; a leap into chill water.

Once acclimatized, of course, the affront is tonic; you're glad you risked all. Provocation becomes stimulation; stimulation nourishes, even as it braces. Safety is, for all its virtue, airless; its redoubts must be quit, only to be regained, and then abandoned again before the hasty scuttle back. Thus we shuttle our way forward, like dancing crabs.

Every day's first sip of wine (after the flaccid afternoon, the stale journey home) is a little like this. All wine, after all, is acid. Even the low-acid ones, the Condrieu or Gewürztraminer with an insouciant pH of 4, are three grand notches short of chemical neutrality. The further you descend towards a pH of 3, the sharper the shock, the cooler the pool, the more polar the gale.

This wine's colour is a kind of mercury, pointing to what lies ahead. An absence of gold, drained away to nothing, leaving just a glint of silver, a suspicion of green. Nose into the glass, toe in the chill water. Fresh. What does 'fresh' smell of? Lemon juice, separated from the oils of its skin: raw, bare. Or ice. Not cubes, but the frozen fringe of a trickling winter stream: no reeds, no plant matter, no muddy carp. Just water rushing over stones, arrested in part by water turned stone itself.

Why is it that a shy scent of this sort can engage the attention so, or set the mouth watering even before the first sip? There's no yeast here; it's flayed plant, stripped juice. It's the presence that is almost an absence: the clearing in the boreal forest, filled with cold light, with crusted snow. All the same, our noses must gauge something here that is not found elsewhere. There are other Chardonnays from cool places that do not smell like this, even if their point of difference is simply a more assertive aromatic presence. Here we feast on an ice-jewelled absence.

You taste the juicy driving sourness. The tongue plunges in, then splashes and shakes the mouth into life like a wet dog bounding into a warm kitchen. This is the taste of shivering. That, in a way, is all there is: it's Petit Chablis. We might, as we smelled its aromatic absence, have imagined water running over stones, and water turned stone, but there is no particular stoniness in the wine to dignify its austere, close-shaven, convict-like almost-fruit; no texture, no layers. There is just the confrontation, the shock. Lemon juice again, without spurting fragrant lemon oil, without cream, without layers; bitter lemon, unapologetic with it. Terrific. It took all summer to limp its way, like Magwitch in irons, to a 12% ripeness. Just the job. Your mouth is alive again, and the redoubt is empty. You're out; you're on.

Crioux is a kind of brand (though there is a *lieu-dit* of this name, which has nothing to do with this wine); Fèvre's Didier Seguier blends it from assorted parcels of purchased fruit. I bought this bottle in a supermarket for 12 euros or so. I waited a couple of years before opening it. I don't know why. I can't say it's improved, though there's no evidence of decline, either. Perhaps the general profile of 2016, a relatively fresh one, encouraged me.

The back label alludes to the familiar tropes of Portlandian and Kimmeridgean: lost semi-eternities of slow-dropping tropical bliss in the late Jurassic. It would be more useful to say that this is a wine of the highest, coldest hill sites and their hard, rattling cap rock, not of the warmer spots with their richer, yellowy, fossil-thickened marls. There is wine in here from above the forest above Les Clos. Though also, to be accurate, from cold clays in Lignorelles. And from sandy or silty patches when they wash up at the edges of the region, before the vines dissolve into fields of swaying green wheat. It's the wine of marginal land, of disappointed hopes.

But good Petit Chablis dashes hopes no longer. Our planet's intelligent life, as we now recognize with dismay, has inadvertently duplicated the effect of the volcanic provinces of even deeper time than the Jurassic, layering carbon dioxide into the atmosphere as effectively as the belching Siberian traps of the Permian-Triassic boundary. It's easy, if you drink wine, to taste global warming. Wines are getting richer, Chablis included. There's even a new roundness in the cheeks of their starveling cousins. The unbalanced have found equilibrium, while the perfectly balanced begin to totter. And what, after all, do we want from Chablis? We want a shock in a glass, the taste of shivering, and a jewelled absence. Petit Chablis, shaven-headed as it is, may do this better today than much Chablis.

Of course that's not all we want Chablis to do; there's a music in the marls that percussive cap rock will never give you. Every great wine has its own *genius loci*. These spirits don't steal willingly away – since there is no other place for them to go; tear the *genius* from its *locus*, and it can only curl up and die. Chablis can only be Chablis in Chablis. Just give, if you haven't already, Petit Chablis a new chance.

Not Quite the White Queen:

1999 Corton-Charlemagne, Bonneau du Martray

If you like red burgundy, the Côte d'Or will already be an obsession. Irancy and Mâcon Rouge speak plainly of their origins, but few would reach for them in preference to a bottle of Vosne. Mercurey and Givry Rouge jump a little higher, but their Premier Cru claims remain indulgent. All the action begins at Marsannay; by Santenay, the credits are rolling. What happens between the two is as action-packed as *The Godfather*.

White burgundy, by contrast, is a different matter. Greater Burgundy is white-wine country, extensive and intermittent. For Chardonnay, that descent from northern Chablis all the way down to the last vines of Mâcon, tiptoeing into Saint Amour, is a chronicle. The wine world offers few comparable examples of a single grape variety teased through so many nuances of climate and soil, from Petit Chablis at its sharpest and sourest through to the puffy pillows of Pouilly-Fuissé, which loll about like dolls made of honeycomb. Somewhere in the middle stands Corton-Charlemagne, beautiful yet thin-lipped, sculpted yet silent: the enigma at the heart of the journey.

Enigma? Well, it isn't Montrachet. It isn't quite the white queen. No one gets to taste Montrachet often, but even a sip or two of a competently made, semi-mature bottle will tell you what you need to know, which is that this one vineyard can be a synopsis of the rest. Montrachet is a banquet at which almost everything is served. It can be as stony as Chablis and as matronly as Mâcon – at the same time. It's not difficult to make a case for its being the most nourishing, the most complete white wine in the world. You might not want to bother to eat with it at all. Whatever Chardonnay can achieve in Burgundy, Montrachet seems capable of reflecting in the mirrors of its eyes. Every ambitious white burgundy on the Côte d'Or aspires in some way to that multivalence, that capaciousness, that richness of resource.

Every white burgundy, that is, except Corton-Charlemagne. Cool, pristine, aloof, saintly, sometimes virginal, Corton-Charlemagne doesn't really want to be a banquet. It's not exactly stony either, though there should always be a focus and a finesse to it. Many find it 'mineral'. It certainly doesn't want to be matronly, or a doll: how vulgar. So what does it want to be? Taste it young, and you may be hard put to say. Inscrutability is all. Taste it a little older, and the enigma begins to unfold. You may be allowed a secret or two.

As the vineyard is over six times as large as Montrachet, it's not difficult to find a bottle with this name on it, but the reference is surely Bonneau du Martray, with 11.5 hectares of Grand Cru land just here. This includes 9.5 hectares of Chardonnay in a single parcel, part of which lies in the upper hill slope En Charlemagne, facing the westerly hills, and part of which lies a little lower down in Le Charlemagne, whose gaze is more southwesterly, looking across to the early-rising les Vergelesses. Majestic, both: the hill of Corton is a natural carousel whose vineyard height (280–330 metres, compared to Montrachet's 250–270 metres) commands the countryside as a general might survey a battlefield. But the vines at this hidden end of the hill emerge only stealthily from the morning shadows. The soil warms slowly. Later, as the tide of dusk rises, the vines clutch like shipwrecked mariners at the evening light; by vespers, those of Les Vergelesses across the valley have long slipped into night's cool oblivion. Jean-Charles le Bault de la Morinière, who formerly farmed this land prior to the domaine's sale (to Stan Kroenke) in 2017, had it anatomized into nine different soil types; he vinified 20 separate *cuvées* before making the final blend. That blend, though, is a synopsis of the place in the way that no other Corton-Charlemagne can be. It is, as he says, a vineyard of light and not heat. Heat makes a banquet; light illuminates the virgin.

What secrets can you find in the 1999? Its colour is a synthesis of silver and gold. I remember trying this wine when its silver was shot with green, long before it dreamed of gold. Aromatically, back then, its finger was pressed across its lips; there was a sappy tautness, but little else. Now, 10 years later, the tide is rising: honeysuckle, lime. All there, all understated still, but deftly disposed and more compelling, somehow, for its restraint. (The *Mona Lisa*, you recall, is not a large painting.) When every detail is as fine and as well-proportioned as these are, time spent in scrutiny quickly dissolves. Back comes the lime on the tongue, lifted with linden; it's found a little glycerol; the sense of richness and fullness swells and amplifies as the wine lingers. Poised: elegant, refined. It is not, as Montrachet is, a meal on its own; it needs the company of food. The reserve, though, has gone at last. Taking the chronicle of white burgundy as a whole, this may be its still centre, its calm and constant heart.

Bathing Without Washing:

2005 Châteauneuf-du-Pape Blanc, Réservé, Château Rayas

We shepherd our bottles through a drinking life, casting an affectionate eye over the flock from time to time. As the years accumulate, we put on a white coat to monitor each bleating glass flask, intuiting some tenderness which might indicate that the moment has finally come to reach for the corkscrew. These are our wines.

And then there are other people's wines, the ones we have no idea we will meet, the wines about whose past we know nothing until a kind friend or generous acquaintance glides a glass in front of us. There's no monitoring or mental preparation to be done; there's no investment in anticipated pleasure. No lip-licking. If such wines are served blind, as this wine was served to my fellow guests and me around a dinner table in Riga in late September 2020, the encounter has an immaculate purity to it: just the drinker and the liquid.

What's it saying? Guessing games usually follow, about which I am wary, since the game itself proceeds to dominate the encounter. Our interest, in truth, lies not in identification but in meeting, listening, searching, appreciating; in coming-to-know. Both form and function are best surveyed in the sunlight of innocence. Identity casts a long shadow.

The liquid was gold in colour, aromatically unflamboyant, unshowy, but warm and clean and comforting in a homely kind of way. I took a sip. Thick; it was thick. Unctuous. Tongue-coating. This I found lovely, not least because it came for me at the end of a full month of wine tasting, and my tongue was sore; here was balm. I felt the wine more than tasted it. It was like sinking into a bath without struggling to wash my tired limbs.

After a while, though, the image that came to mind was that of a patterned carpet. This wine seemed to resemble a cherished carpet: close-grained and seamless, dense with work. Professional instincts kicked in. I began fumbling for analogies; almonds, hay, aniseed. These aromas came and went; you could read them (and others; I wasn't jotting) like motifs in the carpet's pattern. They didn't matter in themselves but deepened interest in the whole; they kept drawing the drinker back in. There was little acidity in this wine; acidity was irrelevant here. It was a celebration of texture, of wealth, of wine marrow, of sweet fullness; its balance lay in faint tannin napped in glycerol, but more significantly in a quiet, gently articulated aromatic expression of Mediterranean summer wealth. It was a wine of warmth. I felt warmly about it.

This, I think, was the first bottle of white Rayas (celebrated, rare) I've ever had the chance to taste. There are just a couple of hectares of Grenache Blanc and Clairette in these sandy, pine-punctuated vineyards. The marrow comes from Grenache, and the aromatic whispers from Clairette, an underrated variety for warm places on earth. Both are picked ripe though not exaggeratedly so, then vinified in big old wood and aged for some months in stainless steel. Its grandeur didn't lie in concentration or intricacy; instead it lay in the wine's unfussy self-sufficiency, its unapologetic breadth, its acceptance of its own nature. A warm, soft Mediterranean white in which oak and artifice play no role, and in which the conventions of white-wine aesthetics play no role. Just itself.

Of course it's called 'Rayas' and is therefore allowed to be itself, even applauded for being itself. This, surely, is what every wine producer is hoping and aiming for. This is why successive generations toil for year after year. Let the intrinsic qualities of the wine-place object sing out and create their own climate of appreciation, their own language of aroma and flavour. Given enough time and some inner distinction, the language will be learned, spoken, relished, loved; lustre will accrue. But those of us met together that evening around a late-summer table didn't taste 'Rayas', at least prior to the wine's revelation; we just tasted a rich and soothing dry white wine.

Could such a wine have been made outside Europe? Perhaps in California, where wine creators are ready to let things be themselves, but elsewhere only rarely. Elsewhere, actually, this white wine wouldn't meet expectations, and wouldn't inspire confidence; elsewhere it would be too much and not enough. The wine would have to be taken in some direction or another; it would have to be given edges and hooks and handles, and have a flavour narrative engineered into it. It would need more shape, more balance… and end up with so much shape and so much balance that it would no longer unroll like a carpet across the tongue, or fall on a sore tongue like balm.

I've often thought about this problem, and feel sympathy for those who are working in the new places, where every distinguished wine's inner language is, at first, just a jangle of unfamiliar phonemes. The language has yet to be learned; and without unusual confidence and vision on its creator's part, there is a risk that it never will be. It will be given the clatter of some other borrowed and inauthentic language; or its singularity will be so provoking that its creator loses faith, moves on, starts again, replants, grafts over. Rayas Blanc, in this sense, teaches courage.

Very Like the Cuckoo's Call:

2005 Rioja, Gran Riserva, La Granja Remelluri

It was sunny, to begin with. Amaya Goñi brought us water, and we sipped it at a table in the walled garden. There was, though, change in the air. As we made for the vineyards, white clouds edged over the mountain: vapoury buckshot. The tissue of birdsong thinned; a moist stillness fell.

Is Remelluri a 'single vineyard'? Not really. It's a small synopsis of the Cordillera Cantábrica foothills that Jaíme Rodríguez and his son Telmo have turned into 192 gardens. The mountain carries on slithering down about the gardens, as any protective mother should. Some of the gardens are 30 rows wide; some three. The journey between them is a hike, and we took Txuspa, the estate terrier, who was quickly lost in that labyrinth of scent adventures that only a dog and a mountain can understand. A cuckoo hailed a mate, its call the definition of soft clarity. The light was milky now. I wished I could have climbed up to the ridgeline above, for the view. Perhaps, though, it was better that I didn't. I expected to see the wide Atlantic with its white foam horses and misty sea frets. The reality has to be less dramatic than that; the sea is over 60 kilometres away. But what's 60 kilometres when the ocean runs clear to Ouessant, to Bantry Bay and to Greenland?

I have, I think, underestimated Rioja for 30 years. Never disparaged it; every bottle made my mouth water. But all I saw was a forest of brand names and age statements, dressed up in fishnet stockings made of gold thread: Crianza this, Riserva that. It was hard, sometimes, to taste the land inside the age statement. Things have changed. There was jolly Miguel Angel de Gregorio a few days earlier, beaming at me across a massive oak table in the heart of his restored palace in Briones, a bottle labelled Allende Rioja (and nothing else) clamped in his hand: 'We sell wines, not calendars.'

I tasted the 2005 Gran Reserva in the library at Remelluri: a little book-lined room in a beautifully restored house whose stone steps were first contoured by monkish feet. I sat by the open window, looking across the vineyard over which the drive unspools. The clouds were grey now, and darkening further; the white haze of the sun had been squeezed like toothpaste down the valley, beyond Logroño; the Atlantic was coming, over the mountain.

The first few May days in Rioja in 2011 had a dreamlike quality, principally because every street, every field and every courtyard was filled with drifting seed-heads: a reef of coral spawning under a full moon. This in turn made me remember Andrei Tarkovsky, dead this quarter century, whose film *Mirror* changed the way I saw the world when it unexpectedly hit me, broadside, in 1980. Tarkovsky filmed stones under the running water of a river, or the wind coursing through a field of oats or ruffling a birch copse, and left you feeling more deeply moved than after the cumulative violence of every one of last year's action thrillers. He saw being inside existence. He would have loved these seed-heads. I saw them for him. And now the storm was coming at Remelluri. In the distance, across the valley to the west in what was now an eerie indigo haze, a distant dog was barking: another Tarkovsky motif. The wind continued to rise; the walnut tree out in the vineyard flailed; the chimneys gagged; the roof-tiles whistled.

And I tasted the wines from these gardens under the mountain, at somewhere between 600 and 800 metres up in the air of northern Spain, where ripeness comes only as the season closes, but which brings Tempranillo to a perfection of soft clarity very like the cuckoo's call. The Gran Reserva is made from the oldest vines (60 years), cut with Grenache and a little Graciano, nurtured with a couple of years in oak. Dark, rich, smouldering, sappy: a scent of burnt stones, of crushed plums, of blood, of pulverized brushwood and wild flowers, all stroked by cedar (you can see what sent the phylloxera-stricken Bordelais scurrying down here).

The palate, golf-ball tight at this stage, made me think of plant essences when I tasted it at Remelluri: the Hieronymites of the past, walking the mountain, searching out its apothecary virtues as the locals still do near Chartreuse today. I've tasted it since and it evokes darkness: not the lurid darkness of the storm, but the sweeter restorative darkness of winter rest under the snows, and of the time that we must give to time to create anything of worth (book, garden, cathedral). It has an inner glow, too, though, and a wealth behind its prodigious grip, power and concentration.

The summer solstice is almost upon us now; I know I haven't tasted a more impressive wine this year. Tempranillo in this high, closed, pale-soiled valley, screened from the sea but at the same time ventilated and aired by the sea, is one of the world's great variety–terroir combinations, as this wine and others prove. As I tasted in the rising storm, indeed, it was hard not to levitate just a little: a final Tarkovsky motif, and perhaps a metaphor for the extent to which beauty can rearrange reality, if you sit quietly enough to let it.

Forest Whispers:

2011 Château-Chalon, Vin Jaune, André and Mireille Tissot

It's winter. La Réserve Thomas, Lyon; mixed company, granite light. Lunchers shuffle in, un-muffle, disburse warmth; servers dart about in preparatory rituals. Our large group gathers critical mass. Eyes flick down onto phone screens; absence usurps presence, a few desultory conversations aside. Time freewheels. Then Stéphane Tissot and his wife Bénédicte walk in.

Bottles fly from boxes, and corks seem to pull themselves unaided. Time accelerates: the Tissots are heading north, whereas we are heading east. Nobody says as much, but the conviction grows that there is no time to be lost. Stéphane, unintroduced, takes the floor, begins to talk, smilingly, bubblingly; the bottles do the rounds. Yellow wine splashes into glasses; scents of bread and leaf and sour fruit mingle with the now-fading aromas of morning coffee. The little screens are set aside and fall dark; eyes light in their place. There's a fumbling for notebooks. He tears, rips, surges through 14 different wines, each with its story: a torrent in spate. I do my best to harvest the nuances and amass the details, but it's like trying to stuff cats into boxes; the details scamper off, the nuances scratch, and then we're on to the next wine...

Two decades have passed since I last met Stéphane Tissot, yet time doesn't seem to have diminished that fierce energy and optimism, that seethe of ideas, that profusion of projects. The difference is that his vineyard holdings have more than doubled – so there is more to serve to us, to tell us, to lavish on us. Not every wine is successful; that I remember from before, too. But the great wines, the *vins jaunes* and the other *vins de voile*, are finer than ever. Did I ever realize *vin jaune* could be this good? I fish one conclusion out from the spate: his Arbois *vins jaunes* are indeed different from those he makes in Château-Chalon.

Wait, though; perhaps you've never been to the Jura, in which case I owe you a description. Clay soils give farmers options; wine regions where clay predominates are rarely monocultures. Vineyards sometimes seem an afterthought in the Jura: they're a way of using well-exposed slopes of moderate or poor fertility. Flatter land nourishes cereals; cows cud their way about the richer pastureland and the higher plateaux; orchards punctuate the rest. From 600 or 700 metres the forest takes over, climbing athletically. Vineyards here occupy nearly 2,000 hectares; locals say they could plant 9,000. But Comté cheese sells well, and dairy farmers covet the land, too. Jura grass is gorgeous. I rose early that next morning, to hear water seeping from the hill, to see the violet mist puddling the cold valley, to smell the smoke and the byres, to watch dawn sunlight lick the frost from every green blade.

Another 20-year memory: walking from the edge of the village of Voiteur up the steep, grassy vineyard slopes beneath the hilltop village of Château-Chalon. It was springtime on that earlier occasion: late April, suddenly warm. I counted 13 varieties of wild flower around the vineyards; an elderly peacock butterfly came to rest on my knee. The knock of cowbells hung in the air. This is where Savagnin, a sometimes gaunt old aristocrat of a grape variety, ripens slowly over a measured, temperate summer, its roots buried in sticky blue-grey marl. Château-Chalon is tiny: just 60 hectares of hill slopes in the four villages of Château-Chalon itself, Domblans, Menétru-le-Vignoble and Nevy-sur-Seille. Arbois, by contrast, is much bigger: 12 villages and 766 hectares lying 30 kilometres to the north. Savagnin is planted on cool grey marl there, too, but the fact that most of Arbois's vineyards are planted with red varieties suggests a little more July warmth in the air.

Savagnin is late-ripening in the Jura. It's harvested as ripe as possible, though up here that might mean only 13% natural alcohol; it's vinified, does malo, beds down in old casks. Sometimes an air space is left; sometimes not; in either case, one eventually develops, and is followed by a thin film of yeasts, a *voile* or 'veil'. After six years of solicitous restraint, bottling follows, into the exquisitely dumpy little 62-centilitre *clavelin* bottle. Sometimes things lag or go wrong along the way, and the delinquent wine is hauled off for earlier consumption as a traditionally styled (ie, faintly oxidative) Savagnin. The cellar conditions matter, too; ventilation is vital, and cooler temperatures favour the Château-Chalon style while greater temperature variations furnish an Arbois thumbprint. Alcohol levels tend to rise as the wines mature, especially in Arbois.

Stéphane Tissot's 2011 Arbois *vins jaunes*, at any rate, seemed magnificently demonstrative: the nutty En Spois; the peaty La Vasée, a dancing bear; mellowed-out Mailloche and buxom Les Bruyères. They paraded though the glasses. And then the 2011 Château-Chalon: suddenly a counter-current. Quietness fell in the glass. There was nuance, cream, subtlety, forest whispers; spring on the move. In the mouth, always that bolt of acidity – and, as with great Riesling, all the drama of flavour is acted out inside the acidity. This is a young Château-Chalon, so the forest mushrooms, the umami beat, have barely begun; instead there's a crackle of early summer fruit, of plants trodden underfoot, of crushed acorn and scuffed heather, with a dandelion-bitter aftertaste. For all the elegance, it hangs there, driving and long: stored electricity, slowly leaching its juicy yet caustic charge.

The Antidote:

2010 Madiran, Cuvée du Couvent, Domaine Capmartin

The weather? Here in Languedoc, it must have rained heavily at the close of November 2012, since the photographs I took in early December show my sons hurling small, wind-snapped branches into the swollen river Hérault. There will have been gathering darkness at the days' end, of course, as the northern half of this tilting planet leaned out towards the rest of the universe, dragging night into our lives like a sleeper groping for a misplaced blanket.

Other photos tell me that I was in Burgundy in mid-November. Here's a dreary picture of the Romanée-Conti vineyard: mute, drab, brown, grey, snuffed in mist, lifeless. You can see the top of the stone cross, but not much further. My fellow gawpers are all wearing woolly hats and scarves. If it wasn't for the masonry, it could be the Marmandais.

No wonder I came home and ordered (my records tell me) nine bottles of Madiran. Three were the 2009 Prestige from Château Viella; three were the 2010 Vieilles Vignes from Labranche Laffont; and three were this wine. They cost about 13 euros per bottle, delivered by the end of that month, and I've made no better wine purchase over the last six years. They arrived, sat in the rack, gathered a bit of dust, got jostled from time to time, watched life unfold around them. Every time I pulled out a bottle, though, it came good: dark, dense, deep and dependable. This was the last survivor, drunk on January 2nd 2016: wonderful wine.

It's not actually obligatory to drink Madiran in winter. It can inspire in spring: keep going, it seems to say, don't give up, everything will be worth the effort. In summer, by contrast, served with a light chill, it acts more as a memento mori: black, forbidding, as shocking as the skull on the desk, incongruous yet illuminating, reminding the drinker (as no rosé ever can) that life will soon become much more difficult. Sensually speaking, it most perfectly echoes autumn, mimicking the aromatic messiness and textural litter of the natural world as everything sets about falling and decaying, while humans attempt to scold a little order into the scene with flame and smoke. But winter, it's true, is when Madiran performs best. Then it's the antidote: to cold, to drained light, to exhaustion, to the fear that there will be no return, to the terror inspired by the indifferent stars. No red wine is more consoling, more reassuring, more fortifying. It will brace your struts and buttress your walls. The brute of a wine is at its most humane and giving in winter. It's a candle with a flame of blood. It's a life force, liquefied.

A small formality, by the way: Madiran requires forethought. I've never had a Madiran that wasn't better with 24 hours of air inside it. The tannins don't exactly soften, but they then find a harmony and equilibrium with the wine's insistent acidity. Freshly opened, a bottle of Madiran is like a stored tent, stuffed tightly into a bag, its poles and canvas all there in economical but senseless disorder. By day two, the elastic inside the poles has jolted them into shape, the canvas forms a little home, and the guys are pegged tautly enough to keep the wind at bay.

And now a confession: I didn't make a tasting note. I didn't think I was going to need to; it wasn't meant to be that good a bottle. Only later did I realize that this wine had, after all, been an event in my life, but by then it was too late to hymn its parts. 'I'll be surprised if there's a wine I actually enjoy more than this all year,' I jotted retrospectively, hunting about for an adjective or two. 'Freshly opened, very good; the day after, grand. The dark countryside and soul warmth in a glass. Splendid purity, depth and balance. Get a case of the '15.' That's it.

Here's another Madiran note, from a wine I tasted in the autumn of 2015. 'Startlingly dark: saturated black-red. Earthy, warm, some lingering oak sweetness but balanced now, with plum fruits and drifting savoury smoke. On the palate, youthful and intense: tight, taut, close-grained, with splendid tannic depths. Powerful, searching, perfumed, textured and authoritative.' That was another wine which left me enraptured, and another wine which improved on day two. A more expensive Madiran, this time, though I'd been given it: the 2002 Château Montus Cuvée Prestige. What I'd point out, though, is that these magnificent wines disdain the passing of the years; the 2010 and 2002 were almost coevals. Both were, in 2016, still 'young'.

You may, for all I know, order classed-growth Bordeaux and Grand Cru burgundy monthly; you may have a magnificent cellar where tissue-wrapped bottles idle away the decades in cool tranquillity. But, fortunate reader, you're a human being, too; you must have your low moments, your winter discontent, your nocturnal frights, your intimations of mortality. May I recommend a few bottles of Madiran?

Some Useless Notes

What's the answer? I'm not sure, but here's the question.

Every year, in the grey heart of mid-winter, the Domaine de la Romanée-Conti (DRC) brings its most recently bottled wines to London. Aubert de Villaine, the Domaine's superintending craftsman, shows them to the press, the wine trade and to private customers and sommeliers at the dockside offices of the United Kingdom agent Corney & Barrow. Needless to say, the invitation (on card thick and significant enough to exclude window draughts, fill cavity walls and substitute for carpet underlay) is treasured, and I try to be there, despite living 650 kilometres away. The wines are genuinely thrilling. I take notes, and invariably want to use them for an article. But who, exactly, would the article be for?

Those in a position to buy the wines, it seems to me, have absolutely no need for press guidance, since declining any proffered DRC would be the most financially stupid thing it is possible for a moneyed human being to do in a given calendar year. It must be wondered, too, what percentage of those buying the wines will eventually feel financially spruce enough to spurn the dizzying return on their investment and drink them, at maturity or otherwise. For all that, I know that the agents strive to find genuine drinking homes for the wines. A secondary market exists. It's also affecting that the tasting happens at all, since there is assuredly no need for it; the wines would fly

112   SOME BEAUTIFUL WINES

without any help from foil cutter or corkscrew. Many lesser domaines are meaner with tasting opportunities.

In the teeth of such existential doubts, I'm going to persist in describing the 2012 DRC wines shown in early February 2015. They are singularly beautiful wine objects, after all, and tracking the play of their lineaments might teach us something about wine beauty more generally. They are, too, a sort of ideal to which all red burgundy aspires – and red burgundy itself is an ideal towards which much, perhaps most, fine red wine aspires, whatever its variety and place of origin, that ideal being one of limpidity, grace, balance, and the untrammelled expression of a site and season. So here goes.

The 2012 burgundy vintage wasn't a great one. If you drew up a checklist of every difficulty a burgundy wine-grower might face during a season, then 2012 saw most ticked (episodic cold, rain and hail, with attendant downy and powdery mildew, *coulure* and *millerandage*). Skipping between the puddles, though, came periods of generous warmth, notably in June, in August and in much of September. Resources are not wanting at DRC, and a gimlet eye on the vineyards throughout, plus a late harvest, meant a small but healthy crop. (Very small: 11 hl/ha for the Corton, rising to 27 hl/ha for Grands Echezeaux.)

Sure enough, the wines taste cool, contained and shapely. In a way, that's why I wanted to describe them: their characters seem more than usually scrutable in 2012, when the steam of a generous summer's warmth isn't hissing through them, misting the glass. The optics are polished from the cradle.

Corton definitely set the vintage tone: very sappy and fresh, almost shocking, with billowing raspberry perfume. It was a wine of military bearing; severe but deep. Echezeaux immediately whisked you away to another village and another *côte* altogether. Suddenly you could smell summer at work in the air: the sweet fresh fatness of hay and straw, and the fruits now more plum than raspberry. On the palate, too, the fruit style was richer than Corton, and the textures more gratifying; a resonant earthiness corralled the finish. I almost forgot it was 2012.

Grands Echezeaux seemed, if anything, a little less ripe (it was picked earlier): fruits back to raspberry with – mmm! – some violets, and a lovely washday-fresh lift to it. It then splashed onto the palate with mountain-stream force. The fruits, you realized, weren't all red, but had a little black in them too, and there was magnificent baseline grip (hurrah for stems). Dense and mouthcoating, but very elegant and dapper, ready to brighten the worst day.

There's a decided key change when you come to the Romanée-St-Vivant: it's quieter, more stealthy, more cat-like; all deft brushstrokes and soft fur. On the palate, it's less firm and pushy than those boisterous Echezeaux boys, and the ripeness goes back a click, leaving it slim-bellied; we stay in the red-fruit register throughout. A wine of disposition, not accumulation.

Then into Richebourg, and the volume returns: it's an aromatic wine, though the aromas are exuberant and impressionist rather than finely detailed: a raspberry blast; something burr-like and autumnal. The palate changes in your mouth, from the cool initial impression of the vintage to a plume of fruit in the mid-palate; finally fiery in the finish. Ample tannins, but polished.

La Tâche is the Kublai Khan of the set: exotic and spicy, with musk and sandalwood mingling with the fruits. On the palate, it's the great gatherer, bringing together much of what is in the other wines and stocking it all in good warehouse order; the tannins are the biggest of all, but they seem the softest of all, too. I decided I couldn't spit this wine, but by then it had melted into my mouth anyway.

So how does Romanée-Conti follow La Tâche? By outdoing it in purity and aromatic finesse (if Richbourg is nose-filling, Romanée-Conti is nose-lacquering). Pure fruits and bay leaf, but without any of La Tâche's spice; vapoury, aerial. It was another wine that seemed completely locked on to the vintage style: fresh, pert, alert, spring-like, crystalline; almost lunging in its intensity. Nothing but those fruits and violets on the palate, and very fine tannins, though less thickly articulated than those of La Tâche and Richebourg. If you're looking for kinship, it's really Romanée-St-Vivant's very beautiful elder sister.

There you are: useless notes, but a sketch of terroir in action in the world's most inspiring vineyards.

The Two-Pin Dinner

Here's what happened. Six of us tackled (but didn't finish) eight bottles. They were worth in excess of £9,000 – but they weren't. The final zero (and then some) came courtesy of two bottles, one of which had originally cost around £11, and the other of which had been a gift. No one around the table was rich; we all loved wine. The purpose of the dinner was to burn the infamous price tags in the flames of our enjoyment.

Let me, though, start more than two decades ago. I first met Frank Ward when he was writing a wine column for *The European* in 1990 (this Maxwell- then Barclay brothers-owned newspaper lasted under eight years, and Frank's uncompromising refusal to trivialize his wine-writing meant that his own tenure there was shorter still). I've never met anyone who accords more importance to the act of tasting and drinking wine than Frank and his wife Lisbet, a fine cook.

Dinners at their house, atop the steep shingle beach of Deal, are the most civilized of treats: unpretentious (Frank grew up in Wolverhampton); un-nerdy, without duelling references to further vintages, producers, collectors and tastings; but unhurriedly open to the beauty and poetry of what might be in the glass and on the plate. The other guests on this occasion were the composer David Matthews and his wife Jenifer.

Frank himself began life as an artist in Paris. Lisbet (who is Swedish) qualified as a midwife, which entitled them to a tiny flat back in Sweden, so they moved there, and after a spell looking after their baby daughter, Frank began to import wine to Sweden. 'It was uphill all the way. Going to sell to the Swedish Monopoly was like going to the Kremlin – you had to face all those hard-faced men. I offered them DRC, but they said it cost too much and no one would buy it.' Eventually he made a living importing burgundy producers like Rousseau, Tollot-Beaut and de Vogüé, chiefly for restaurants.

'But I've never been comfortable with selling wine. I prefer passing wine on to people.' He tastes more as an artist than a merchant.

He remembers buying around 10 cases of different 1982 Bordeaux *en primeur* – from O W Loeb. Anthony Goldthorp, who was running the company at that time, urged him to buy a case of 'a new Pomerol' called Le Pin – at £130. 'After it arrived, I tried a bottle. It was very oaky and tannic, not seductive at all. I couldn't see what all the fuss was about.' Two bottles drunk shortly afterwards, courtesy of Armin Diel in Nahe, confirmed the profile; Frank forgot about the rest of his case.

Some years later, he noticed its extraordinary price rise. He then slowly sold off his other bottles, one by one, to furnish further purchases (I know of no cellar more like Ali Baba's than Frank's). 'Then there came a point when I said "For heaven's sake, I'm a wine lover!" It would be terrible if there was none of this left to appreciate. Hence this evening – a demonstration that good wine is for drinking by those who love and appreciate it.' When Frank invited me, I suggested we also drank the 1998 Le Pin that I had been given, in an act of great generosity, shortly after it was bottled. Hence our two-Pin dinner.

These circumstances were liberating; we didn't have to worship the label or grovel before the wines' reputations or a host's munificence; we could just... enjoy.

The 1982, the first vintage for these newly planted Merlot vines (on just one-third of a hectare then), was lovelier than I had expected. It proved two things. One is that a grand vintage and fine site will produce wonderful wine, despite the 'primitive conditions' in which owner Jacques Thienpont remembers working. The other is that, at least in the best parts of Bordeaux, wines that seem forbiddingly oaky and tannic in their youth need be neither of these things in their maturity. This was actually the darker-hued wine of the pair, but everyone's idea of a dream Pomerol: sweet, soft, unctuous, glycerous, creamy and beguiling. It glowed; we lapped it up, as cats lap milk.

The 1998 (two hectares by now) was a showier wine on the nose – all truffles, white mushrooms and ripe plums. It had much brighter acidity, an acidity I almost found disconcerting; those who crave freshness might prefer it. Frank and I tried both after breakfast the next day: they had held the air with assurance, and their characters remained clearly defined.

Where does the Le Pin myth come from? Both, we decided as we tracked their progress over those hours, were exuberant and exotic wines, brightly plumed and alluringly contoured, like carnival dancers: how can you not like that? They weren't dense Latour, intricate Haut-Brion or sombre Montrose; nor are they meant to be. Add rarity to the plumage, a lustrous appellation and a large dose of herd instinct among those of high net worth, and you have the formula for an absurd price. It was our great good fortune to meet them, one evening in a house atop the steep shingle beach of Deal, as wines. Not legends.

A Rosary of Reasons:

1882 Colheita Port, Ne Oublie, Graham's

I've tasted 19th-century table wines on a few occasions: half a dozen bottles, perhaps. In most cases, the experience was rather like viewing saints' relics in obscure Sicilian churches: these were strange objects locked in glass whose gift to venerators was principally an emotional or spiritual one, since they now bore no resemblance to the living things they had once been.

An exception? There was one: the 1865 Clos Vougeot fished out by Joseph Henriot from the stash he found at the Château de Beaune when he moved in in 1995. There was a little flesh on the bones; there was a bloom of fruit on the spare cheeks; the cellar had not yet become a catacomb. The Montrachet of the same vintage alongside it, by contrast, was mummified, sunken and sallow; time and oxygen had stretched its skin into grotesque contortions. Set aside our respect for venerability, and in truth even the Clos Vougeot was unexceptional old wine made exceptional by the fact that it was very, very old. I feel honoured to have swallowed the fermented juice of grapes harvested three months after the premiere of *Tristan und Isolde*. As a drink, I would have preferred the 1999.

None of the above is true of fortified wines. The greatest 19th-century wines I have tried have all been fortified – mostly vintage Madeiras, but not all. They need no apologies, no excuses; there is nothing reliquary about these bottles. The wines ripple with the muscular ease of scaffolders, married to the intensity of poets and the rigour of emeritus professors of logic. They are indeed the best of the best. It's hard to guard casks and bottles for that long in our disorderly world. Keeping them out of the jaws of time means great expense. We would otherwise drink 19th-century fortified wines on a regular basis.

I was reminded of this on a dark, wet night during the winter of 2011, sitting in Rui Paula's waterfront restaurant in Folgosa do Douro with Paul and Jane Symington while the rain drummed down on the roof. 'I've got something I want you to try,' said Paul, once the main course was over, and he ran out to the car. He conferred with the staff; they assented without demur; new glasses were brought; and into them was poured an unctuous black wine with green glints.

What did it smell of? What didn't it smell of? You can't create complexity of this order in under a century or so, I suspect. Caramel, treacle, hessian, straw, lavender, camphor, coffee, chicory, crushed acorns, salted bacon hock… I stopped there, but the game could have gone on for another half-hour. There was a cleanliness and a cut about the wine, though, which was testament to 130 years of exemplary stewardship. It sat in the glass like an aroma mill, idling out scents that began to perfume the air around us. Perhaps my memory is playing tricks, but I seem to remember diners at nearby tables turning towards us, sniffing, incongruously aware of a new and alluring sensual presence in the room.

I was prepared by now for a palate explosion. I got one: the wine was salty, deep, profoundly aromatic, sweet and acidic, too. Despite prodigious wealth of flavour, it was seamlessly harmonious, thick yet almost silky, its spirit smoothed into the wine to the point of invisibility. Apples and cinders, burnt raisins, thyme and pomegranate, creosote and apricot skins, liquorice and treacle, chocolate and toasted almond: off it went again, ceaselessly murmuring its rosary of sensual reasons as to why staying alive might be a good idea. It was almost as if the wine had been out and about for all of this time, wandering the hills and the plains and the entrepôts, gathering sackfuls of scent and flavour as it travelled.

It was, in fact, the Symington family's oldest Colheita wine, dating from 1882. The family believe it had originally been purchased by the first Symington to work in the port trade, Andrew James, sometime in the 1920s. He would have bought it because it bore the date of his arrival in Portugal. As a Scot, of course, mere sentiment alone would have been inadequate: he would have tasted its qualities, wished to see them secured for the company, and driven a fair bargain. Whose farm? No one knows. After perhaps 40 years in the alternating heat and cool of the Douro, the three casks moved down to Vila Nova de Gaia, where they have stayed (nowadays housed in the Warre lodges) ever since. The wine has seldom if ever been refreshed, so its ageing process is closer to that of a Madeira than a typical Colheita port. A single bottle has left Portugal only once (to be sampled chez Robinson); none has been sold, either. I admire the family's restraint in not wolfing the lot back in 1982.

In 2012, the Symingtons bottled one of the three casks under the Graham's label, christening the wine with the Graham family motto Ne Oublie. Should you ever be in a position to ambush one of the 656 bottles, don't hesitate. This is no mummy, no museum piece, no doubtful fingernail in a dusty glass case, but a synopsis of life and time in the finest fettle.

120   SOME BEAUTIFUL WINES

CHAPTER FIVE

A TEA BREAK

The Cup that Consoles

Water is humankind's favourite drink, and the universal drink of the animal world. This is hardly a surprise, living as we do on the blue planet, tracing our ancestry to sea life, and being composed chiefly of water ourselves. Tea comes next. There are no geographical and few cultural bars to its consumption; Muslims, Christians, Buddhists, agnostics and atheists happily sip tea together (only Mormons and some Jehovah's Witnesses spurn the offer). Tea is much more widely drunk than wine, not least because of Islam's proscription of alcohol. The Turks are the world's largest per capita tea drinkers (3.16 kilograms per person per year in 2016); in Britain, around 40 percent of the human daily fluid intake is tea.

Both tea and wine are drug-laced water: tea contains the world's most popular drug, caffeine, while wine contains the third-most popular, alcohol. (Nicotine, for the time being, divides the two.) Caffeine is far more toxic than alcohol: 5 grams would kill you, whereas anyone who drinks half a bottle of 12% abv wine for dinner will have consumed 36 g of alcohol without notable ill effect. The average cup of tea contains just 30 milligrams of caffeine, though, and the average cup of coffee 75 mg. Weight for weight, tea leaves contain more caffeine than coffee beans, but a much lighter load is used in the drink's preparation. The effects of small doses of caffeine (an increase in metabolic rate and neural activity) are less evident to both users and observers than the celebrated effects of alcohol. They're quietly significant nonetheless.

Both tea and wine, thus, are old friends to humanity. They punctuate our days and nights; they bring us refreshment and solace. Life would be less agreeable without their familiar pleasures. If I had to choose between the two, I'd choose tea – yet tea is little known to most wine drinkers. Let me make its case.

I Histories

The pair are Asian. Wine's origins seem to lie in Transcaucasia [*see* Chapter One], where wild *Vitis vinifera* vines grow abundantly. Tea is native to the zone that includes the far south of China (Yunnan Province), Laos and Myanmar. Wild *Camellia sinensis* plants continue to thrive in the remote terrain here. It's easy enough to create a rough tea garden in parts of southern China by simply clearing away other plants and leaving tea bushes to flourish. *Vitis vinifera* needs extensive selection and breeding (as well as grafting onto American vine rootstocks) to be usefully fruitful; not so *Camellia sinensis*, which was planted from seed until the 1970s. Even today, the finest pu-erh teas in Yunnan Province are made from wild tea trees, many of them hundreds of years old. In 1961, a tea tree perhaps more than 1,700 years old, and over 30 metres high with a trunk girth of a metre, was found in Yunnan.

Plants this important to humanity, of course, need the sustenance of myth. No sooner had Noah stepped from his ark 'upon the mountains of Ararat' than he 'began to be an husbandman, and he planted a vineyard'. The exact means by which lofty, rampant wild vines were disciplined into the fruitfulness so swiftly enjoyed by Noah ('And he drank of the wine, and was drunken') will never be known, but since the jar samples containing wine residues found at Shulaveris Gora and Gadachrili Gora in Georgia's Lower Kartli date back 8,000 to 7,800 years, it would seem that wine is tea's older sibling. The mythical origins of tea stretch back a mere 4,400 years to the legendary Emperor Shennong ('the Divine Farmer') who sagely noted that boiled water was safer than lake or river water to drink. One day his servants allowed a few leaves to fall from a tea bush into the Imperial Kettle. The Emperor hazarded a sip or two of the infusion: delicious. A myth of greater enchantment has Bodhidharma, the Buddhist monk who brought Chan (Zen) Buddhism to China in the sixth century, cut off his own eyelids to avoid falling asleep during meditation. The eyelids rooted; tea bushes grew from the sleepy flesh.

The first tentative written reference to tea occurs in the earliest collection of Chinese poetry, the *Shi Jing* or Book of Odes, whose poems were written between 3,100 and 2,700 years ago; tentative, because the ancient ideogram thought to signify tea might also designate other plants. The sophisticated Greek winemaking cultures implied by the many references to wine in Homer's *Odyssey*, composed at around the same time (between 2,800 and 2,700 years ago) are more assured. Most start the tea clock with the *Cha Jing*, the Tang-Dynasty masterpiece known as the *Tea Classic*, written by former circus clown Lu Yu between 760 and 780. Lu Yu was a kind of Chinese Columella whose work included horticultural and manufacturing instructions, from which we can deduce that systematic tea cultivation and consumption were already well-established, and probably had been since the Three Kingdoms period (220–280).

After Lu Yu's great book, more than eight centuries followed during which tea was principally a Chinese product (shared with Korea and Japan), and its cultivation and consumption became a matter of astonishing refinement. A substantial library of 'Tea Classics' was created during the Song (960–1279) and Ming (1358–1644) dynasties of which perhaps the best known is the *Da Guan Cha Lun*, or *Treatise on Tea*, written by the Song-Dynasty Emperor Huizong in 1107. Huizong was an aesthete and polymath who painted, wrote poetry and played the *guqin*; he invented the style of calligraphy known as 'Slender Gold'. He also neglected the army, leading to invasion and the subsequent collapse and demise of the Song. Having led a life of luxury and sophistication, Huizong was eventually reduced to the rank of a commoner and died, a captive, in Manchuria. His *Treatise* included material on what we could properly call tea terroir and tea processing, as well as laying down criteria for tea competitions involving a form of blind tasting. He described the Song form of the tea ceremony in great detail.

The first European reference to tea occurs in Ramusio's *Navigationi et Viaggi*, published in Venice in 1559. Tea was auctioned in Amsterdam in 1608; 50 years later, it became a trader's treat in London. 'That excellent and by all Physicions approved drink called by the Chineans Tcha, by other nations Tay alias Tea,' boasted proprietor Thomas Garway in 1658, 'is sold at the Sultaness Head a cophee house in Sweetings Rents by the Royal Exchange London.' The civil servant Samuel Pepys drank his first cup two years later, in September 1660: 'I did send for a cup of tea (a China drink) of which I had never drank before.' That was just three years earlier than the diarist's celebrated first taste of 'Ho Bryan' (Haut-Brion), and six years before Arnaud de Pontac sent his son François-Auguste to open London's first gastropub, the 'Pontack's Head'. Tea and fine Bordeaux, in other words, reached London simultaneously.

The tea trade continued to be China-dominated for another century and a half. The Honourable East India Company maintained a monopoly on it that lasted until the 1830s, when the fact that the Company was dishonourably paying for the tea with profits from opium smuggling brought about, in part, the demise of the arrangement; the monopoly was beginning to grate with rival British merchants, too, and Parliament voted it down. The race was soon on to obtain seeds and plants from within Fortress China and plant them elsewhere – at which point it was discovered that tea was also indigenous to Upper Assam, 'within the Honourable Company's Territories'. (These indigenous plants, *Camellia sinensis var assamica*, have proved identical to the Da Ye variety found in parts of Yunnan.)

The progress of tea growing outside China and its nearest neighbours was initially fitful. Eventually, however, India rivalled China, and Sri Lanka (formerly Ceylon) and Kenya became major producers, with scores of other countries producing smaller amounts of tea. Over six million tonnes are now produced every year; China produces 2.4 million tonnes, with India producing 900,000 tonnes and Kenya 305,000 tonnes [2021 figures]. *Camellia sinensis* is, in principle, a subtropical plant; most of China's wine is produced further north than its tea. The plant is hardy, though, and anywhere that a warm summer combines with ample rainfall (1,300 millimetres (mm) a year or more) and regular cloud cover offers the potential for tea cultivation. The long days of dry, sunny heat so enjoyed by *Vitis vinifera* are inappropriate, though, for a jungle plant whose commercial crop is leaf rather than fruit. Sun ripens fruit; clouds and rain nourish leaves.

Historically speaking, two technological innovations have marched arm-in-arm with the geographical expansion of tea growing. The first was the sales initiative of a New York tea merchant called Thomas Sullivan in 1908, who decided to send out samples of his teas to customers in small silk bags. The second took place at Amgoorie tea estate in Assam in 1931, when Sir William McKercher and his assistant F G Johnson created what they called a CTC ('crush, tear, curl') machine. The tea bag and the CTC machine have, between them, come to dominate many tea markets. In the process, tea drinkers around the world have grown unfamiliar with China's extraordinary panoply of tea types. It's as if wine drinkers had no idea that France and French wine existed.

2 Cultures

All tea is made from the *Camellia sinensis* plant, and the striking differences between teas are due to origin, cultivar, harvesting date and processing method. Most teas exist in a wide spectrum of 'grades', too, from the very finest whole leaf examples via broken grades to what are known as fannings and dust.

Camellia sinensis v *sinensis* and *Camellia sinensis* v *assamica* are the two fundamental varieties of the tea plant. The stronger, maltier v *assamica* is used in Assam and, in part, in Yunnan, Sri Lanka and Kenya; the more delicate v *sinensis* predominates in China, as well as being used in Darjeeling.

Many different cultivars ('cultivated varieties') of these tea varieties exist, and it is these cultivars that are the true equivalent of what the wine world calls grape varieties. (A variety should grow true to seed, whereas a cultivar will not necessarily grow true to seed and needs to be reproduced by other means such as cuttings – so 'grape varieties' like Chardonnay and Syrah would be better called cultivars.)

Just as different wine appellations in France may share the same grape variety, so different tea types in China are based on certain common cultivars. Casually, China claims '10,000' tea types; there are certainly many hundreds in commercial production. A contemporary Chinese *Book of Famous Green Teas* lists 135 types within this style alone. Little of the Chinese literature concerning tea cultivars has yet been translated. The same cultivar grown in a different location will produce a different tea, even if processed in the same style – so any Chinese familiar with the nation's tea culture will have no difficulty understanding the French concept of terroir.

There are seven fundamental Chinese tea styles, and a grasp of these is the simplest route to understanding Chinese tea. These styles are, in increasing order of strength of flavour, white tea, yellow tea, green tea, oolong tea, black tea and pu-erh tea. Teas infused with flower blossoms (usually based on green tea) constitute a further tea type, often called scented tea.

White tea (*bai cha*) is the easiest of all teas to process: it simply consists of sun-dried or warm-air-dried leaf. The leaf does not undergo firing, steaming, bruising or oxidizing. The most celebrated of all white teas is the light, feathery Silver Needle (Yin Zhen) producing in the Fuding area of Fujian Province: this is based on the Da Bai or Da Hao cultivars, picked in earliest spring (before the sap has risen) as downy buds alone. Any tea in the world, though, can be processed in a 'white' style if wished. White teas are gentle, subtle, teasing and quenching.

Green tea (*lu cha*) is a vast family of teas based on a number of different cultivars – two celebrated examples would be the Long Jing 43 or Jiu Ken cultivars used to produce Dragon Well (Long Jing) tea. The leaves are picked at various points in the spring, with the most prized qualities being those picked before the Qingming spring festival. The picked leaves are withered for a few hours to allow the cell walls to weaken so that the moisture in the leaf can evaporate smoothly during the firing process, but the aim is to avoid oxidation and thereby preserve green colours and the aromas and flavours associated with this. For the finest China green teas, the leaf is then fired in a dry, hot wok, by hand: the tea worker swirls and lifts the leaves to keep them moving and ensure they don't burn. Chinese green teas of different types look notably different from one another, and much of the skill in firing consists of shaping the leaves in an appropriate way to the tea style. (Pellets of green tea are known as gunpowder in English, or as 'pearl tea', *zhu cha*, in Mandarin.) Green tea can also be kiln-fired, and Japanese green teas are fired by steaming, which gives them a distinctive umami character. After firing, the tea is rolled, and a final drying period (over charcoal for the finest and rarest green teas) concludes the process. Great green tea (like Long Jing) is, quite literally, 'garden fresh': the weighty, vividly green leaves seem to smell of chlorophyll, and the flavour is leafier than any Sauvignon Blanc wine. (The dusty, straw-like 'green tea' sold in most tea bags, by contrast, is a poor shadow.)

Yellow tea (*huang cha*) is picked in spring and initially wok-fired in the same way as green tea. The aim with yellow tea, though, is to produce a tea with less of the sappy flavour that characterizes green tea. After this initial firing, the tea is steamed, heaped and covered, then slow-dried at a very low temperature (traditionally having first been wrapped in yellow 'cow skin paper' or *niu pi zhi*). This process pales the naturally green tea, and the end result is a wan, silvery green with a smoother, sweeter, creamier and less grassy flavour than classic green tea. Yellow tea is rare, even in China, as green tea made from the same sources is easier to make and to market.

Oolong, black and pu-erh teas differ from green tea in that they all undergo some element of oxidation during their processing; this is why the pristine green colour is lost. This oxidation is sometimes called 'fermentation' – though, in contrast to wine, the transformation is accomplished by chemical and not biological means. No yeast is involved.

Oolong tea (*wulong cha*) is semi-oxidized. After picking, the leaves are withered as they are for green tea, though in this case they are tossed intermittently during the withering process. They are then placed in a drum and rotated to bruise the outer edges of the leaf and begin the oxidation process. Once a sufficient level of oxidation has been achieved (which varies greatly according to the type of tea produced), the leaves are then gently fired before being compressed into a cloth ball before repeated firing, drying and, in some cases, baking.

Some oolong teas are almost green while others are dark brown or ash-grey; some are tightly rolled into pellets while others resemble long, dry, crinkly tongues or spears of leaf. No tea type, though, is capable of greater aromatic refinement than this one, and oolong can evoke a huge repertoire of allusions from peaches and apricots to flowers and crushed stones (called 'rock tea' in Chinese).

Black tea (*hong cha* – which literally means 'red tea') is fully oxidized. After picking and withering, the leaves are bruised to the required degree by machines that roll the leaf to and fro. Once the oxidation is complete, the leaves are kiln-fired. There is a wide variation in black tea types within China, from the finest, needle-like 'hair tip' Keemun Maofeng to coarse, low-grade black tea. Most black teas from Yunnan have distinctively earthy, savoury or malty tones, but the finest wild types (from the forested Daxue Mountain) can rival rare oolongs for perfumed finesse.

Pu-erh tea (*puerh cha* or 'dark tea') is the only tea type whose processing involves maturation, as fine wine does. Like bottles of Latour or La Tâche, the greatest cakes of pu-erh can be aged for many years after sale, and 50- or 60-year-old examples command astonishing prices (though purchasers are paying for age itself: there is little of the vintage differentiation that is such a hallmark of wine production).

Authentic pu-erh is grown exclusively in Yunnan Province, and often picked from wild trees. (Cheap 'pu-erh', by contrast, is produced in Fujian as well as Vietnam and Laos, from cultivated bushes.) The fundamental cultivar used is called Da Yeh (or 'big leaf': an *assamica*), though it exists in many local and clonal variants in the province. After withering in the open air or in a well-ventilated space, the classical process of making pu-erh involves wok-firing followed by sun-drying. The leaf is then immediately pressed into cakes and matured in warehouses in Guangdong or elsewhere, where local microflora will 'ripen' these cakes very slowly, over years or decades. This is Sheng Pu-Erh, meaning 'raw' or 'living' Pu-Erh. In youth, the tea has a pungent, powerful and assertive flavour of savoury, leathery style; with age, it grows darker, richer and more mellow.

There is an alternative, speedier way of making pu-erh that involves storing the leaves in large piles in warm, humid rooms locally, subject to the action of local yeast, moulds and bacteria for a month or two before being pressed. This is Shou ('cooked' or 'ripened') pu-erh. A wine analogy would be between Madeira aged by *estufagem* compared to Madeira aged by *canteiro*. Some secrecy accompanies the making of cooked pu-erh. It's less expensive than raw pu-erh, less subtle, and has less long-term ageing potential. It does, though, quickly attain an approximation of the classical rich, dark liquorousness acquired by Sheng Pu-Erh only after decades.

Flower teas (*hua cha*), finally, are made by an elaborate process of layering green or black tea with the blossoms themselves. The petals or flowerheads (jasmine, rose or osmanthus) infuse the tea with their scent, and are later removed and discarded save for a few cosmetic strays. Essences are never used for high-quality flower tea. China has also developed an extraordinary art, a kind of vegetable origami, involving the creation of tea and flower blooms tied into the shapes of flowers themselves, of animals or of other shapes such as stars. One of these dried flower tea shapes is placed in a glass teapot or vessel, where it unfolds in the hot water, often making an entirely new shape as it does so. The effect is like watching a slow underwater firework.

Green tea is dominant in China and Japan, whereas in almost all other producing countries, black tea dominates. Whole-leaf black-tea production, as described above, is called 'orthodox' in opposition to tea processed by CTC machines, which delivers a chopped, granular or particulate leaf. Orthodox black tea from all sources is customarily divided into grades. A common division would be into four whole-leaf grades, of which the best would be SFTGFOP (Special Fine Tippy Golden Flowery Orange Pekoe), then three broken grades, two grades of fannings and finally 'dust'. CTC teas, by contrast, are graded into brokens, fannings and several dust grades.

India still has a lingering fine-tea tradition, notably the headily perfumed first- and second-flush orthodox teas from Darjeeling: the only black teas to rival great Chinese and Japanese green teas in terms of pristine plant-fresh mimicry. Tippy, early-flush versions of the much maltier, darker and stronger Assam teas provide unrivalled black-tea complexity. Indeed most tea-producing countries (and certainly India, Sri Lanka and Kenya) produce superb black tea, but only as the best unbroken orthodox grades. CTC versions and orthodox fannings and dusts, by contrast, tend to dominate exports. The culprit is the tea bag. Almost all tea bags are filled with CTC tea – or fannings and dusts more generally. This is ideal for cheapness and strength, when black tea is to be drunk with milk; much less so for subtlety and quality if drunk without milk.

3 Health

Tea is healthful. Indeed some studies suggest that tea is a healthier drink than water, especially for those whose diet is low in fresh fruit and vegetables. All tea brings health benefits, but green tea appears to be the most beneficial type of all. Adding milk (and sugar) to tea mitigates those benefits by inhibiting antioxidant absorption. Tea contains a number of useful compounds including fluoride, zinc, folic acid, manganese and vitamins B1, B2 and B6, but the principal 'active ingredient' as far as its health benefits are concerned is the one it shares with red wine: tannin. 'Tannin' is perhaps best described as a family of compounds whose chemistry is close to that of gallic acid (GA); tannins are commonly measured as if they were gallic acid or GA-equivalent. These compounds occur naturally in the bark of trees, especially oak; they help protect the tree from fire, insects and bacteria. Those trained in the indelicate task of tanning animal skins (which, once the putrefying flesh had been excised, originally required human urine to help remove hair fibres and animal faeces mixed with water to soften the skin) use wood tannins to convert the skin into leather. The tannins do this by interacting with the proteins in the skin. The same process is at work when you eat food with red wine, or add milk to black tea. Tannins, in fact, are common in the plant world: as well as tea leaves and grape skins, most berries contain them, as do persimmons and pomegranates. Wine tannins are usually called proanthocyanidins; tea tannins are called catechins. Both are classified as flavonoids, and have antioxidant and other effects in the body that, many studies suggest, can help prevent cancer, heart disease, bowel disease and neurodegenerative diseases.

4 Consolation, service

The philosophical flavour of tea is very different from that of wine, though each drink brings us solace and invites us to drink something beautiful. Alcoholic wine is elevating, stimulating and emotionally rousing, breaking down inhibitions and conveying a sense of togetherness to irredeemably separate beings. Conversation, song, physical interaction, ritual sharing, the partaking of the divine common to both the Dionysiac mysteries and the Christian Eucharist: all conspire to efface the pain of imprisonment within the ego.

Tea also provides an escape from the ego, by different means. There is no mood alteration; instead, there is only the scent and flavour of leaf, plant and earth, accompanied by a mild charge of caffeine and the reassurance of warm liquid nourishment. Caffeine is a stimulant – but tea's effect seems to be that of an alert calmness, perhaps due to the presence in tea of other alkaloids such as theophylline and theobromine, and the amino acid L-theanine, which are thought to have relaxing and calming effects. Tea can induce contemplation to those unpractised in meditation techniques, and even acts as an aid to meditation for those trained in meditative traditions. In place of shadowy Orphism and terrifying Dionysiac rituals, in place of the elevation of Christian communion and the warm bonds of Jewish ritual, and in place of the passion, debate and action to which secular wine drinkers may be roused, tea propels the drinker towards non-action (*wu wei*), simplicity (*pu*), compassion and the doctrine of being in emptiness central to Taoism and shared by Buddhism. This is tea's consoling force: a place of illuminated quietness where lost perspective might be re-gained.

What of the tea ceremony? For the Chinese, this usually means *gongfu cha*, or *gongfu* tea service, first mentioned by Wu Lu in the eighth century. *Gongfu* means 'great skill', and the aim is very similar to that of a host serving a series of fine wines in beautiful decanters and glasses for a dinner. It is not, in other words, primarily symbolic and intricately codified, as the Japanese tea ceremony is; it is, rather, pragmatic and designed to show fine tea at its best. The principles of *gongfu cha* underlie all service in China's tea houses, and are practised in Chinese homes. The teapot and teacups, to Western eyes, appear minute and the amount of tea used in the pot colossal, but the principle is that of repeated infusions (four or five for green teas, and up to 30 for an aged pu-erh); the skill lies in the tea server ensuring that temperature and strength of liquor remain ideal for the drinkers throughout service. The purity and temperature of the water (below boiling for green tea, boiling for pu-erh) are important, and the elegance of the accompanying utensils and trays adds to the pleasure of the experience, as do the hand-gestures of the tea server. The surroundings, too, should be both calming and beautiful.

Japan's tea ceremony is tea's philosophical pinnacle, though it is much misunderstood. Its Japanese name – *chado* – means 'the way of tea'. There are many variants (some can last four hours); it implies a particular domestic architecture (guests and host arrive through different doors, and the room needs a scroll alcove and ideally a sunken hearth); not only do tea practitioners need to master the intricacies of tea production, but costumes, calligraphy, flower arranging, ceramics and the use of incense are all important. The guests, like the host, have prescribed gestures and actions to follow. Where, one might wonder, is the simplicity in all this?

It lies in the overarching modesty of the undertaking, properly understood. I can't do better at this point than quote from Kakuzo Okakura's *The Book of Tea*: the ideal introduction to tea philosophy. 'Teaism,' as he calls *chado*, 'is a cult founded on the adoration of the beautiful among the sordid facts of everyday existence. It inculcates purity and harmony, the mystery of mutual charity, the romanticism of the social order. It is essentially a worship of the Imperfect, as it is a tender attempt to accomplish something possible in this impossible thing we know as life.' Making a cup of tea is the most banal of actions, yet *chado* seeks to endow this action with universal significance. According to Okakura, 'it expresses conjointly with ethics and religion our whole point of view about man and nature. It is hygiene, for it enforces cleanliness; it is economics, for it shows comfort in simplicity rather than in the complex and costly; it is moral geometry, inasmuch as it defines our sense of proportion to the universe.' The ritual prescriptions of the ceremony are a way of preserving the advances of others, but it is a 'way' among many other ways, a path among many other paths, and it is the act of embarking on the way that matters, rather than the following or linking the prescriptions (the signs, the waymarks, the cairns) themselves. 'Tao' means 'path', but (Okakura again) 'The Tao is in the Passage rather than the Path'. This is close to the fundamental engagement of the true philosopher as defined by one of the 20th century's leading practitioners, Martin Heidegger: '*Alles ist Weg*' ('all is way'). [*See* Chapter Nine.] Heidegger's *Holzwege* ('woodland trails': paths that do not pass through a forest but rather lead more deeply into it) are given, we might say, a literal form in the gestures of the tea ceremony; they lead us towards the *Lichtung*, the 'clearing' or emptiness in the heart of the forest where we can contemplate, feel or find the quiddity of things. Or, better still, the being of being.

134   A TEA BREAK

CHAPTER SIX

INTERROGATIONS AND IMPIETIES

The Illuminati of the Bottle

I have an Asian acquaintance, successful, single and wealthy, in the upper echelons of accountancy – and a wine lover, which is how we know each other. We became Facebook friends, but I disappointed him. 'You don't post about wine,' he complained. 'It's just politics.' That was true, back then; now I don't post at all. In the interests of fairness, I took a look at his page and his posts, but could find very little about accountancy. It was just wine.

One of wine's least congenial aspects is the tyranny of the geek. Those who climb aboard the wine bus have an oath of allegiance thrust into their hands. No one reads the small print. You shove it into your back pocket and merrily sit down to the next tasting or dinner or masterclass. If you do look through it all in a later moment of boredom, you'll come across the following clause. 'By joining our informal organization, you accept that wine is an absolute good. You accept that it is not only a superior beverage to every other, but is also a subject of all-consuming interest and importance, occluding and expunging every other topic whatsoever, and enjoying right of conversational pre-emption at every hour of day or night.' Once on the bus, you'll also find you have been issued with burgundy-coloured spectacles that prove strangely hard to remove. The world looks pleasant through them; few, thus, lament the disconcerting loss of detail in the field of vision that wearing them entails.

Why so? Wine is a social lubricant, so it's no surprise that it colonizes post-professional evenings, even for those who have been professionally chained to the tasting bench all day. For most wine drinkers, indeed, it's a kind of gleeful symbol of liberation from work, so the idea that it might be work (and thus, like Larkin's squatting toad, a source of oppression) would seem unfathomable. Because it can be collected by eager hobbyists, and because there is no limit to the visceral detail that inheres to the subject, it attracts minds that prefer name checking, date lobbing and score flipping to all other forms of exercise.

The expense of fine wine makes flaunting it a status-enhancing game for rich boys and girls, a drama of esteem played out on aeroplanes and in restaurants and at all the 'smart addresses'; witness the photographs of bottles, labels, glasses of business-class champagne and winery name plaques that litter social media. There's also a kind of machismo of wine: it's not uncommon to hear pumped wine pros or geeky ultras boast, Don Juan-like, about the number of samples they might assay during *en primeur* week, or on a regional research trip, or over the course of a year. The more, of course, the better. And we haven't even got on to the big swinging dicks among the old wine crowd – but let's not go there.

The arcane language doesn't help. It reinforces the idea that wine geeks are a kind of sect, the Illuminati of the bottle, who aren't so much communicating with each other as exchanging secret codes. This, of course, is a source of public amusement out at the interface – but not more. That's the pity of it. Once you've had a laugh at the language and the self-delight involved in retailing this body of arcana, wine geekdom is dissuasive. The uninitiated walk away, muttering 'not for me'. The earnest, impressively researched blog posts go unread, save by other Illuminati.

A glass of wine is not a wholly autonomous object. It's not just a score and a cluster of adjectives. In addition to its geographical identity, it has an economic weight and a cultural presence; these thicken it and make it strange, at least potentially. They drag on its presence in the world. These are what we might grab at and lunge for. That's where the humanity of wine lies.

Professionally, I must engage with the search for the best, but with every year that passes I grow more conscious of its fallacy, the fact that it cannot exist, and would not matter in any case even if it did exist. Only difference exists.

Wine can salve the anguish of the dying, but it can also kill in its own right. We can all name some it has killed, and think of others whose lives it has abbreviated, or killed in part. This wrestle with the dual nature of Dionysus ('most terrible, yet most gentle to mortals': Euripides' summary in *The Bacchae*) is genuinely interesting for every drinker: a true shared experience.

Wine is a beautiful commonplace object in a disorientated and dangerous world, but it is not wholly disengaged from that world. How do we feel about drinking a glass of Tokaji shortly after Hungary's proudly illiberal prime minister wins a third term in office based on an anti-Semitic election campaign or a fourth term based on the erosion of democratic rights? Should we seek out Turkish wine or not, knowing that Turkey's president jails writers, journalists and jurists at whim, but knowing also that Turkey's wine producers are unlikely to support their president and are indeed engaged, when they make wine, in a professionally courageous act? How would French wine have fared in the world had it been the Putin-admiring nativist Marine Le Pen and not the wine-loving internationalist Emmanuel Macron who won the 2017 French Presidential election, as 10.6 million French voters wished, or the 2022 French Presidential election, as 13.3 million French voters wished? On January 20th 2017, America acquired its second wine-producing president, but the contrast with the first was striking; the second is a teetotaller who has declared that Mexicans (such as those who patiently tend his vines over the steamy Virginia summer – and indeed those who tend most of the USA's vines) are 'drug dealers, criminals, rapists'. Wine loves China and China loves wine – but its people can't say what they think, or vote for whom they wish. Jail awaits those Chinese who 'pick quarrels and provoke trouble' – though when confronted by corruption this is a journalist's (even a wine journalist's) duty. Is Crimean wine Ukrainian – or Russian? 'Wine, like money, likes silence,' a Crimean wine grower told me when I asked him this question in 2014. 'Nature is also a confrontation between the strong and the weak, and about the balance between the two,' his fellow grower reminded me. After Russian war crimes in Mariupol and Bucha, will former leaders of wine-exporting nations be happy to stroll through the vineyards of Crimea with Russia's leader, as Italy's Silvio Berlusconi did in September 2015? And how far has land reform got in South Africa's manicured winelands?

Too much is at stake to neuter wine, to shave and starve and clip it into ineffectual and self-referential aesthetics alone. It is dangerous, it faces dangers, and it is never more needed than at times of danger. We should allow it this messy destiny; even celebrate it. This may be of interest to the unIlluminated.

Disarming the Mafia

It's time to own up. Deep breath. Here we go.

A couple of times every year, some pleasant, sincere and meritorious enquirer will ask me for my favourite food-and-wine recommendations, for my general philosophy on food-and-wine matching, or for some specific wine ideas for serving with festive turkey, chilled gazpacho or barbecued spare ribs with cracked-pepper-and-blue-cheese sauce. I usually reply, politely enough, that the subject bores me, that I have nothing of interest to say about it, and that my own approach is to eat whatever's going, and drink the wine I most fancy, in a spirit of easy-going gastronomic anarchy. Generally it all works out fine.

I then feel like a philistine, a fake and a party pooper – for five minutes, after which I forget the whole business. But a flurry of renewed queries recently made me think that I can't really go on like this: the moment has come to explain myself.

I don't deny that 'perfect combinations' exist. I agree that combination A is generally better – or worse – than combination B. It's beyond doubt that most dry wines are best enjoyed with food. I love flavours, and creating and combining them in cooking. The subject matters.

In my view, though, the matching itself eludes prescription, and is best approached with a little common sense on a case-by-case basis, embracing the serendipity that the contingencies of life imply, and discussed spontaneously if wished at table with fellow meal participants but under no other circumstances. Here's why.

Let's suppose you have experienced the felicity of a perfect combination, and wish to pass it on to others. Everybody cooks dishes differently, so 'the same dish' from any non-industrial kitchen will never taste the same twice. (The results even vary when two people use the same recipe, or when the same person cooks a dish on two occasions.)

Take lasagne, for example. How much tomato? From a tin? Tomato paste? Ready-made sauce? What sort of meat have you chosen? How fresh? What fat content? How seasoned? Did you add stock cubes, sugar or wine? What about the béchamel: spices and seasonings? Cheese on top? What sort? How long did you cook it for? How sloppy or firm was it? Did you burn the edges? These things might all turn a perfect combination into a disappointing one.

The same – as you all know – is true for wine. Your lasagne might be perfect with the 2018 Vignes du Tremblay Moulin-à-Vent brought from Eric Janin's Romanèche domaine on your return from a Provençal holiday three years ago. That doesn't mean it will be perfect with Tesco's 2021 Beaujolais-Villages. Useful information on a combination means specifying appellation, vintage and producer for the wine and ingredients and preparation method for the dish. These are preposterous and impractical levels of detail, and you'd come across as tragic for spelling them out.

Even then, it's only perfect for your mouth. For many years, my wife and I couldn't find any successful food-and-wine combinations for my father-in-law. Then we discovered Blanquette de Limoux Méthode Ancestrale, which he loves. With everything. Some people like Aussie Shiraz, with everything. Some prefer Pinot Grigio, with everything. They can't all be right, but they are – for them.

There are even problems with classic combinations. Oysters with Chablis? Great: the Chablis is doing the contrastive work otherwise accomplished by a squeeze of lemon juice. But what if you've already given the lemon a good squeezing? Then the juice might fight with the Chablis. Add some of that tempting Tabasco as well, or some insane vinegar and diced shallot, and it all quickly gets nasty.

The 'holiday-wine scenario' is too clichéd to bear extensive repetition (you know, rosé retsina + lamb @ Zakynthos shoreline taverna + luminous September evening versus rosé retsina + lamb @ basement flat in Doncaster + damp November evening). It proves that the perfect combination in one place and at one moment can be a comprehensive failure in and at another. There is more than tastebuds at stake here.

Away from perfection, though, the plain fact is that many dishes go well enough with almost anything (notably those made with pork

140   INTERROGATIONS AND IMPIETIES

or chicken), and most dishes have far greater wine latitude than the recommendation mafia would suggest.

Let's sum up: the perfect combination is beyond recommendation whereas a decent combination has no need of recommendation. If you do start issuing the banal counsels you see on the back of supermarket wines, you either risk shutting off some interesting alternative possibilities for those who misguidedly take such advice as gospel, or you create havoc by being inadequately specific. Most famously, of course, when you declare that a particular wine goes with 'cheese'. Cheese where I live often means Roquefort, which is delicious (if over-salty) in its own right, but which annihilates all known wines. Yes, even Sauternes. Roquefort can make a glass of water taste disgusting.

So there you are: wine, food, enjoy. That's it.

Hot and Bothered

The 2003 vintage in Europe was shocking. Shockingly hot: the first great blast of climate change. I was in Champagne in late August. Chaos: growers raced back from abbreviated beach holidays to find bunches desiccating on the vines. I saw Pinot grapes in Aÿ as hard, and as flavourless, as plastic. Those who had worked most assiduously, with leaf trimming and bunch positioning, lost most.

A few days before leaving my then-home in Hastings for Champagne, I'd opened a bottle of Bandol. Thickly textured and densely allusive, though not wholly comfortable. Disaggregated, somehow. I put it in the fridge overnight, without thinking.

The next day: revelation. 12°C meant tightened sinews and unexpected poise. The tannins (ripe and sensitively extracted) coped easily. Most astonishingly, the chill seemed to have uncovered an unexpected vein of fruit flavour in the wine. In its 'hot' state, at 24°C, that fruit had been little more than balancing acidity: a kind of camshaft. Drop 12°C, and the camshaft became a bough, clustered with dark, taut sloes. It was good wine at 24°C, but much better wine at 12°C.

Since moving to Languedoc in 2010, I fridge-chill all red wines, all summer. In winter (often colder here than in Hastings), I leave them outside the front door for nocturnal cryo-sedation rather than submitting them to the corruption of our underfloor heating.

How many millions of bottles are disfigured by heat in service every year? If you serve a £50 bottle of wine at the wrong temperature, you throw away £40. No wine, even the broadest chested, will sing at over 21°C. The more a wine warms above that temperature, the more its component parts begin to slide away from one another. Only refrigeration and air-conditioning make the appreciation of wine possible in tropical latitudes. (Yes, this adds to wine's carbon footprint – so long as we continue to generate electricity from fossil fuels.)

Wines, though, know nothing about refrigerators or thermostats. Temperature, like happiness, is a continuum. A macho fridge at 4°C or a centrally heated room of 21°C are not the only alternatives. Most wines except the sweetest are at their best between 10°C and 16°C, which is neither the temperature of your fridge nor the temperature of your living room. The red wines I bring inside in winter at 6°C are far too cold – but within the hour they'll be through 8°C to 10°C, then 12°C; every sip, in fact, will be taken at some subtly different temperature to the previous one. A lower starting point means more drinking pleasure, and more insight into the wine, too. Experiment with the gamut; interrogate it. Persist.

You may take flak from guests. This is an area where popular opinion is entrenched. I first learned my wine-drinking habits in rural Norfolk, where (50 years ago) it was thought essential to roast red wines in front of open fires or torture them, through their fundaments, by sitting them on top of stoves and hobs for an hour before drinking. The practice lingers wherever change comes slowly, wherever houses are old, stone-walled and chill: wine as tepid soup. (At the time, it tasted good.)

Nor are northerners alone in dogma. I was travelling one hot July day with a merchant friend in Tuscany. We asked the proprietress of our roadside restaurant to chill the hot bottle of Chianti she had just brought us. She leant over us, her soft hazel eyes widening as the sweat trickled from her temples, and waved a plump, moist forefinger in our direction. '*I vini rossi non si bevono freschi,*' she said emphatically, spelling it slowly out to these idiot Englishmen: you don't drink red wine chilled! Then she turned and swayed majestically back into the kitchen.

Drinking with the Valkyries

One drawback of a decade lived far from London, with its comfortably cool cellars, its perennially damp and draughty climate, its 'wine houses', its resilient traditions, its ancient political allegiances, its winter darkness is that – I'm missing port. Bizarre: France, where I live, remains by far the largest market for port; the French drink more than the Portuguese. Most of the port drunk in France, though, is unambitious. A simple glass of fruity fortified wine is not what I'm missing.

What I'm missing is more exciting than that. It's the wine drinker's equivalent of zorbing, wing walking, base jumping or any other extreme-sport metaphor you might choose to shiver over. What I'm missing is the chance to drink young Vintage port.

The idea behind Vintage port is that it should LAST A LONG TIME, and the best the longest. My youngest brother was born in 1963, and he still has shapely Sandeman Vintage port with his birth date on to pull out for special birthdays.

In order to create wine of this sort, those vinifying Vintage port have to adopt the most unfashionable winemaking strategies in the world and… holy cow, the results are good!

The wine has torrents of alcohol, half of it added as high-strength grape spirit, and the fruit is pummelled to annihilation as quickly as possible during a break-neck vinification period of extreme if carefully controlled violence (perhaps cage-fighting would be the best metaphor of all). The fashion nowadays for every other red wine on the planet, by contrast, decrees slow, gradual, gossamer-fingered extraction – indeed little more than 'maceration' if you can manage it, and the less alcohol, the better. Vintage port remains unapologetic. Power, tannin, extract, explosive fruit, density and ferocity: bring them all on, baby.

Remember that port is fortified when it is only half-way through its fermentation period, and at that point, it says farewell to its skins, its pips and its stems (if stems have been used). Extraction is then over. Finito! Forget the 45 days of fermentation and post-fermentation maceration many Barolo wines undergo: Vintage port may only have a week to grab and stash everything it will need in order to see out 50 years in a bottle. Extreme force is necessary. Shock and awe: trembling grapes. Merciless human feet were perfect for the task, but the new era of pistons, plungers and robotic treaders working sleeplessly round the clock in temperature-controlled *lagares* (treading tanks) in the Douro may be even more effective. Vintage port quality has never been finer.

That's not what I want to tell you, though. What I want to say is this: ignore anyone telling you not to taste and drink Vintage port in earliest youth. You should drink it, soon. Act precipitately.

By all means store a few bottles pending 'full maturity' if you wish, and appreciate it in a state of subtle, graceful and polite refinement, sagely tutored by time. That's a pleasure, too.

But you won't fully understand it unless you have tasted it young, in its 'Ride of the Valkyries' stage, when it comes hurtling out of the glass and puts the screamers on you. Yes, it can be challenging. Yes, it's black in the glass. It smells of steamrollered plums, strimmed nettles, Earl Grey and an accident with a pepper grinder, and it tastes like sweet, vinous magma. But it's also the product of a company or a farm's oldest, wisest vines, carefully cosseted, from long-proven vineyards, and usually made with a blend of largely indigenous grape varieties. Quality is quietly there, like a store of hydrogen, feeding its solar force. Don't wait until later, when it's become a red giant or a white dwarf: open that stellar bottle now. Wine offers no other experience like this.

144   INTERROGATIONS AND IMPIETIES

Of Jellyfish and Guardsmen

What do we mean by 'a grape variety' or (more properly) 'a cultivar'? Do such names on labels inform us about the taste of wine – or about the longing for conceptual simplicity?

The more I read about the subject; the more I taste wines from 'the same variety' produced in different places; the more that I consider the technical distinction between variety and mutation (a clone being a propagated mutation with beneficial traits); and the more that DNA insights reveal genetic links between varieties that make absolutely no sense whatsoever in relation to aroma and flavour; then the more questionable our attachment to the notion of variety begins to seem.

I understand its viticultural inevitability – and it's hard to find an easier route to wine knowledge than by tracking grape varieties. They seem to offer a kind of grammar of wine. Those names and their flavour profiles… they're just so tempting.

When you start to put wines in your mouth, though, the system begins to collapse. The more you taste, the more it collapses. Too much 'varietal thinking', in other words, may inhibit and shackle wine appreciation. If we were to regard place and the cultural traditions of place as the primary translators of wine flavour, and variety as secondary and anecdotal, we'd be wiser wine lovers.

Of course it's interesting to know that Gewürztraminer and Savagnin or Pinot Noir and Pinot Gris are, genetically speaking, 'the same grape variety', and that the only difference between them is one of mutation. It doesn't alter the fact a great Alsace Gewurztraminer is wildly different from a varietal Savagnin from Arbois or the Côtes du Jura (let alone *vin jaune*). The former is exotically perfumed, languid on the tongue and almost devoid of acidity; the latter smells either coolly and reticently fruity or intriguingly tangy, and the acidity can hit your tongue like an axe. I once tasted the poised and athletic 2005 Clos Saint Jacques from Rousseau (a red Grand Cru burgundy) at the table of a generous friend. The 'same variety' as Zind-Humbrecht's balsam-and-honey-laden 2010 Clos Saint Urban Rangen de Thann Pinot Gris? Not in any sensual universe I know.

What we learn from this, I think, is that the implications of genetic damage or errors in the DNA of a single variety can be far more consequential, to the human nose and mouth, than the DNA boundary markers between varieties, even though that damage or those errors might be minute or insignificant in the DNA profile as a whole. It's, um, weird.

The paradoxes aren't restricted to mutants, though. A couple of weeks prior to writing this text, I tasted (in the same afternoon) a Tannat from the Alta Mesa AVA in warm Lodi shortly before trying a barrel sample of the 2012 Vignes Préphylloxériques, a Tannat produced from a tiny, ancient parcel in Saint-Mont by the Plaimont Producteurs co-operative.

No mutational tension here, in other words; it's the same variety. Once again, though, the wines were unrecognizably different from one another. The former was soft and untannic, trembling like a jellyfish, rich with burnt blackberry; the latter was invigorating, resonant and profoundly tannic, more guardsman than gelatinous zooplankton. Not only were they different in flavour analogies, but they were a shocking structural contrast. I was tasting two places, and two wine cultures. Other varieties grown in each place would surely have told the same tale. The variety, in fact, was an impediment to understanding.

Are we really illuminating New Zealand's Marlborough Sauvignon by continually benchmarking it against Sancerre or Pouilly-Fumé? Mendoza Malbec is a different prospect to Cahors; Rutherford Cabernet and Margaux will never stroll hand-in-hand. Tasting Chablis is irrelevant if you want to make (or enjoy) a white wine that happens to come from Chardonnay grapes grown in Tuscany, Margaret River or Napa. China's Cabernet Gernischt is 'the same as' Chile's Carmenère – but in another sense it isn't. The wine world begins to acknowledge this paradox, in fact, with the dual names 'Syrah' and 'Shiraz', or with 'Pinot Grigio' and 'Pinot Gris'. Producers of each, in new global locations, carefully consider which name to use depending on the style of wine they wish to make (restrained or demonstrative respectively).

We pay lip-service to place and origin, but we continue to organize our wine thinking, and build our wine aesthetics, around the superannuated and treacherous varietal model. Bring on the post-cultivar age. Origin and culture are what matters. Why make a fetish of what is no more than the third most important thing about a wine?

Wine's Drab Roses

Shortly before Christmas 2018, a 92-year-old Briton died in the same Shropshire village in which he had been born. That implies a quiet life – yet his name is well-known around the world, at least to gardeners and rose-lovers. David Austin was the greatest rose-breeder of his times, responsible for creating more than 240 new roses (including one called Chianti and another called Comtes de Champagne). As I read the accounts of Austin's life and work, I was struck by the contrast between the world of roses – where breeding innovation is not merely welcomed but championed – and wine creation, where most producers rely on a tiny pool of long-established cultivars (varieties), despite their often poor disease-resistance, weak site aptitude and increasing climate discomfort.

I don't want to make facile comparisons. A rose plant is an end in itself, a finished product, enjoyed for the appearance and scent of its blooms, and valued for its performance abilities. A vine variety, by contrast, is more like a tool or an ingredient: something that the wine grower uses to maximize the agricultural potential of any land that has (or might have) a wine-growing vocation. Because so much wine is sold by variety, though, and because a combination of variety and location is thought to define the potential of a wine's sensual profile, these cultivars matter.

Whenever I've had a chance to talk to geneticists and breeders working in this area, their frustration at the timidity and conservatism of wine producers, legislators and drinkers is tangible. Vine breeders are in no doubt that, without recourse to genetic modification, they would be able to breed fungal disease resistance into the varieties we already use, thereby sparing soils and river systems significant annual chemical pollution. It would be possible to breed other advantageous traits into existing varieties, such as the ability to achieve full physiological ripeness at lower sugar levels than at present, to ripen later, or to be less susceptible to problems such as *coulure* or *millerandage*. Why not, too, breed for better aroma and flavour?

David Austin wished to combine the beauty of scent and visual subtlety and classicism of old gallica, damask and alba rose varieties – but dispose with their tendency to disease and leaf-loss, and their habit of flowering only once a year. This he did, by drawing sparingly on the genetic material of floribunda and hybrid tea varieties with immense patience over a long life. Vine breeders around the world could do as well, indeed perhaps better, given modern gene-editing techniques and the latent genetic diversity hidden in refuges such as Portugal, Italy or Georgia.

Much, though, is ranged against such work. It takes decades. Varieties of this sort, furthermore, would have to have new names – so they would immediately be confronted by legislative problems in Europe, where only certain named varieties are permitted in zones that enjoy protected geographical indications. Both inside and outside Europe, consumer resistance would need to be overcome. Wine drinkers are conservative; wine enthusiasts and fine-wine collectors rigidly so.

For all that, change is inevitable, at least in Europe, since the EU means to eliminate copper from agricultural use (its use has been extended until 2025 at reduced levels of 4 kg/ha per year). The only way out of the impasse, especially for organic growers, will be to breed new, resistant versions of existing varieties. Champagne, for example, has been working on just that for Chardonnay, Pinot Noir and Pinot Meunier since 2010. Rigorous sensory analysis is necessary before adoption, but who wouldn't like to see an end to blue-leaved vines, stinking June vineyards and copper-laden soils?

More importantly, though, why assume that varietal innovation must mean the loss of some fabled ancestral quality? Might it not rather be the case that our reliance on a small number of 'international' varieties, most of which find themselves inappropriately planted in alien environments, delivers colossally disappointing wines to the world's drinkers? In 2016, just 17 varieties accounted for half the world's plantings. Merlot was the second most widely grown variety in the world, Sauvignon Blanc the sixth and Pinot Gris (largely labelled as Pinot Grigio) the twelfth. In each case, standard versions of these varieties are wildly adrift of what the variety can produce at its best; they veer between anodyne and lurid. Can we really say that we have the best of all possible wine worlds at present? I doubt it. There is enormous genetic diversity and resource hidden in global vineyards. We do little or nothing with it. We're content with our drab roses.

Beyond Best

In early 2016, I realized something had changed in my relationship with wine. I didn't want the best any more.

What? How can anybody not want to taste, enjoy and own the wine world's summits? Explain yourself...

The best is now unaffordable

Notions of 'affordability', of course, are relative: that's obvious. Personal circumstances are all, and a particular price for a bottle of wine is either affordable or unaffordable in relation to one's wealth as a functioning economic unit (as an individual or a family). In the interests of journalistic transparency, I've made an annual disclosure of earnings on my own website from 2011 onwards (http://www.andrewjefford.com/disclosure/) – so by consulting that you can, if you wish, approach what follows with some relevant figures to hand. All of these GBP figures are calibrated for 2016 – but differentials have done nothing but widen since.

I first bought 'the best' in 1983, when I purchased a case of Château Pichon-Lalande 1982 for £9 a bottle, equivalent to £28.71 in 2016 figures (allowing for inflation). It was wonderful wine, and at that price I never had qualms about drinking it: bliss.

I have subsequently bought 'the best', but the prices have risen steadily. Pichon-Baron 1990 at £30 a bottle (£60 allowing for inflation); Bâtard-Montrachet 1995 from Sauzet at £69.50 a bottle (£117); Château Margaux 1996 at £97 a bottle (£164); La Fleur Pétrus 1998 at £45.62 a bottle (£72.54); Lynch-Bages 2000 at £40.15 a bottle (£61.03).

Per bottle prices for the latest releases of these wines vary from around £100 a bottle for Lynch-Bages 2015 to £400 a bottle for the Château Margaux 2015; and a young vintage of the Sauzet Bâtard is going to cost at least £200, so we can say that the prices of 'the best' have certainly accelerated ahead of inflation. When inflation is taken into account, my current earnings are about 27 percent less than my two best earnings years (2000 and 2008), and those earnings now largely support a family of four. I only mention these circumstances to point out how the affordability of 'the best' can easily be obliterated, which is why most of the purchases mentioned above have been re-sold: wines like these are now too costly for me to buy and too valuable for us to drink.

Any income of over £60,000 per year puts its earner in the top seven percent of the UK working population, so I am already much better paid than most of my compatriots, as well as an immensely privileged individual in a global sense. Yet for 'the best wine' to be truly affordable for those with children to support, I think you'd need to be in the top three percent of UK earners, bringing in more than £91,300 per year before tax. Ideally, you'd be a one-percenter (£159,000 per year plus): those people own 21 percent of the UK's wealth – but must surely own a much, much larger percentage of all the country's top wine.

The best is overpriced

If a particular commodity is high-status, sought-after and limited in supply, then 'the best' will always be disproportionately more expensive than other quality categories of that commodity, by virtue of nothing more than its rarity. Footballer Paul Pogba (who moved on August 9th 2016 from Juventus to Manchester United for a record transfer fee at the time of £89 million) was not 89 times better than a professional footballer whose transfer fee at the same moment was £1 million, or infinitely better than a player on free loan. He was better by an incalculable number of small increments, and justified his fee because those slight incremental improvements are very hard for the managers and owners of football clubs to locate in a single individual. Wine is no different. The best must necessarily – by any value-for-money standard or (if you prefer) objective assessment of quality increments – be overpriced. If affordability of 'the best' is a consideration (as it will be for 97 percent of Britons), forget fine wine: it's not worth it.

The best isn't interesting

Let me be clear: I don't mean that great wine cannot offer sublime drinking pleasure. It can, and if any of my one-percenter friends offer me a glass of Cheval Blanc or Musigny, I count myself fortunate and revel in the experience. I would love to be able to drink these wines at home, informally and thoughtfully, a couple of times a year.

Such wines tend to be tasted reverentially amid formal surroundings, though; they are often (in my opinion) over-aged by their owners; and it requires no great intelligence, originality and tasting ability to single them out for praise, or lavish them with points. Because of their status, they are often accumulated and served en masse at grand, showy horizontal or vertical tastings where full, profound and leisurely appreciation and enjoyment of their qualities is impossible (*see* pages 180–82). In other words, tasting great wine can often be a pre-programmed, ritualized experience. It may be exquisite (because of the secular sanctity of the ritual rather than the taste of the wine), but it isn't necessarily interesting.

Whereas if you sit down with an old friend in a restaurant in Heraklion, and he suggests you try a bottle of Yiannis Economou's 2006 Liatiko, and you discover that it looks and tastes like some kind of kinky, low-acid cousin of Barolo, and its aromatic sweetness (sniffed amid the restaurant scents of burnt sage and grilled octopus) makes you think for some reason of Byzantium, and its savoury qualities and lush tannins bond perfectly with the roast goat and bitter foraged wild greens that the Egyptian-Filipino waitress has just brought you... well, all of that is interesting. In 20 years, I may well be dead. I want as much interest as possible in my tasting life before I die.

The best is somebody else's decision

Sometimes I adore 'the best' wines that I'm served; sometimes their strengths seem to me to be gestural and button-pushing; on rare occasions I think they're an out-and-out swindle. But the point is that they are always someone else's definition of 'the best': a committee verdict by the world's one-percenters, working in co-ordination with a few centuries or decades of tradition.

After 40 years of thoughtful and questing wine drinking, I now know the kind of thing I like to buy for my own drinking – as opposed to the much broader spectrum of wines that I would hope to appreciate professionally. If it's red, I want some kind of palpable and detaining tannic presence (based on skins or stems, of course, not oak or powder) and textural wealth; I don't relish unripe, prominent or exaggeratedly structural acidity; I'm looking for a certain sobriety, challenge or allusiveness of aroma and flavour, and sometimes a strange sort of viscerally appealing comeliness (typical, for example, of Pomerol or of some Napa Cabernet). If it's white, I want discretion and subtlety, a closeness of grain, a little teasing aromatic intrigue. (Or its visceral opposite, especially from Condrieu and Alsace Gewurztraminer.) The non-fruit flavours we habitually call 'mineral' are usually welcome.

Purity and limpidity are outstanding virtues in wines of either colour. Originality of flavour is preferable to banality, though on its own it does not guarantee merit. I don't want too much fruit in wines of either colour; I don't want any palpable oak at all; I don't want violence of flavour, garish balances, or the lack of drinkability that goes with these things. I don't want wine to smell like cider or beer.

These are my tastes; yours may be quite different. But whatever they are, you can probably eliminate three-quarters of all the wines commonly considered 'the best' in different categories by arriving at a calm understanding of your own preferences, and by hunting them down wherever they might be found. Given my set of tastes, it's not difficult, for example, to find wines which deliver much more profound satisfaction than many of the world's 'bests' by hunting round for outstanding sub-€25 bottles in Alsace, Bordeaux, South-West France, Roussillon, the Southern Rhône Valley, Italy, Austria or Georgia. And when 'the best' is your decision – then it really is the best.

Nature in All Her Glory

When I wrote *The New France* (2002), I found myself repeatedly using one phrase in chapter after chapter: 'non-interventionism'. Oddly, it has no French equivalent. I wouldn't even know how to translate it into French.

Books are written for their readers, which in this case meant English-language wine lovers and wine creators. France was generally out of favour at the time, criticized for its legislative rigidity and qualitative inconsistency. The Southern Hemisphere and California, by contrast, were in the ascendant, and their 'reliable' and sometimes interventionist wines widely acclaimed. But everyone in both hemispheres was claiming that they wanted to make terroir wine, or 'wine of place'. That was, correctly, considered the future of fine wine.

I could see an anomaly – so my use of non-interventionism was to underline a fundamental truth of terroir, one so unthinkingly accepted in France that no one ever bothered to mention it. Which is this: if you want to make a wine of place, you have to respect that place and what it delivers to you in terms of raw materials. Place, variety and season are all inscribed in the chemical constituents of the must. Intervene and adjust them if you wish to make 'a better wine', but do so knowing that you will efface the sense of place and season as a consequence.

A decade and a half later, this is widely understood. If I was writing the book again, I doubt that I'd even mention this rather awkward phrase. But we've all gone much further now – beyond where the buses stop, and on into the dark forests and craggy uplands of 'natural' wine. Sometimes the sun sweeps across these uplands, to thrilling effect; sometimes the forests are drenched in mist and rain, and are a miserable place for a wine drinker to find herself or himself. The natural-wine premise is absolute non-interventionism: nature in all her glory.

There is, though, another anomaly here, as Australian wine thinker Brian Croser has pointed out: even absolute non-interventionism should not mean non-winemaking. Bottled nature needs help to be glorious. As so often, the analogy of winemaker-as-midwife is apt. If midwives cross their arms, do nothing and let nature take its unimpeded course, the levels of death in childbirth will soar. (I would have no sons, rather than two.) Fundamentalist non-interventionism is, like all absolute beliefs, a disaster.

'Paradoxically,' Croser wrote in a letter circulated in 2018, 'it takes a high degree of knowledge, a power of informed observation and a large capital investment to be truly and successfully "non-interventionist" in growing grapes and making fine wine.' He's right – though smaller and less well-funded wine-growers might perhaps hope to replicate the 'large capital investment' with unreasonable doses of hard work.

How about trying to come up with a workable definition of what successful non-interventionism might mean? The two key points would be, as Croser suggests, 'knowledge' and 'observation'. Growers need knowledge to understand what is happening in a vineyard or a fermenting tank at every moment, which in turn implies constant scrutiny. A wine grower is on sentry duty from bud-break to bottling, and you can never have enough knowledge or experience to inform what you are observing. Non-interventionist winemaking means proactive inactivity: maximum respect for raw materials combined with minimum tolerance of deviations as must ferments to finished wine. When it's time to act, act you must.

To harvest the very best grapes that place and season permit, at the perfect cusp of ripeness, will often mean a summer of incessant work. To ferment the juice of those grapes in a limpid and transparent manner means

154   INTERROGATIONS AND IMPIETIES

close-focus analysis, patience, spotless hygiene and, in most cases, restrained use of sulphur to avert the chronic spoilage or homogenizing faults that will efface terroir even more comprehensively than winemaking adjustments.

It's our great good fortune as drinkers that almost every fine wine from both hemispheres is now made in this way. Natural wines, by contrast, are often proudly confrontational; it's for you to decide if they're delivering profundity and purity, or abusing your trust.

Like winemakers, drinkers too need to be alert – to the truths of undogmatic pleasure.

Auction Fever

Why buy wine at auction? Careful comparison of prices suggests that auction purchasers enjoy paying over the odds – and that's before they've found handfuls of extra money for the alarming 'buyer's premium' (and local taxes). A decade ago, I thought that the emergence of international fine-wine broker-merchants like Farr Vintners and its competitors would soon put wine auctioneers out of business. Far from it.

Do the paddle wavers not bother with – or forget all about – their homework? Just so, and willingly. Auctions fill a psychological and social more than a commercial need.

Stocking your wine cellar is now a solitary, even a lonely activity. You scan websites; compare prices; check point scores; send an email; make an electronic transfer; file an invoice. There might be the odd phone call to someone urbane and plausible to discuss provenance, but you could easily assemble a grand collection to sit beneath your former Georgian vicarage in Hampshire (or private residence on Hong Kong's Peak) without a single handshake or broached bottle. It's a bit, um, sad.

Then the auction room beckons. Auctions, like restaurants, are a form of social theatre. There is a narrative; there are performers and players, even improvised scripts; and those who take part step into the spotlight of a society ritual. It's where you 'come out' as a collector. It's poker for rich softies. It's about raised pulses and primal urges; buyers tussle over prize lots like portly stags in combat during the rut. Small wonder the homework goes out of the window.

The rare auctions I have attended in London in the past have been run with almost painful sobriety and deferentially pursed lips, while the annual Hospices de Beaune auction in Burgundy (which sets the price for the new vintage) tends to be a characteristically French blend of glamour and tedium. There is, though, another way, as I learned at the 'Napa Valley Vintners Barrel Auction for the Wine Trade' held in mid-February 2013.

'Fritzy and Urse' (Napa Valley auctioneers Fritz Hatton and Ursula Hermacinski) were strangers to pursed lips and tedium. Fritzy got it all going with plenty of whooping and hollering ('I feel the energy in the room like never before, woo hoo hoo!') and was frank with shy bidders ('20? 20? We're already at 22. Get him a cup o' coffee…'; or 'How much? How much? 10? You can do better than that…').

Urse was more of a tease ('C'mon kitty cats' is a phrase you don't often hear in London's King Street or New Bond Street), but 'It's cash money, I'll take it', and a bang of the gavel followed by 'thank you. Rock on!' had indubitable West Coast panache.

And rock on they did. Here's the enigma. These buyers were wine merchants – cool heads on intimate terms with bottom lines – and the proceeds go to the Vintners for their promotional activities: not exactly a charity to drain wallets on waves of compassion. Most of the wines were from the difficult 2011 vintage, yet even so the sale very nearly broke its own record. The paddle-waver in front of me bid for Lot 47: 60 bottles of the 2011 Shafer Sunspot Vineyard. His friend filmed him on his iPhone throughout. The early flock of hopeless bidders fell away as the price climbed past $30,000 (for just 60 bottles); he himself shrugged his shoulders and gave up, smiling wryly back at the iPhone, as it went past $40,000. The 60 bottles eventually sold for $50,000, or around $833/£550 per bottle – in other words, four times the price of the newly anointed 'Parker perfect' 2010 Château Pape-Clément.

I tasted as much as I could before the sale, and was bemused to see what I felt were wines of refinement and poise, like the 2011 Cabernet Sauvignon from Spring Mountain Vineyard or the Corison 2011 Cabernet Sauvignon Premiere Reserve (which included some Kronos), fetch much less than the monstrous Bevan Cellars and Boswell 2011 'We Will Rock You' (made, Russell Bevan assured me, with a 42% *saignée*): 120 bottles knocked down at a staggering $625 a bottle. It's only my opinion, but I felt that this awesome but undrinkable wine was very nearly the stuff of nightmares.

It all made Bordeaux seem cheap – but hey, it's an auction, folks were there to see and be seen, and (as Fritzy assured us) 'we're trending on Twitter above NASCAR and the Oscars, woo hoo!'

The Party's Over

The relationship between rock, soil and wine flavour is little understood yet widely acclaimed. There's a long-held European belief is that nothing matters more than the physical medium in which vines are rooted, and growers will often dazzle visitors with their command of exotic geological detail. Outside Europe, the notion that a distinguished site is the key to wine quality is rapidly gaining traction. 'Let the vineyard speak' is an unquestioned ideal, no matter how difficult this action may be to define.

For writers, meanwhile, it's party time; the tasting-note air is thick with 'liquid rock', fossils, flints, seashells, pumice, tuff, granite sands and flaking schist; fruit flavours command most respect when infused with slate, lime and marl. Into this exciting if dangerous environment steps a dark figure with a whistle: Professor Alex Maltman of Aberystwyth University.

Maltman is a civilized geologist of rigorously scientific temperament. His specialism was sediment deformation (he took early retirement in 2004, though he continues with some teaching duties). Away from the ocean-bed day-job, he spent 40 years reading about wine, and 30 years growing grapes and making wine – in Wales, so you can tell he's not easily dissuaded. After four decades of quiet chortling, he decided that enough is enough; out has come the whistle, with a series of papers published since 2003, Maltman is calling time on the wine world's geological fantasies.

The publication of these papers in the *Journal of Wine Research* and other academic journals initially meant a restricted audience, though Maltman has subsequently published *Vineyards, Rocks, & Soils: The Wine Lover's Guide to Geology* (2018), and has also written widely for *The World of Fine Wine* and other wine journals in recent years.

Maltman stresses that he is 'not claiming that there is no such thing as minerality, that vines don't take up minerals from the soil, or that vineyard geology is irrelevant. Clearly, the geology defines the water and nutrient supply crucial in vine growth, providing there's no irrigation or fertilizing.' As a wine-lover, too, he says he understands and recognizes the un-fruity components in flavours of certain wines (like Chablis, Mosel Riesling, white Hermitage, Santorini Assyrtiko, Priorat or Douro reds) about which mineral descriptors are commonly used.

He demolishes any literal connection, though, by pointing out that single-element nutrient minerals in solution (as cations) are very different from complex, usually insoluble geological minerals, which have zero or low levels of cation-exchange capacity. Any mineral solutes present in wine, he says, exist at levels well below the threshold for detection, and if they could be tasted would taste unpleasant anyway; furthermore, as far as flavour creation in wine grapes is concerned, 'the real action is up on the vine', via photosynthetic processes, rather than down in the roots. (And wine grapes, of course, are simply the raw materials used to create a processed product; the 'wine flavours' we know are the product of fermentation.)

We surround ourselves, therefore, with fairy stories. He cited a mailing from the The Sunday Times Wine Club, stressing that their Saint Chinian-Roquebrun is special because it comes 'from a terroir that's 100% unique. The secret? Schist. As the experts will tell you, some rocks make better wine. There's the limestone that forms the Côtes of Burgundy. And of Right Bank Bordeaux. Chalk in Champagne. The gravels of the Médoc and Graves. And down south, "schist" – the geological equivalent of

Viennetta ice cream… Comes in green, purple, brown and black, all stuffed full of tasty minerals.' He calls this the 'passive-descriptive approach'. 'You describe the geology and wine from place A (preferably with lots of nice maps, pictures and big words) and then the geology from place B where, oh!, the wines are different! You then take it as read that it is the geology that is responsible for the differences, ignoring everything else and making no attempt to explain what it is the geology is supposed to be doing. It's so misleading, at so many levels.'

Maltman's painstakingly argued critique made me aware of the difficulties inherent in drawing any direct inference about aroma and flavour from vineyard soil and geology. I'm happy to use 'mineral', 'stone' or 'earth' in a strictly metaphorical sense, to allude to a certain sensorial repertoire we associate with worked earth or rocks, just as we use 'cream' or 'cassis' in similar metaphorical sense. Note, though, that the beautiful and seductive scents of warm worked earth, wetted stones or the 'petrichor' aroma of soil after rain derives from organic compounds in the soil or on the rocks, not the minerals themselves, which have no sensorial identity at all.

The problem with wielding these metaphors, though, is that if I describe a wine whose vine is growing in slate as 'slatey', the metaphor is quickly gobbled up by the literal image, and the trusting reader assumes a direct line of transmission.

We need to wield these terms with care, then. What we can all agree on is that such non-fruit uniqueness exists in wines from certain places, and that as Maltman says 'it is conceivable that physical geological factors do have some role in giving typicity'. The transmission role from geological minerals to nutrient minerals is complex, though, and it is still far from clear whether tiny variations in nutrient minerals (by further complex transformative processes) eventually play any kind of a role in the acquisition of aroma and flavour compounds in wine grapes.

There is, in sum, no granite in wine. Party time, ladies and gentlemen, is over.

Call in the Plumbers

Appellations have a problem. Not existential: they're a fine idea, since they help small producers go to market with a meaningful name. They're also necessary: value in the wine world is principally based on origin, and appellations guarantee origin. The problem is the same one that you have with your car or your house: appellations need maintenance to work well. They're not getting it.

Many French appellations were created in the 1930s. It was a decade of execrable weather, economic depression and political foreboding: life couldn't have been tougher for growers, or more different from today. Another flurry of appellations arrived in the 1950s: a happier time, but economically testing. There were more in the 1980s, as former VDQS wines won promotion to appellation status – but by then the best sites were mostly long acclaimed, and hopeful new arrivals have often found the going hard.

In the last 40 years, everything has changed. Economic conditions have improved today; fine-wine regions have prospered beyond the wildest dreams of previous generations. For modest wines, global competition is now fierce. Consumption patterns have changed. The weather, meanwhile, has warmed for all. Many Northern European regions are benefitting from climate change – but there are evident threats, from heatwaves, drought, storms, hail, disorderly weather in general and (paradoxically) spring frost. Everything about most appellations now needs revision, notably their permitted varieties and blends, and their internal and external boundary lines.

Change, though, creates losers as well as winners. Losers mean lawyers and legal challenges. It's all too difficult. It doesn't happen.

Ground-level evolution continues anyway, leaving legislation looking inadequate. In Anjou in July 2020, for example, I discovered that a schist-soiled region famed for sweet white wines and semi-sweet rosé is fast mutating

160   INTERROGATIONS AND IMPIETIES

into a vanguard region for dry Chenin Blanc-based terroir whites and Cabernet Franc-based reds. Quarts de Chaume may be the Loire's only official Grand Cru – but the suite of chic Anjou Blanc *parcellaires* produced within its boundaries is just as interesting and finds a readier market.

In Châteauneuf-du-Pape in May 2021, I found a renaissance of the older, 'forgotten' varieties like Vaccarèse, Counoise, Muscardin and Picardin. No more blow-out showstoppers based on centenarian Grenache aged in oak, but instead wines that feature every permitted variety (white and red alike), whole-bunch fermentation for freshness, with some use of concrete and earthenware jars in place of new oak. Grenache, meanwhile, is being regarded more circumspectly since 'ripeness' implies lofty alcohol statements on labels, and the increasingly uncomfortable Syrah is no longer an automatic choice for these warm vineyards. Individual vineyard rankings are changing.

There is, though, a key difference between these two regions. Châteauneuf was France's pioneer appellation – the process got under way in 1894, and the rules were first drafted in 1923. They're wonderfully flexible. The rules of later appellations, including those of the Loire, grew steadily less flexible: the French mania for over-legislating now leaves them hamstrung. Appellations across southern France, for example, desperately need Châteauneuf's freedom of action to make blended wine or varietal wine as wished, to call on a wide range of varieties and to modify or change plantings within workably large zones. They haven't got it; they're stuck.

Fine-wine zones like Burgundy, meanwhile, could produce much more desirable and saleable wine with cautious boundary modifications that reflect the realities of today's climate. Some believe, too, that complantation of, for example, Aligoté with Chardonnay would produce fresher and more complex white wines as the climate warms. But Burgundy's stuck, too.

Without maintenance, nothing lasts forever. Time to call in the plumbers.

In Praise of Young Wine

I'm old. Too tired to party – yet awake in the small hours. Anxious about minutiae. Reluctant to leave the house without a warm pully and a scarf. I think that concludes the investigation.

You can call me mature if you like. What, though, would it mean? Wise? Every age brings its own energy and insights to the world – yet the elderly can make ill-advised decisions, forget what matters while repeating what doesn't, and impose the tedium of their shrinking world on all about them.

You can see where I'm going with this. Wine changes with time, and a bottle of fine red wine aspires to the same life span as a human being. Bottles of wine, though, get used up with more rapidity than human beings expire; the older ones are rarer. 'Vintage wine' in common parlance means older wine; and everybody knows the old ones are the best, just as they know that a dog is for life, not just for Christmas.

Wine, come to think of it, is required to be a sort of liquid pug, which comes yapping and tumbling out to perform delightful party tricks the moment we pull the cork, whenever that may be. A cellar is a personal kennel, packed with these objects of emotion. We lavish them with love and affection. We know all their names. We want to look after them, to bring them out to mark our own special occasions. Anyone who stores wine is a wine investor. We're investing wine with our hopes and our trust; we're acquiring a stake in future happiness. It's a wager that the worst will not happen, the house fire or the motorway pile-up or the catastrophically positioned brain tumour; that there will be a hearth and a home in years to come, and friends to share peace and plenty with.

You may, of course, be a sophisticate with the cognitive apparatus required to decode cellaring challenges. You will know that Picpoul de Pinet should be consumed 10 minutes after purchase; you can take a view on the ageing of Condrieu, marshalling support or citing exceptions depending on which way the argument is drifting; and you will consider me suspect for declining to store any Vintage port for longer than a decade, or for preferring a 2010 classed growth Bordeaux to a 1989.

I can see quite clearly, of course, when we sit down with the bottles and you patiently explain it to me, that the best 1994 Vintage ports really do 'drink better' than the 2017s. I'm going to agree with you that Bordeaux ages more reliably and more successfully than any other wine on the planet, and that it's a shame to miss out on the successes. If you've still got any 1990 Cheval Blanc to share with me, I'll revel in its benign glow. I've often pointed out that disposition is a superior quality in wine to accumulation; I'm a fierce advocate of drinkability, the quality too many tasters forget, and forget to taste for. That's all reasonable.

But... I love young wine, perhaps unreasonably. I love youth in wine, and everything that goes with it: the energy, the excitement, the flesh, the vivacity, the extravagance. Texture in wine is a particular delight. The profoundest pleasures in red wine are derived from tannins, assuming that those tannins are the consequence of a season spent ripening in the summer sunshine, and drawn unhurriedly and unfrenziedly from the slow bath of vinification. I love to feel them on teeth and tongue, giving the fruit a dignity it can acquire in no other way, and somehow evoking (both by texture and by strangeness of flavour) the natural milieu in which vines find themselves. Who doesn't like to be gripped, to be seized, to be clenched in this way? Who doesn't enjoy being invaded by a young wine, and having your head turned, your horizons altered, your composure rattled?

Acidity in wine is never better than in youth, when it, too, remains spliced to generous fruit contours, indeed when it seems to bubble and froth with fruit itself, like a gurgling baby with milk. I can't claim that a wine's aromatic allusions are maximized in youth, since great old wines can be scented and resonant, too; but the very lack of serenity and harmony implied by youthfulness is a joy in itself, as you can pick out so much in the merry mix. Sometimes those aromas may be incoherent or contradictory but they're always exuberant, whereas the smiling serenity of old age can sometimes be a little featureless, a bit uneventful, a touch toothless.

That's the nub: the old bottles aren't always good, and weren't always worth keeping. The invariable reverence may be misplaced. The emperor's old clothes can be scandalously scanty, too, yet the mere fact that he is there, still tottering before us, slack-fleshed and antique, awes us into gestural praise.

It's not always like that, I know; one rapturous encounter with 'maturity' can compensate for a few laborious flops. My rule, though, is to take the fun before the fun sets off south. As an elder, permit me to advise you that, as often as not, 'mature' really does mean 'old'. And old isn't what it was – when it was young.

Wine Is Also a Dream

We were in Côte Rôtie's La Mouline, the students and I, looking down through the reddening leaves of this little vineyard, beyond each succeeding terrace wall, and finally over what appeared to be a leafy cliff edge that plunged straight down into the gardens, the swimming pools and the back yards of the village of Ampuis below. Philippe Guigal, whose family owns it, was in ruminative mood.

He told us (echoing a famous Schubert song) about the 'three suns' that growers in Switzerland's Valais say ripen their vines: the sun in the sky, the sun reflected off Lake Geneva and the sun still glowing, come darkness, in the terrace walls and stones. Côte Rôtie, said Philippe, was a little like that, though the Rhône couldn't quite compete with the lake. We harried him with the technicalities that obsess students. He smilingly parried them. He told us that the most important words in the Guigal cellar were 'slow' and 'motion'. He told us they weren't obsessed by pH and never acidified their wines. He said that non-malo Viognier was non-interesting wine. And then he said this: 'Wine is also a dream.'

Yes Philippe, I thought in the silence of my hotel room several hours later. This is true.

Wine producers know their wines intimately, like parents know their children, and like married couples know each other. They know them mundanely – as grapes, juice, smells, problems, frustrations, anxieties, difficulties. Most growing seasons are a series of crises; winemaking delivers a set of unpredictable and unruly ferments. Lesser wines often outshine brighter wines in the noisy playground of an autumn cellar. Producers must wonder, sometimes, how it is that the reduced, unbalanced, turbid or plain boring young wine run off from a tank or barrel might, one day, justify a price tag of hundreds of pounds, euros, dollars a bottle.

Or does it? Many studies have shown consumers preferring less expensive wine to more expensive alternatives. Celebrated studies by the Princeton economist Richard Quandt and others have demonstrated the fallibility of expert judgments about wine and the inconsistency of results from different wine competitions. (Type 'wine' and 'bullshit' into your search bar and you'll quickly marshal the evidence.) What wine magazines call 'blind tasting', remember, is nothing of the sort. True blind tasting would mean that nobody taking part, including the steward, knew anything whatsoever about the liquid being tasted; black glasses would be used; and some of the samples would be duplicated as controls. This would almost certainly produce results of meaningless chaos, even with panels drawn exclusively from the ranks of Masters of Wine and Master Sommeliers. Visiting Martians would find the wine circus an amusing example of the human propensity to overcomplicate what is simple, and to behave in a delusional manner for emotional reasons.

You could argue, in fact, that what matters most about most wine – and all of the wine scrutinized and written about by wine writers – is its dream force. I'd define this as the ability to induce reverie, to inspire aspiration or hope, and to promise (even if it finally fails to deliver) exceptional sensual gratification. In other words, that which wine traders trade and wine collectors collect, and about which wine writers write, is not simply 'also a dream' but principally a dream.

The dream begins because wine is an alcoholic drink. The ethanol in wine alters brain chemistry, engaging the emotions and modifying the drinker's mood. (Brain chemistry changes during the dreaming process, too, thanks to the action of compounds such as melatonin and oxytocin.) Wine writers tend to ignore the alcohol in wine, or to regard it as an unwelcome hazard and a blemish if palpable, yet the truth is that if wine wasn't an alcoholic drink, its dream force would instantly evaporate, and its emotional appeal shrivel. Alcohol is most important.

Wine commands our attention because it commands our emotions, and the way in which it does that is the first building block in our mental construction of a wine's personality. We cannot feel about a Mosel Kabinett ('pure, pristine and filigree') in the same way we feel about a Châteauneuf-du-Pape ('warming, rich and powerful') – principally because the latter is twice as strong as the former, as we will realize after half a glass. But after three glasses of either, we are emotionally engaged with the wine in a way that we will never be with fruit juice or a soft drink, no matter how subtle.

The second element of wine's dream force is its cultural depth. The magnificent text that in part marked the birth of the European literary tradition (Homer's *Odyssey*) brims with acts of wine-drinking. Indeed its plot at one point relies on wine's intoxicating effect. Odysseus and his men blind the Cyclops by plunging a burning olive-wood stake into his single eye only because he is dead-drunk (and covered in vomit: a mixture of wine and half-digested human flesh). The world's largest religion in terms of number of followers asks worshippers to sip wine at the moment of greatest significance in its key ritual. Office workers heading out for a glass of Pinot Grigio after work on Friday aren't consciously thinking of either an oral narrative poem in ancient Greek or of the Christian Eucharist – but both are there nonetheless, oneirically, quietly haunting the act those office workers are about to engage in.

Wine's history is there, too, clinging like barnacles to the hull of the dream, and sinking it more deeply into our consciousness. Pepys drinking Haut-Brion in the Royal Oake, the Prince de Conti and La Pompadour squabbling over what we now call Romanée-Conti, or Napoleon quaffing Chambertin (diluted with water) en route to disaster in Moscow: all add to the dream force of each wine. This happened. Geoffrey Chaucer's father was a wine merchant, yes. If Falstaff could rhapsodize sherris-sack so memorably, it was because the actor-playwright William Shakespeare took pleasure, seated with friends in London's late-16th century taverns, in tasting it, drinking it and noting how its '*nimble, fiery, and delectable shapes*' become '*excellent wit*'. As we can do; the same.

The history of critical evaluation is a mill of dreams, too. When you prepare to draw the cork on a New Year's Eve bottle of Château Léoville-Las Cases, you will remember that the brokers of Bordeaux sagely considered it a 'second growth' back in 1855. You will, in part, be drinking that dream of approbation when you find the wine good (and better than a 'mere' Médoc like Château Potensac, made by the same hands with the same care). Of course, there are modern equivalents: a bottle of Grange comes freighted with the dream of an Australian winemaker who secretly carried on trying to create Australia's answer to great Bordeaux, despite having been forbidden by his bosses to do so. Every bottle of Stag's Leap Wine Cellars SLV Cabernet Sauvignon reminds the drinker of that Rubicon of critical evaluation: the Judgement of Paris.

I'm loath to admit it, but the notion of terroir, too, has as much to do with wine dreams as wine reality. Is every bottle of Sancerre signally different from every bottle of Pouilly-Fumé? Of course not, but the dream of place insists we think about them in a different way, and insists that both are different from Sauvignon de Touraine. Saint Chinian grown on schist must be different from Saint Chinian grown on limestone; ditto for Savennières and Saumur. The dream, here, is a kind of ideal, like a morally impeccable life, to which all must aspire though few if any conform.

Even something as simple as a glass bottle has dream force – heavy, glossy, strong but fragile, made of melted sand, and often now embossed, too. We need to abandon glass, since it costs the climate dearly; the dream will make it hard. One reason for the tenacity of cork closures over what seem to be more efficient alternatives is that this chamfered piece of oak bark from a Portuguese or Sardinian forest has a dreamier hold over drinkers than a metal cap with a plastic liner. Bottle labels – intricate, resonant, code-laden – create their own dreams. Never underestimate their power. Most wine producers are foolishly insouciant about them.

You could even argue that the dream modifies our reaction to the taste of the wine. Few drinkers enjoy their first sips of wine. If you're planning a dry January, remember that when seasoned drinkers take a break from wine, they're sometimes disconcerted on returning to it, and struggle to like it again. Wine may not, in fact, 'taste nice'. It is an acquired taste. We need the dream to urge us forward, to prompt our response; only then can we come to understand it and enjoy it.

Am I pointing all this out to belittle the liquid itself? Not at all. Terroir exists; quality exists. Critical assessment is, in the end, the voice of the market: the greatest wines are those found so over the longest period by the greatest number. Dreams cannot save a wine that doesn't deserve its reputation. What Philippe Guigal meant by that little 'also' is that no wine can ever be separated from the dream force that accompanies it. Wine drunk under true blind-test conditions, or wine reduced to its existential, dream-stripped residuum, couldn't be enjoyed. We need (and have paid for) the dream, too. The dream is always part of the pleasure. It may, indeed, be most of the pleasure.

CHAPTER SEVEN

WINE SHADOWS

The Crazed Giant

It may be the event wine growers fear more than any other: a wanton act of destruction by a crazed, machete-wielding giant. This 30-metre-high hooligan strides, eyes rolling, through your vineyard in a matter of minutes, lunging, slashing, slicing and flailing senselessly, shredding the vines and whatever they may be carrying. Then he's gone, rampaging over the hill, leaving you to gasp at the wreckage.

Ok, there's no giant. It's just ice, pelting out of a high-energy cumulonimbus cloud, but the effect is the same. It took seven minutes for Provençal grower Raimond de Villeneuve of Château de Roquefort to lose his entire crop on July 1st 2012. 'I can still see myself running around the vineyards up to my knees at times in streams of hailstones, petrified, blue with cold. All that ice on still-warm ground created great veils of white mist.' He made a doom-laden tour of his 24 hectares afterwards. 'I knew I wouldn't even get the hint of a harvest.'

The same thing happened in 2013, at around five in the morning on June 17th, to growers in Vouvray, Montlouis, Touraine and Chinon. François Chidaine, the president of the Montlouis growers, lost all his Vouvray and 40 percent of his Montlouis – hail hit for the second year running. Some of the stones were as big as hen's eggs. Without financial help, he says he may have to quit. Some growers in Burgundy's Côte de Beaune villages of Volnay and Pommard were hit three years running, in 2012, 2013 and 2014; the total loss to Volnay's Domaine Lafarge in those years was an entire single crop. When Château d'Issan in Bordeaux's Margaux saw half its crop destroyed by hail in both 2008 and 2009, the cost to the owners was two million euros. French agriculture loses half a billion euros per year to ice pellets.

What's to be done? The two main prevention techniques adopted at present are cloud seeding (with ground-sited silver iodide smoke generators, or silver iodide or dry ice dispensers attached to light aeroplanes) and hail canons, which don't fire shells but simply generate shock waves. These shock waves are said to travel though the cloud, disrupting hail-formation and making the pellets fall as slush or rain.

The idea behind seeding against hail is to increase hail nuclei in the cloud and thereby decrease the size of the hailstones, making them more likely to melt on the way down or fall harmlessly. As it happened, 34 of these generators were installed in Burgundy at the beginning of June 2014, and were used in that summer's storms. The hailstones were considered smaller than those that had fallen the previous year; perhaps they would have been bigger without the silver iodide. The effectiveness of anti-hail techniques can't be gauged, though. It's an experiment for which no control is possible.

I stood in the vineyards of Eisenberg in Austria's southern Burgenland at the end of June 2013, shortly after the crazed giant had rampaged through there (on June 22nd). Slashed leaves, blistered stems, scarred bunches; the broken tissues were already browning and drying. What to do?

'For the next couple of weeks, nothing,' said local grower Dr Stephan Oberpfalzer. 'The vines are in shock. Then we'll have to re-prune somehow. The big worry is that the vines might be affected for next year, too.' 'We're not a region for hail normally,' said fellow grower Thomas Straka: 'But in the last years it's been getting worse and worse. There hasn't been hail like this in Eisenberg for 70 years. It was the first time,' he reflected, wryly, 'I've ever heard our village's name on the radio.'

They're used to all of this in Mendoza, where the spectacular afternoon thunderheads that pile over the Andes regularly let rip with *la piedra*, as hail is called there. Hail is so predictable in Argentina's sub-Andean vineyards that the vines are netted against it (though the nets block out between 10 and 30 percent of the sunlight); another strategy is to own vineyards in different zones to minimize catastrophic loss. Argentine insurers, of course, decline the risk.

If you can find insurance, according to Stephan Oberpfalzer, the cost is €1,000 per €15,000 of crop, with insurers reimbursing the percentage damaged minus a 10% excess. Amazingly enough, in Austria the government pays half of the premium for growers. After an attack, though, no insurer will offer cover for the following year – and in any case, some growers still consider hail insurance a luxury.

What if you're trounced? The only positive outcome of a visit from the crazed giant is human solidarity. No fewer than 35 different Southern Rhône and Provence domaines got together to help Raimond de Villeneuve out in 2012, and together they created three 'Grêle' (hail) cuvées for him, which he sold to tide him over until his own 2013s were ready.

Only Endure

'I was screaming,' remembered Janet Trefethen, 'and then I woke up. My body had registered the earthquake before I was conscious. John was in North Carolina and I was home with my dog. The dog and I went outside and watched the swimming pool rock back and forth. I looked down and saw that my feet were all bloody – I'd run out of the house over broken glass. I got into the truck and drove down to the winery, still in my flimsy nightie. The gates were locked and I couldn't open them. All the power was off. I was worried about fire. The winery was in a sad shape – leaning four feet to the west in the middle. If the earthquake had carried on for another two minutes, it would have been total collapse.'

It was Sunday August 14th 2014, shortly after three in the morning, when a magnitude six earthquake shook the southern end of Napa Valley. It was caused by movement of the West Napa Fault, a small part of the gigantic San Andreas Fault system. The earthquake injured 200 people, one of whom later died (she'd been hit by her falling TV), and caused up to $1 billion's worth of damage. Trefethen's wooden winery was built in 1886; its pioneer lines and reassuring colour, like coral sand, made it a familiar overture for those driving up Highway 29. After the quake, as Janet said, it took on macabre fairground 'fun house' distortions – but held up. A week ago, I walked around inside it and saw its new quake-proof structural refit: a happy if expensive end to the story (despite being a National Historical Landmark, the building was uninsured when the quake struck – as no insurer would take on its risk).

Earthquakes are a hazard of Pacific rather than Atlantic winemaking – countries in the 'Ring of Fire' experience 91 percent of all of the world's earthquakes. This is never far from the minds of those making wines not just in California, Oregon and Washington, but in Chile (which has experienced three of the nine worst earthquakes in recorded history) and New Zealand, too. The earthquakes on February 22nd 2011 in Christchurch and on September 4th 2010 in Canterbury were stronger still than the Napa quake (6.3 and 7.1 magnitude respectively), and the Canterbury quake far more deadly, with 185 fatalities. Atlantic zones aren't immune, though: within Europe, Portugal and Italy are just two winemaking nations to have experienced catastrophic earthquakes in the past.

Together with hail, an earthquake is one of the most unpredictable disasters to affect any wine producer. It's hard for those of us not involved in an activity exposed to risks of this sort to imagine how we might react. Almost all winegrowers, though, do what the Trefethens did – which is take a deep breath, roll up their sleeves, and begin to make good the damage.

We should all feel gratitude for that since, as Trefethen's CEO Jon Ruel points out, 'the one thing you can't build is history'. Janet Trefethen mentioned how, after bracing and painstaking restoration, the winery seemed to find its 'structural memory'. You can extend this analogy, I think, to the activity of winemaking itself: every wine region has its own 'cultural memory', and the acquisition of experience over the length of decades cannot be duplicated. If the disaster-struck gave up and moved on, that wealth of experience would be lost.

At the time of my visit, I tasted three superb Cabernet Sauvignons at Trefethen – from 1975 (poised, perfumed, sweet-fruited and cedary), from 2003 (another Cabernet with remarkable aromatic complexity, lift and freshness) and 2013 (bright, sturdy, floral, with the same combination of aromatic complexity and natural poise); the winery has been an exceptional performer at the Decanter World Wine Awards in succeeding years. These wines underline what a fine location Oak Knoll is – for satisfying yet texturally rich Cabernet that expresses the warmth and generosity of Napa in a lively, graceful and un-caricatural manner. 'The way we farm now is so different from the way we farmed in 1973,' stressed Janet, alluding to the winery's first commercial release – but I'm sure the 2013 wouldn't have been as good without the experience of 1973. Just one lesson: endure. Whatever it takes.

Burning Vines

The 2019–20 Australian Bushfire season ('Black Summer') burned 18.6 million hectares, or an area more than three times the size of the island of Ireland. The vineyard region I know best, the Adelaide Hills, was grievously affected. Around a third of the 2020 crop was lost and some 1,100 hectares burned, including vineyards and wineries I remember well from the 15 months my family and I spent living there between 2009 and 2010: those of Geoff Weaver, James Tilbrook, the Henschke vineyards at Lenswood, Petaluma and Bird in Hand.

We register the facts; imagining what losses like this must feel like is harder. Creating a vineyard and a winery business for a small-scale, ex-Oddbins émigré like James Tilbrook is much more than a job: it is a life in its near-entirety, truly a life less ordinary. Imagine everything you have put your efforts into – not just your physical and mental labour but your passion, your creative forces, your vision, everything you fought for and cared about – is destroyed in a few hours. Vines, winery, bottle stocks (the proof of those efforts): the lot.

Geoff Weaver's loving engagement with his landscape took the form of brushstrokes on paper as well as the growing and fermenting of wine grapes: the cabin next to his vineyard was an artistic refuge as well as place in which to shepherd wine creation into being. Geoff lost 30 years' worth of his landscape paintings in the fire. He tried to defend his holding against the flames but was beaten back, down to the dam at the lowest point, where he was picked up by a friend.

Australia, we know, is a land of fire. Vegetation becomes fuel every summer. Hot winds from the interior meet cool ocean air: storms, lightning, ignition. The open, low-lying landscape offers little topographical resistance, either to the weather systems or to a fire train. Everyone is conscious of this. I remember friends who lived up on Green Hill, on the cusp between Adelaide city and the Hills region, building an underground shelter in their garden, so if fire cut them off they could crouch in the lap of the earth until it passed overhead. No Australian sleeps in the countryside in summer without thinking about an escape route.

Indigenous vegetation has evolved to cope with (and in some cases exploit) fire. The vine may not be native, yet it too (akin to certain species of eucalyptus) hides adventitious buds beneath its cambium. Anyone planting a vineyard in Australia knows that fire may come for it. The damage that fire does is a matter of chance: the more quickly it passes, the better. Perhaps most of the vineyards affected by the recent fires are recoverable with a season's loss of crop. If the fire tarries, though, you are looking at seven years lost, aside from the cost of re-establishing the vines. The smallest are hit hardest. James Tilbrook had spent over a million Australian dollars, he estimates, on establishing his four-hectare vineyard and winery, plus stock; the vineyard is insured for AU$100,000.

Fire, I fear, will be a wine theme of the 2020s, and not just in Australia. Where I live in the Languedoc is acutely vulnerable, like all Mediterranean biotopes: Catalonia, Portugal, South Africa, Chile and Argentina all now live with constant fire risk. Wildfires and droughts are as perennial a challenge in California as in Australia. A warming world ups the risk, perhaps to the point at which the economics of viticulture become senseless: another small reason for making atmospheric decarbonization humanity's principal goal over the next decade.

Is human resilience a function of the biotope too? Everything I know about Australians suggests it might be. The friend who picked Geoff Weaver up was Brian Croser. 'Geoff looked and smelled,' Brian told me, 'like Father Christmas having come down the chimney head-first, but he was unharmed except emotionally. I said to him that he can paint all the lovely places in the Adelaide Hills, the Flinders Ranges and Fleurieu again. And this time he can get it right.'

Wine's Transactional Flaw

Gallus gallus domesticus is the commonest bird in the world. You may have a dead one in your fridge right now, along with half a dozen of its unfertilized eggs. You may even have a few live ones, contentedly imprisoned in your yard.

And then one day, leafing through a book of poems, you happen to read that

> *The Hen*
> *Worships the dust. She finds God everywhere.*
> *Everywhere she finds his jewels.*

and things change. The commonest bird in the world becomes radiant. You know her better. Perhaps you know her for the first time.

I don't want to labour the point. We all have our favourite poems, or paintings, or pieces of music: works of art that drench us in electricity, help us see anew, see aright, see further, feel more deeply, melt in empathy. This experience is common, sublime and necessary; part, most of us feel, of being fully human. A life shorn of these experiences (though many such must be lived) makes a daunting prospect.

Enjoying great wine is like this. Suddenly there are scents and flavours in a glass that writhe us upwards: provoking, beautiful, haunting. We want to tear into them, not just to savour but to understand. We wire ourselves mentally to the place they came from, and find ourselves in love with that place as much as with the wine, since this beauty can only have come from that place. Further explorations beckon. Soon we have mental mycelia in place, threading the humus of this culture; they set us working and set to work in us; we digest our earth through wine. Our relationship with the planet grows deeper and fonder through this emplaced inebriation.

We are creator-curious, too: what were the gestures that brought this beautiful thing into being? These are a matter of craft, not art. Ted Hughes

176   WINE SHADOWS

(the quotations in this text come from his poem 'The Hen') began with a sheet of blank paper; he was the poem's entire maker; that is art. The viticulturist and winemaker, by contrast, solicit and later fashion a gift of nature; they are co-makers, co-workers with skies, with hillsides, with yeasts. The artistry and the brilliance is mostly nature's, though it would not exist at all without the gate-keeping craftswoman or craftsman.

Note, though, that we appreciate the great poem and the fine wine in a similar way: part-analysis, part-awe. Both reward our intense attention. It is this experience that lies at the heart of whatever you want to call the common passion wine lovers share. This is the joy of wine; this is what unlocks its world of difference. It is here that you find its richness and sustenance and nourishment. Such nourishment isn't quite identical to that surrendered by a work of art, since the ingestion of ethanol is involved, but there is kinship: it is at the very least a disreputable cousin. Ethanol alone is not responsible. White Claw Hard Seltzer will not take you on a similar journey.

> *She rakes, with noble, tireless foot,*
> *The treasury of the dirt.*

There are, though, two classes of artistic experience, two ways of nourishing ourselves on works of art: the disinterested and the transactional.

For most of us, great art is free, or almost. You can spend an hour in front of Vermeer's 'Lady Standing at a Virginal' or Caravaggio's 'Supper at Emmaus' in London's National Gallery for nothing. Streaming services make great music near-costless; a second-hand copy of *War and Peace* can be had for 99p. The works of William Shakespeare are downloadable in a few online minutes. The Hughes estate still enjoys copyright on his *Collected Poems*, but the book costs £16.99 and this poem occupies one page out of 1333, so its price is 1.27 pence, and it will illuminate the rest of my days. Costless enjoyment of great art, by the way, is one of the enormous privileges of contemporary human life; this was rarely true in times past. (Save when stumbling into cathedrals.)

If you want to own 'originals', of course, the case is different. Were an authentic Caravaggio or Vermeer to come to auction, and should you have the perfect spot for it in your living room, you would need well over £100 million. A complete copy of Shakespeare's First Folio was sold for $9.98 million in New York in October 2020. First editions and signed copies of books and records find a ready collectors' market; there's kudos to having heard the greatest musicians perform, regardless of ticket price; those denied the experience will always be assured that the live version was superior to the recording (even when recordings of the live performance fail to back the assertion). Private ownership of a great painting, furthermore, snuffs out its wonder for the world as the gavel falls. The canvas in question may slide into a bank-vault maw, to be seen by no one aside from bored security guards and anguished conservators until, several decades later, its profit as an 'alternative asset' is realized and its owner financially nourished.

Wine, in a sense, is worse: it is condemned to be transactional. This is wine's curse. You cannot go to the National Gallery and spend an hour enjoying a glass of La Tâche for free. Spotify will not stream it into your kitchen. There is no second-hand paperback version of La Tâche. No one enjoys La Tâche disinterestedly; everyone has skin in the game. The owner plays potentate; the guests are flattering courtiers; every sip is a sacrament at the high mass of wealth and privilege.

The moment that significant pecuniary value attaches to an aesthetic experience, it begins to tarnish. Infections set in: elitism, snobbery, fashion, the clique, avarice, exclusion. Of course La Tâche is an extreme case, but the difference with a £20 Gigondas is one of degree, not kind; the problem is that there is a price tag at all, since some noble bright enquiring spirit is always excluded. Innocent aesthetic enchantment belongs only to those for whom the price does not matter.

> *With her eye on reward*
> *She tilts her head religiously*
> *At the most practical angle*
> *Which reveals to her*
> *That the fox is a country superstition,*
> *That her eggs have made man her slave*
> *And that the heavens, for all their threatening,*
> *Have not yet fallen.*

There are many sad ramifications for wine, which should bring joy and happiness. Chief among these is that its discourse is drenched in considerations of cost and value, of distribution, of sourcing and of transaction. Much wine writing is consequently doomed, both by those commissioning and consuming it, to be shopping list after shopping list, bottle shot after bottle shot, suggested purchase after suggested purchase, hurried along the transactional mill race with a froth of superlatives. The dullest thing about any wine is its price tag, yet price is always there, torturing the wine and poisoning its aesthetic nourishment. The better and more aesthetically interesting the wine, the more exclusive the drinking circle – and the stronger the poison. Critics and writers rarely pass comment on this, writing as if La Tâche could indeed be streamed into your kitchen by Spotify, yet it makes those of us who write about fine wines the high priests and priestesses of exclusion.

Can wine's transactional flaw be subverted? It can't. We're discussing a fastidiously crafted object from a unique patch of earth and a single seasonal cycle, not a reproducible work of art. Of course it must be transactional; it would be idiotic to argue otherwise.

Rather than a flaw, then, this is really a kind of tragic destiny. Wine is, almost alone among comestible products, one whose appreciation is destined to have something in common with the appreciation of works of art. It is that which makes its colossal inequalities seem unjust.

Drinkers can respond. We can decide to spurn wine hierarchies, and refuse to exchange £50 or £80 for a wine when one at £18 would provide just as much aesthetic nourishment: my own drinking life has been one long amble through the foothills, yet the thrill of discovery has only grown with time. There has never, in human history, been a time of greater wine endeavour, not all of it misguided. We can mock the pretensions of luxury, and refuse to participate in the silliness of its discourse. We can remain jocund, never taking wine too seriously; murmur 'it's only wine' to yourself from time to time. Aesthetic experiences may indeed be essential to a life richly lived, but in times of crisis or struggle, they're insignificant. We can be open to the anarchic, and to alternative aesthetic languages. Forget obsessions with sulphur and fantasies of purity: this is the real contribution of the natural-wine movement to wine's pool. We might even try asking the rich to share a little more. There are signs that the wine world is almost ready to face its abysmal record on inclusivity; part of the solution surely means addressing the transactional flaw. Perhaps there is a future for something called wine philanthropy.

We should never forget, too, the keystone of wine aesthetics: difference precedes excellence. It's a liberation of sorts.

She is a hard bronze of uprightness.
And indulges herself in nothing
Except to swoon a little, a delicious slight swoon,
One eye closed, just before sleep,
Conjuring the odour of tarragon.

The Curse of the Vertical

Wine lovers are used to thinking about horizontal and vertical, especially when it comes to tasting. A horizontal tasting enables a range of wines from the same year to be compared: the emphasis is on the difference between wines. A vertical tasting looks at just one wine through a range of different years, emphasizing the difference in vintages. That's a useful distinction.

I'd suggest, though, that horizontal and vertical thinking in wine goes far beyond that, permeating our approach to wine more generally – to disastrous effect. We'd enjoy wine much more if we could abandon thinking about it vertically and throw all our energy into thinking about it horizontally. Here's what I mean.

Few of us drink one type of wine alone, to the exclusion of all others. Almost all of those who love good wine love its diversity. No other alcoholic drink matches wine's multitudes. It's a kind of sensual barometer for difference itself, reflecting the ever-changing places and climates in which vines are grown, and the variety of cultures and talents of the craftswomen and craftsmen who vinify it. If I taste wine, I taste difference.

How, though, do we go about sorting those differences?

The best way is horizontally, which means prizing differences as sacrosanct, and giving them our full attention: enjoying difference for itself.

Some differences in wine are well-understood, and comparisons have long been easy and enjoyable to make: a Left Bank, Cabernet-dominated Bordeaux, for example, compared to a Right Bank, Merlot-dominated counterpart; a Barbaresco compared to a Barolo; or a Rioja compared to a Ribera del Duero. In the latter two cases, the principal comparison is between places – close and nuanced in the Piedmontese example, more distant and dramatic in the Spanish. The subtle contrast in place in the Bordeaux example is gently amplified by varietal difference.

The fact that the southern hemisphere is principally planted at present with a small number of 'international' varieties makes the act of contrasting differences in place and winemaking culture and technique straightforward. Chardonnay, Cabernet or Syrah act as reagents for those differences; Pinot Noir, too, for cooler climate locations. Tasting each wine as an individual, in which those differences are inerasably inscribed, is a revealing experience: a Tumbarumba Chardonnay against a Margaret River or Adelaide Hills counterpart, for example, or Pinot Noir from different parts of New Zealand and of Oregon. This varietal homogeneity won't last; after a further century or two, the contrasts will have deepened – but so, too, will our understanding of the differences given sensual form by the wines of the place.

Sadly, though, the horizontal approach is the underdog, at least at present. The near-universal habit of scoring wines has had a catastrophic effect: the vertical approach to appreciating differences between wines is top dog.

Take five well-made wines of interest: all are different. All provide pleasure, of different sorts.

Now give those five wines a score each: suddenly you have a vertical suite of difference. There is a 'best'. There is a 'worst'. There's a 'second from bottom', a 'middling wine' and a 'second best'. There are, in other words, four losers and one winner, as Hugh Johnson pointed out many years ago.

What happens to the losers? Their differences are now downplayed and disparaged. We focus, if we focus on anything, on their 'failings': the things that meant that they weren't 'the winner'.

Never mind that those might be the very things that, on another day and with an unencumbered mind, we might have appreciated most about those wines; never mind that on another day our scores for the wines might have been reversed. Not only have we ruined our experience of the differences between the wines, but we have also erased the opportunities we might have had for deriving pleasure from each.

The negative effects of a vertical approach to wine don't stop there. Too much focus on scores, on winners and on losers fuels price inflation, as the winners or their sales intermediaries ramp up prices. It leads to an unhealthy emphasis on brands and branding; it leads to misunderstandings and simplifications concerning vintages. It leads to price gouging. There are flagrant examples of this associated with white wines of assorted, often modest origin when vinified by Médoc classed growths.

It leads to a burgeoning population of label drinkers: wealthy, status-conscious enthusiasts who sincerely crave 'the best', unaware of how fallible, empty and unsatisfactory that concept can be when applied to wine. It creates perfect victims for the kind of deceit practiced not simply by the fine-wine forgers of the wine world, but by the army of commonplace counterfeiters who have flourished in recent years in China.

You might argue that there are some benefits to the vertical approach to wine. This is true. I wrote 'five well-made wines of interest' in the example above. A vertical approach will help you set aside wines that are not well-made (few nowadays) and set aside uninteresting wines (examples abound). Verticality has a place.

It also, though, needs to be kept in its place: locked up in a kennel. Only the loping, smiling, slurping, drooling, affectionate and limitlessly gentle hound of horizontality can ensure you derive maximum pleasure from the wine world and its beautiful differences. Forget 'the best'. Keep scores at bay, as simply one attribute of a wine among many. Embrace difference.

Scored Rigid

Wine was once scoreless. My 1973 Penguin version of Edmund Penning-Rowsell's *The Wines of Bordeaux* brims with figures – most of them vintage dates and the *tonneaux* of wine produced at individual châteaux in those years. The author has clearly tasted and drunk a wealth of fine Bordeaux, distinguishes châteaux styles in a general sense and makes qualitative assessments – but never pins the butterfly to the wheel with a score. Penning-Rowsell's clubby, discursive assessements follow the model laid down by the one-time *Guardian* journalist, essayist and Edinburgh Professor of Rhetoric, George Saintsbury, in his 1920 *Notes on a Cellar Book*, written in retirement in Bath.

By the late 1970s, though, change was afoot. From September 1952 onwards, a young wine-trade recruit called Michael Broadbent began taking 'handwritten tasting notes, in excess of 85,000, in small, identical red books – 133 to date' (as he wrote in the Introduction to *Vintage Wine* in 2002). Broadbent came to use what he called a '"broad-brush" five star rating system' – which, since no stars equated to 'Poor', could be construed as a six-point scale. Hugh Johnson, a persistent critic of 100-point-scale scores, also adopted a one- to four-star system for 'general quality standing' in his *Pocket Wine Guide*, with the stars appearing in red for 'good value in its class'. *Decanter* magazine, founded in 1975, initially employed a five-star system for its tastings, but later switched to the 20-point scale used by pioneer European critics such as Clive Coates MW and France's Michel Bettane.

'I borrowed it from law school,' Robert Parker told me in March 1995 when I asked him about the so-called 100-point scale (in fact a 50-point scale), which he used for the *Baltimore-Washington Wine Advocate*, launched in the summer of 1978. 'I was dissatisfied with the 20-point system, because it didn't give me enough latitude.' Parker plumbed the scale's lower depths with his reviews of the 1973 Bordeaux vintage: Margaux '73 scored 55 ('a terrible wine ... thin and acidic') and the top-scoring wine, Petrus '73, scored just 87. He mailed out 6,500 free issues and received 600 subscriptions in return, so the wider market effect was negligible – but his reputation soared after his hugely enthusiastic report on Bordeaux '82s was published in April 1983, as American merchants trumpeted Parker's 90+ scores in their offers and shop windows. From then on, the 100-point scale slowly became the international benchmark. *Decanter* switched to its use in 2012 and *Revue du Vin de France* adopted it in 2020.

Does the scale matter? That depends on its practical application. Parker may have begun with the full breadth of a 50-point scale, but scores of less than 80 have been rare in the *Wine Advocate* over the last two decades. This is generally true wherever the 100-point scale is used today.

Of those wines given printed tasting notes in the panel tasting of Alsace Riesling printed in the November 2021 edition of *Decanter* magazine, for example, the lowest score given by any taster was 82 and the highest was 99. This is a typical use of the 100-point scale; few reviewing organizations or critics bother to describe wines scoring below 80. It is, in fact, a full 20-point scale dressed up as something else.

So why not revert to a 20-point scale? Because those using the 20-point scale rarely bother to describe wines scoring 12 or less, so they are using an 8-point scale. (Or a 16-point scale if they resort to half-point graduations.)

In any case, an inflationary scoring spiral (or, if you prefer, 'score compression') is at work among leading critics, though the wine community at large is probably to blame for this. Parker took great pains to stress that scores in the 80s were in fact meritorious: the *Wine Advocate* rubric for 80–89 says that 'such a wine, particularly in the 85–89 range, is very very good; many of the wines that fall into this range often are great value as well'.

Over time, though, undue significance accrued to the 'magic gateway' of 90 points. Retailers report that consumers only want wines with scores of 90 or over. Naturally, ambitious producers are disappointed if their wines score less than this. Producers complain to critics – and critics depend on producers' goodwill for access and support. So in regions without established hierarchies, 'successful wines' tend to be scored at 90 points or more – on a 10-point scale.

For fine wines, meanwhile, this inflation or compression continues – with producer disappointment setting in for scores below 95. Top Bordeaux properties, in good to great vintages like 2018, 2019 and 2020, are now expecting scores of between 96 and 100; the financial consequences of not obtaining these will be significant. For such wines, we're back to a five-point scale.

Along with this goes the normalization of 'a perfect score': 100/100. Think, for a moment, what 'perfection' should signify. It means that the wine is flawless; it means that it's impossible to conceive of anything better. Most of us, I'd guess, might assume that such wines would float over the horizon no more than half a dozen times in a drinking lifetime.

Yet in the 'Weekly Tasting Report' issued by 'JS Wine Ratings' (James Suckling and team) for November 2nd to 8th 2021, there were three such wines out of 332 tasting notes (for Casanova di Neri Brunello di Montalcino 'Cerretalto' 2016, Penfolds 'g5' and Krug 2008). Three 'perfect' wines in one week! Among the 62 red Bordeaux 2018 wines listed by Farr Vintners on November 12th 2021, no fewer than seven have won perfect scores from one critic or another (Haut-Brion, Lafite, Larcis-Ducasse, Margaux, Mouton Rothschild, Palmer and Trotanoy).

Lavish scores and 'perfection' galore at the top end... but if you're a try-harder producer of *cru bourgeois* in Bordeaux's Médoc, you're almost condemned by your position in the Bordeaux hierarchy to a score of 88–90, even in good or great vintages. Age such wines for a decade and then compare them with Chilean or South African Cabernet vintage peers with identical scores: the *cru bourgeois* will seem meanly treated. This is a clear structural problem with scoring mid-ranked wines from large fine-wine regions. Such wines are score-trapped by their positions in those hierarchies.

A consideration of context leads us to two fatal ambiguities in the scoring universe, concerning peer-group and price. Many consumers assume that scores are universal: that every 92-point score is comparable and perfectly calibrated with every other 92-point score. They may also unthinkingly assume that scores are absolute – in other words, that they bear no relation to price. A 92-point Australian Sauvignon Blanc 'must be as good as' a 92-point burgundy Grand Cru. That's what the score says, doesn't it?

Alas, it doesn't.

'Tasting is subjective,' Robert Parker told me back in 1995, echoing both Hume and Kant; does anyone disagree? If tasting is subjective, then scores must be personal, not universal; my 95-point Cahors might be your 91-point Cahors. Parker's *Wine Advocate* rubric, moreover, always made it clear that 'The numerical rating given is a guide to what I think of the wine vis-à-vis its peer group' – and this sensible approach is one de facto taken by all critics (and by the Decanter World Wine Awards, where scores are referenced against all the wines entered into the competition in any given year).

Were this not the case, given that quality in the wine world varies colossally (price following suit), then most tasted wines should receive scores of 55 to 85; a score of 73 or 75 would be a ringing endorsement for a good wine of modest origin and ambition. We don't see this, in part because critics are reluctant to acknowledge the unfairness and elitism of terroir. Some wines are far better than others, and always will be, no matter how hard producers in lesser regions may try. To say as much, though, seems disempowering and even prejudicial to those producers and those regions. We like to give everyone a fair chance, so we bring all wines into the fairy ring of 80 to 100 points, even those that don't deserve to be there.

It's also reasonable to take price into account when scoring. Wine is not given away free. Few consumers have resources so copious that 'the price doesn't matter'. No reflective and price-conscious consumer would realistically expect a 93-point Romanian Pinot at £9.99 to provide the same level and kind of satisfaction as a 93-point Vosne Suchots at £69.99 – and critics, too, do not judge the two wines by the same standards. (Though few dare to put this principle fully into practice, by giving 'the best imaginable' Romanian Pinot Noir 99 or 100 points; in practice, scoring for value tends to dissipate at around the 93 to 94-point level.)

Ask any producer, though, and they will tell you that scores still matter enormously, especially scores out of 100. They point out that not all critics are taken equally seriously. They admit that scores have become inflated, but they still want nice things said about their own wines and won't complain if they receive inflated scores.

My view is that scores are foolish, philosophically untenable and damage wine culture rather than enrich it. What interests me in wine is not squabbling over vertical quality graduations but exploring the vast horizontal landscape of difference, which scores have no means of articulating.

Readers (and editors) like scores, so of course I use them: refusing to do so would be pompous and unhelpful. We exist to serve readers. I understand their appeal as a form of shorthand; I can see that they render wine's complexities beguilingly simple. There's a sort of fun behind scores, too – and wine should be fun.

To know, appreciate and enjoy wine to the full, though, set the score aside, and listen to what the wine has to say to you through the song of its aroma and flavour, texture and shape, origin in place and time. Viewed in that way, 95 may be better than 100, and 89 may be best of all.

188   WINE SHADOWS

CHAPTER EIGHT

WINE IN
A LIFE

Lucky Us

The wine was bright and translucent, despite its walnut hue. Vapoury and perfumed, as we all hoped, though the notes varied by taster: crystallized violets, dried fruits, citrus. Rue, for me (that shrubby herb *Ruta graveolens*, so powerfully scented as to asphyxiate its garden neighbours; here, happily, just a hint). It wasn't a sweet wine, or at least not at first – and barely at last, either. It began athletically, then widened and grew more sweetly ample on the middle palate, before finishing in the dark, dry shadows. Tonic acidity, burnished by time, meant that it was clean, even pristine. Yes, it was old Madeiran Boal, but this was a kind of Kabinett version, all lightness and grace (the Cossart house style). Raisin? Treacle? They were there, but time had gnawed them down into that sober chiaroscuro that seemed so appropriate to the vintage.

Which was 1914. The generous owners of the wine had wanted to open this bottle (the second of three, originally purchased from Berry Bros & Rudd) before 2014 was out; I was one of five lucky guests to share it. We drank it appreciatively, if ruminatively: how could we not? Its fruit had set by the time Gavrilo Princip shot Franz Ferdinand; when the grapes were picked, Austria-Hungary had invaded Serbia, Germany had invaded Luxembourg and declared war on France, and Britain had declared war on Germany. Franz-Ferdinand's nephew Charles proved to be the final emperor of the Austro-Hungarian Empire – and was exiled to Madeira, as it happened, by the Council of Allied Powers, where he died in 1922; he's buried in the airy Funchal suburb of Monte. This must be one of the last surviving truly fine wines (as opposed to noble but expired relics) of the old European order.

We drank the wine as the final month of this 100th anniversary year drew on. That also seemed, in its own way, appropriate, since if there are any uplifting memories of the beginning of 1914–18's catastrophic conflict, then they're connected with the 1914 Christmas truce, when the combatants spontaneously agreed to suspend hostilities and fraternize with each other in No Man's Land. (The generals disapproved – as did a young corporal in the 16th Bavarian Reserve Infantry called Adolf Hitler. In subsequent years, sporadic attempts at a Christmas truce were unsuccessful.)

The best-known illustration of the Christmas truce is that which appeared in the *Illustrated London News* on January 9th 1915, showing a collection of moustachioed officerly types (leavened with a few stubble-jowelled squaddies) puffing on cigars (and cigarettes) as they discuss, let's guess, the finer points of trench construction. There are two discarded bottles to one side of a potted Christmas tree on the snowy ground. One has squared-up shoulders and sides, and must surely be either a whisky bottle or a bottle of schnapps, but the lines of the other are more ambiguous; could it be port or Madeira? Consumed, the picture makes clear, from battered tin mugs.

Not that origin matters. The more consequential the moment, the less consequential the wine.

The very fact that we collect and savour and dream on our precious wines, and then jot a few recreational notes on their personalities, underlines the peacefulness of the times most of us are lucky to enjoy at present. Whether or not the vintage was a good one, who the producer was, and exactly what allusions are evoked by the wine would have been a laughable irrelevance for the briefly reconciled combatants, standing in their atrocious snowscape, in a war that was eventually to cost 16 million lives. With worse to come. The very idea of wine would have seemed a cruel dream to the 70 million or more who died in 20th-century famines in Russia, Ukraine, China and elsewhere.

Changes in personal circumstances, too, can reframe the way in which we see wine, rendering what would once have seemed consequential irrelevant. My parents, now in their mid-80s, have always enjoyed wine in a normally casual kind of a way. My mother now has Alzheimer's, and all the landmarks in her world have been washed downstream; my father, who cares for her, was recently scourged by bladder stones, and subsequently diagnosed with prostate cancer (which he's probably had for a decade) and then bone cancer. Shopping is no longer an easy exercise, and my Dad has taken to ordering the occasional inexpensive case of wine from UK mail-order specialist Laithwaites. We try to chat every evening on the phone.

Eating and drinking is almost the last pleasure left for my mother, and the last activity in which she has a little autonomy (though we have to dissuade her from pouring her coffee onto her breakfast cereal and her wine onto her dinner). My father, though he remains admirably cheerful, needs the psychological restoration that a glass or two of wine at the end of the day can effect. Wine has never meant more to them, or brought more benefit, than it does just now. I was staying with them recently, and my Dad opened what is apparently the 'most reordered red' from the Laithwaite's list, a Côtes Catalanes called Cabalié, made not far from where I live. Grenache from hereabouts can be arresting, but this was a flabby, semi-sweet soup of a wine, its fruit evanescent, without redeeming tannin or extract.

'Gosh, it's good,' my Dad said. We smiled hugely, toasted each other, and knocked it back. Lucky us: still together; still with wine in our glasses.

It's a Tough Job

Grass, as we all know, is at its greenest when an insurmountable fence has been positioned between the observer and the field in which it is growing. The metaphor is never more apt than when it comes to a choice of careers. The insurance broker's life would be transformed if only he could taste the excitement of forensic science, just as the auditor's happiness would swell exponentially the day she began work as an RSPB warden; barristers, as we all know, love to escape from Crown Courts and into the House of Commons, where they can hector each other grandly not only all day but late into the night, too.

There's one career, though, that seems to exercise universal appeal, even for those already practising it: the wine trade. 'You call that work?' josh old schoolfriends on hearing that their wine-merchant friend is off for a 'gruelling' two-week tasting tour of Burgundy or the Languedoc. 'I've been given Chile, Argentina, South Africa and California,' moans the supermarket buyer, aghast at the amount of work and travel dumped on her desk. Sympathy, mysteriously, is in short supply.

Should you, therefore, be suffering from wine-trade envy, listen up. It's hell. Honestly. I've been talking to my wine-merchant friends. Here are all the reasons why a career in the prison service is preferable.

The jet set

Aeroplanes are a fact of life for wine merchants, but business-class seats with complimentary in-flight massage are rare in this low-margin business. Getting up at 3am to climb on a 6am budget airline flight from Stansted is more typical. I've spoken to wine buyers who have sat in the brace position through an emergency landing on the Cape Verde Islands, who have been thrown from their seats in violent turbulence over the Andes and who have slept at airports in Patagonia after the control tower was struck by lightning. Another found himself next to a chatty Evangelical preacher for a 22-hour economy-seat flight to Australia. He was still unconverted by the end.

On (and off) the road

Getting to the destination airport is just the beginning of the journey for most wine merchants. It's particularly easy in the Southern Hemisphere to miscalculate the (usually vast) distances to be covered. One pair of wine merchants I know decided to take 10 days to tour New Zealand wineries by road. A mistake: it takes 10 days merely to drive the length of wine-growing New Zealand by road. 'We always arrived in each wine-producing region so late that all we could do was find a place to sleep,' they wailed. Driving cars into mud, ditches and assorted winery obstacles is common (I've done that – twice); another buyer drove away from a Slovenian winery to see gun smoke and running soldiers in her rear-view mirror as a brief civil war erupted, and had a taxi driver pull a knife on her in Serbia by way of encouragement to find a larger tip.

Accidents, of course, will happen. I've driven into a police car in Spain to avoid an oncoming maniac who'd crossed a solid white line – but emerged unscathed and uncharged. It could have been much worse. 'I was driving the TVR V8 I had recently purchased – the most fantastic car I ever owned – and I had a head-on collision at a sharp bend in the middle of the forest,' remembers a burgundy specialist. 'I wrote off the car and ended up spending 10 days in a hospital in Beaune with a plaster cast from my groin to my neck. A well-intentioned doctor wanted to repatriate me, but with five-course meals plus half a litre of red wine twice a day, and a room overlooking the vineyards, I declined.'

The joy of wine tasting

'I remember nearly crashing my car,' chuckled another merchant, 'on the way back from my first visit to Chablis. I'd tasted high-acid wines from the 1984 vintage at eight domaines that day, and had to dash for an aeroplane. No time to eat, so I bought a bar of chocolate to keep hunger at bay and crammed some in my mouth as I accelerated away from the motorway toll-booth. The pain as the the sugar attacked teeth exposed and softened by acidity was explosive.' Ah, yes: dental problems. 'I'd tasted,' remembered another victim, 'all day at the Loire wine fair after a particularly acidic vintage – then had to go to the Rhône to taste tannic reds. And my teeth turned black. The local chemist suggested a whitener: useless. In the end, I had to have them re-enamelled by a dentist, and ultimately replaced.'

Who buys, wins

Wine merchants by definition travel hopefully – like football scouts, they are always in quest of raw, undiscovered talent. It doesn't always turn out well. 'You either want to buy in huge volumes but know you will barely get enough to shake a stick at – or you find something you can buy a shedload of, but know it's going to be a nightmare to sell.' A perpetual complaint is that peak visiting time is in winter when cellars are at their coldest and the vineyards at their most mournful; diplomatic skills are often required, especially when you realize that the grower you have just spent an hour with is a bungler, 'which is exactly when it transpires he likes you and wants to show you a long series of older vintages'. 'Finally,' admits another merchant, 'we buy the wine, ship it and begin to sample it with our customers. Is that really what it tastes like? God – what have we done? We need to sell pallets of this stuff.'

And so to dinner

You'd think that dinner was the big consolation at the end of the day. In fact, the rules of wine-region hospitality often dictate that 'you have to eat an enormous lunch with one grower, and then drive on to eat an enormous dinner with another one, and so on, daily, for a week or two'. Merchants are quickly Buntered. Food can sometimes be over-exotic, even for the adventurous (like burgers made with brains in Hungary), and you sometimes have to do silly things afterwards – like dance round a bonfire on Saint Catherine's Day. 'I was invited to be first and caught my foot in an old vine root. The result was a trip to A&E and lifetime scarring. Fortunately I was the third they'd seen that morning so I felt a bit less stupid.'

Good food, of course, is worth making sacrifices for. The merchant who wrote off his TVR and was plastered like an Egyptian mummy was nonetheless determined, once the plaster came off, to keep his reservation at Maison Lameloise with a Burgundian grower and a local artist. 'The trouble was I couldn't sit down. So the restaurant kindly supplied a pillow and I knelt at the table, much to the surprise of some Americans who thought that the English took their praise of haute cuisine just a little too seriously.'

Hill Sages

The more vineyards you visit, the more comprehensively you become inured to the lure of vineyard ownership. Yes, that summer lunch under the old *micocoulier* was lovely, but the cold of winter is a different matter. Everything in the cellar is expensive, even before it has broken down. You'll need thousands of vines; each requires personal attention four or more times a year. An invisible army of pests and diseases is out to get them all, and a rising tide of weeds to choke them; you can be sure the weather won't help. Once you've got the fruit ripened, harvested, and the wine vinified and bottled, the final nightmare awaits: selling it to an indifferent world, awash with other people's good wine. All that, plus loneliness.

In February 2013, though, I visited a small vineyard so deftly self-contained, and with such an inspiring view, yet at the same time near a thriving and culturally rich metropolis, that I suddenly felt the call of vineyard ownership for, well, at least three minutes. This was Carole Meredith and Steve Lagier's vineyard up on Mount Veeder.

Carole drove me up. And up. And up some more. When you eventually come out of the forest into the light, 400 metres later, you can see not only right across Napa Valley to the Stags Leap crags and to Pritchard Hill, but also the upper reaches of Howell Mountain and the lonelier corners of Atlas Peak, too. Over the shoulder of the hill, the inner switchbacks of Mount Veeder unfurl like waves, wild yet intimate. The softer slopes of Carneros fall away down valley, while the sunlit bowl of San Francisco Bay beckons beyond. The fog wasn't in when I called, but that must be spectacular, too. I imagined Steve setting out to prune in early winter, looking rather like Caspar David Friedrich's celebrated 'Wanderer'.

How much site research, I wondered, had they done? 'Absolutely none,' replied Carole. 'We bought it as a place to live in 1986. Steve was at Mondavi; I was at UC Davis. UC Davis is flat and hot but has great culture; Napa was cooler and fresher but there wasn't much going on back then. The idea was to live in between – but in between turned out to be flat, hot and had no culture. I said: "I'll commute." We looked at 70 properties. This was number 10, but we hadn't seen enough and it had a comically awful access road and a crummy house.' Eventually, though, the site lured them back. They planted a few vines after eight years or so. 'We had no plans,' remembered Carole. 'But we planted a few vines after eight years, just to have something for us.' The results surprised them, so they 'went commercial' (in a small way: just two hectares) in 1998.

The results surprised me, too. Back in her research days in 1998, it was Carole who proved (with her doctoral student John Bowers and Montpellier's Jean-Michel Boursiquot) that Syrah had nothing to do with ancient cities in Persia, but was a natural Northern Rhône crossing of Mondeuse Blanche and Dureza, so Syrah was a doubly logical choice for them to plant up on the high-sited sandstone and shale soils of Mount Veeder. The couple has planted the black version of Mondeuse, too, as well as Malbec and Tribidrag (though they're still calling it Zinfandel: Carole led the 'Zinquest' which finally sorted out its Croatian rather than Puglian roots). Obviously the USA's greatest living ampelographical researcher and a former long-term winemaker for Robert Mondavi weren't going to stuff up their home brew, but even so I was impressed with the freshness, purity and liveliness of the Syrah (head-turning in the 2010 but still apparent in the 2002) and, especially, by the seductive floral notes and ample, juicy tannins of the 2010 Mondeuse, which seemed more successful than many back in Savoie. 'Mountain' wines in Napa often end up almost as rich as their valley-floor counterparts, and there are cogent terroir reasons why this might be so. The Lagier-Meredith wines, though, were as aerial as any screaming party of swifts.

Life on the hill seems to have brought philosophical serenity, too. 'Our role,' they stress on both back label and website, 'is to safeguard the wine during its passage from vineyard to bottle, and to protect it from too much winemaking.' They have, they say, worked hard and lived cheap. They buy old oak, then 'continue to use the barrels until they begin to fall apart'. They protect their biotope – the little lawn behind the house was dotted with orange flags that Carole had used to signal the wild lupins that had naturally established themselves there. I'd been told about Napa's totally dry summers, but it was only when Carole showed me how the fuchsia-flowered gooseberry and the buckeye had adapted to this by simply dumping all their leaves in summer and going into dormancy, saving their growth cycle for winter, that this became more than merely anecdotal.

A healthy life in a beautiful place. Could I ever manage something similar? I took one look at Steve. He's huge, strong and evidently handy. He knows not only how to prune vines and craft limpid wines but how to put fence posts in and make equipment work, how to drive trash down a vertiginous access road in winter, how not to step on poison oak, and how to capture and re-locate rattlesnakes. No, I couldn't.

An Evening with the Lilac-Berried Mutant:

2008 Gewurztraminer, Herrenweg de Turckheim Vieilles Vignes, Zind-Humbrecht

I seldom feel like Lord Alfred Douglas. This is perhaps just as well, given that the most celebrated of Oscar Wilde's lovers had a life rendered miserable by self-indulgence, given that he was long estranged from a vengeful and violent father, given that he was an anti-Semite who squandered much of his inheritance in libel actions (both as plaintiff and defendant), and given that the mental illness which ran in his family – one prone to a disproportionate number of 'shooting accidents' – was eventually to claim his only son. He was, though, also a poet, and his 1894 poem 'Two Loves', which played a crucial part in earning Wilde his 'gross indecency' conviction and two years' hard labour in Pentonville, Wandsworth and Reading gaols, concludes with the celebrated line 'I am the love that dare not speak its name'.

This is when those of us who love Gewurztraminer begin to empathize with Bosie. In right-thinking wine-drinking circles, there is something a little shameful about admitting that you regularly spend an evening with this lilac-berried mutant, and even enjoy the experience. The 'first love', the sort that fills 'The hearts of boy and girl with mutual flame', would of course be a passion for respectable Riesling – upright, straight as a poplar, its pencil stiffened with acidity, and in most cases properly dry or properly sweet without too much hanky-panky in the middle. Riesling and rectitude are bedfellows (in wedlock, of course).

Whereas Gewurztraminer is doubtful, languid and fin-de-siècle, at best a Rosenkavalier and at worst a Salome, with its head-slicing alcohol levels, its neglect of acidity, its copious flesh, its chaotically unpredictable levels of residual sugar and its uninhibited perfumes, oscillating between rose-garden and bedroom, and occasionally growing more meaty and truffley still until it suggests an uninhibited aromatic account of a full-body massage and beyond. But there you are: I love it. What can you do? There's no point in denying your own nature.

I don't have a lot of patience with the customary criticisms of the variety, unless they originate from unfortunates who have never tasted a good one. (Bad Gewurztraminer, it's true, is one of the most horrible of all wines: pharmaceutical, mawkish, oppressive.) The notion that there might be some set of universal aesthetic parameters to which all white wines should conform is suspect, suggesting industry rather than agriculture, and implying a homogeneity of taste that the diversity of the world's great cuisines effectively demolishes.

I would defend Gewurztraminer (even if I didn't like it so much) for the fascination of its ceaselessly transitioning identity, and the fact that it can find a resonant balance down in the lower depths where acidity has almost disappeared and where extract and tannin begin to drag agreeably on luscious, glycerous fruits. Perfume is always there to lift the wine, no matter how low it has sunk; that's what helps it survey the stars from the gutter. Any universal judgement about sugar levels is misguided, too. Gewurztraminer can be a fine dry wine and a fine sweet one, too, but it's most compelling of all in the middle. That is where you feast with panthers; the combination of scent-saturated sugars with the other components in a densely knitted wine seems to give it a provocative unpredictability of allusion. The danger may indeed be half the excitement. Those who insist on dry wines alone at table are living on a restricted diet.

Is Gewurztraminer an egotist, capable only of shouting its own varietal nature at the expense of terroir? This doesn't bear scrutiny. Try a Gewurztraminer from Schlossberg or Brand, then compare it with one from Sporen or Goldert. Taste them all blind. Involve the family: ask them to be served to you when you least expect. The granite and mica of Brand may begin to throw you off the scent, though it remains warm enough for exoticism; Gewurztraminer from the silicious scree of Schlossberg, though, can seem like a different variety. The archetype in Alsace implies clayey marl, a long season and a speckling of hot days and cooler days. That heady Sporen or Goldert profile is what ignites seduction.

This wine, in fact, is grown off the hill on gravels mixed with loam; there's no stony complexity here. It comes, though, from old, low-yield vines in biodynamic cultivation teased and tugged to sumptuous ripeness (with about 20 percent botrytized fruit), then vinified with the care and patience typical of Olivier Humbrecht. The result is not individuated in the way that a Grand Cru might be – but for sheer completeness, extravagance and exuberance, this yellow wine is regal. Aromas ooze from it: honey, ginger, jasmine, old rose. Its sugar is carried almost pertly, thanks to the fruit-dense acidity only a long season in the field can deliver; the rich alcohol wrapped up in all those other things gives it lovely glide on the tongue. There's something fiery in its heart, meaty in its depths, chewy in its texture. And carnal in its nature.

I challenge anyone to sip and then walk away. It would be unnatural, even perverse.

Tears and Threats:

2003 Tokaji Aszú, 6 Puttonyos, Disznókő

A mysterious omission in the generally dithyrambic world of wine writing concerns the impact of small children on a drinking life. Believe me, it's considerable.

They don't, of course, drink wine themselves, but their manifold needs and wants will ensure not only that you have less money to spend on wine but that you also have much less time to devote to the contemplation of its qualities and virtues. You'll often find yourself, indeed, trying to appreciate the year's work of a favourite wine grower in the middle of a storm of gratuitous incivilities: flying objects, tears and threats, vituperative arguments, encroaching spillages. My sons view the wine in the glass either as a kind of vaudeville poison, or as a substance of interest only to adults (thus by definition uninteresting). Bottles will be downed like skittles, wherever they stand; glasses will fall prey to flying wooden Kapla tiles, high-velocity small metal vehicles, and foam-rubber bullets fired from point-blank range. Leave your treasured decanter in the cupboard at all times.

Having a few friends round to dinner is, for most, the ideal way to enjoy wine. Small children make it difficult, since much of the evening is required to feed them, wash them and narrate them to sleep. As they get older, they stay up longer. Soon you are faced with the choice of either beginning dinner so late that the adults themselves require tucking up in bed rather than feeding; or 'eating with the children' – which means surrendering to their conversational dictates, enduring their fidgets, and sooner or later arguing about what percentage of your carefully prepared, artfully presented and now congealed dish it might be appropriate to label as 'disgusting' and thus consign to the biowaste bin before wearily getting out the tubs of ice cream.

The twin dangers are that you either lose the taste for wine altogether, or start gulping it as the readiest antidote to domestic bedlam.

We have, though, found a workable compromise. You invite your friends round 'for tea' (*un goûter* here in France): the ideal meal for children, since most of it is sweet and can be consumed on the hoof. They gorge themselves to satiation, then clear off upstairs or outside to engage in the usual malevolent and destructive acts inspired by sugar, Hollywood and the computer games industry. At that point, you get out the wine.

Perfect! But what wine? Given that your salivary glands are still working to sluice away the remnants of cake or tart, this is not the ideal moment for a great Barolo; even a village Chambolle would crash. It should, in fact, be a sweet wine. The hour isn't quite naughty enough for a voluptuous Sauternes, nor are you likely to have the requisite serenity of mind for a crystalline Spätlese. Madeira or an old Oloroso Dulce would certainly front up to the moment, but laying about treacherously drinkable fortified wines when extensive child conflict-resolution duties still beckon, as well as a possible detour to local accident and emergency facilities, is best avoided. Following extensive trials, in fact, I can report that the ideal wine to be served at this point is Tokaji Aszú.

The dainty little half-litre bottle, the mysterious light amber hue, and the flurry of exotic diacritics on the label all arrest the attention, even of the harried. You can pour it into any kind of strange or whimsical glass and it will feel right and you will feel civilized and grand, as if you were a delegate at the Congress of Vienna. The scents of misty autumn are reverie-inducing and will whisk you to the River Bodrog: the ultimate elsewhere. The cleansing appley acidity will expunge the final traces of sponge. Then the wine's own sweetness, so much more sombre and profound than that of gâteau thanks to beneficent botrytis, will slowly perfume your mouth. The wine's alcoholic afterthoughts begin to lift everyone's spirits, elevating the general conversational level. Before you know it, you are no longer discussing *Kung Fu Panda 2* and have switched to Jiří Menzel's *Closely Observed Trains*.

This graceful and beguiling Tokaji seems to be entering that state which eludes many parents: a serene middle age. There is so much in its aroma: sweet fruits and a twist of barley sugar too, the freshness of lemon verbena and heady linden blossom, mouth-watering umami, a punnet of white mushrooms. There's a tickle of oxidation: just enough to evoke nuts and staves and bungs, but not so much that the other aromas are flattened or cowed. With an aroma like that, no one need rush into the glass – but when you do, there's a surprise waiting. The wine is less sweet than you thought: there is brisk apple, and green plum, and fresh green grape, too. It's smooth and mouth-filling, but that intensity of fruit extract gives it tenacity, even pungency. All of the honey lies behind, resolving the acidity, supporting it, coating it, only to dissolve so that the acidity emerges once again towards the wine's end, carrying the flavours long after you have swallowed. The lime blossom is back then, too, haunting the finish as it haunts summer nights across the villages of Central Europe.

The children may also be back, of course. Post-Aszú, you might be ready to love them again.

Knowing and Loving

The winter darkness slipped around the house like a greatcoat. We sipped Blandy's 1964 Malmsey, and ate Monika's homemade Madeira cake. There was a small pile of beautifully bound guest-books in front of us. 'Here, look at this one,' said Michael.

It was the entry for December 6th 1997. 'The end of the week,' he read, 'when the media proclaimed dinner parties to be passé, with guests resenting the effort of getting there and hosts resenting the effort of preparation. Our riposte was an evening that frothed with good humour, laughter and bubbly conversation from the guests' arrival at 7pm to their departure at 2am. A real tonic of an occasion.' They both smiled, with almost childlike delight. Me too. I'd been a guest there often enough to picture the scene. If there is one invitation in London it would be misguided to turn down, it's an invitation to dinner with Michael and Monika Schuster.

We've all given dinner parties, and we've all been on the receiving end. It can be done well or badly. Aptitude, experience and intuition are essential. Pulling it off with aplomb is administratively and psychologically complex. I try, but comparing my chaotic efforts with the Schusters' is like pitting a neighbourhood bistro against a Michelin Guide fixture.

Why so good? There are three prerequisites, first of all: a nice house, good cooking and a stash of great bottles. The house bit is subjective, I agree, but all the usual hazards (too cold, too hot, hideous furnishings, slavering pets, petulant children, cigarette addiction, scented candles and an unquenchable passion for Elton John) are averted here; indeed the Schusters' house is light, cosy and elegant, a rare combination. They do have a cat, but at nearly 22 it has lost all ability to slaver. Males generally monopolize most of the kitchens I know, but not here: Monika is artful proof of the worth of the Grand Diplôme from the Cordon Bleu Cookery School. And then… they have three cellars: his, hers and the business one. The business one? More on that in a minute.

He was born and brought up in Kenya. His parents were Christian Jews from Frankfurt who fled the Nazis. Michael still has the guest-book of his mother's family, and to anyone who loves music, it makes remarkable reading. His maternal grandfather, Paul Hirsch, was an industrialist who collected music manuscripts; a quick flick through revealed the signatures of Igor Stravinsky, Richard Strauss, Paul Hindemith, Wilhelm Furtwängler, Edwin Fischer, Erich Kleiber, the Busch Quartet… including handwritten musical quotations (though not what they thought of the Sauerbraten or the Hochheimer Kirchenstück Spätlese). The Hirsch Collection is now a British Library treasure; it took several train wagonloads to get it out of Germany, the Nazis having failed to recognize its value in time. Michael himself is a French horn player who performed in the same orchestra as a young cellist called Charles Windsor during schooldays at Gordonstoun. Monika, by contrast, is an Austrian who was brought up by her shoemaking grandfather Richard Thar and his hotel-chef wife Theresia. As a little girl, she used to sit beside her grandfather, handing him wooden nails to tap into the shoes. She says she always wanted to be a *schuster* (the German word for shoemaker) more than a chef. Now, of course, she's both.

204   WINE IN A LIFE

'M and M' are something of a wine-trade institution, but with a unique position. After an early career as a schoolteacher, English teacher in France and then wine merchant, Michael ran a wine school called Winewise for 35 years, which, in addition to providing friendly and clearly structured beginner's classes for all comers, also acted as an occasional weekend crammer to lash would-be Masters of Wine through the many-hurdled horrors of their practical exam. In terms of exposure and experience as well as ability, Michael is one of Britain's finest wine tasters. He also writes (look out for the excellent *Essential Winetasting*) and is a valued wine judge. It would be easy for the partner of someone like that to be overly deferential. Monika (a former pupil) rarely defers: she just tells him he's wrong. That's why she has her own cellar, goes to tastings under her own steam (of which she can build up quite a head), and has her own wine specialisms.

I mentioned 'prerequisites' for dinner party success above, yet it's the intangible things, the 'postrequisites' if you like, that set the Schusters aside. They are fun to be with: how do you quantify that? They are open-minded, unintimidating, unpretentious, anti-materialist. They like people, and think about them. (Monika has made a list of every guest's likes and dislikes, and always tries to cook 'something which people wouldn't cook for themselves'.) They are generous with their cellar, but not alcohol bullies: no one need drink more than they want, you can always pour away leftovers in order to try something else, and they serve jugs of water (three-quarters filtered and one-quarter sparkling). 'I don't buy still water in bottle any more,' says Michael; 'I think it's immoral.' Not all guests are wine-lovers, or even particularly wine-literate, and the conversation ranges widely over many subjects other than wine. All that they ask of their guests is a bit of active participation. 'That,' says Michael, 'seems to me to be an implicit "rule of the game". The art of conversation requires you to be interested in the person next to you. That question-and-response skill is simple enough, but it does require a bit of effort, which not everybody makes.'

As we dabbed up the last crumbs of our Madeira cake and drained the dregs of the 1964 Malmsey, we set about thinking what the word 'connoisseur' might really mean. 'Knowing and loving,' I suggested, was as good a definition as any; merely knowing implies a chilliness of spirit, while merely loving implies a lack of respect for the subject. Paul Hirsch and his cherished music manuscripts came to mind. So, too, did his grandson, his Austrian wife, and the bottles under their London home that, professionally and personally, they love to share.

The Ethnologist in the Cellar

Co-operatives are such a familiar part of the wine landscape, particularly in Europe, that we tend to forget what extraordinary hybrids they are: not just commercial entities with a social dimension, but collections of individual entrepreneurs who have agreed to pool resources and efface individuality for the common good.

Nowadays, these mixed roles prove challenging. Co-operatives may be institutions of vital social significance in their villages, but they often struggle to make commercial headway, not least because pride, ambition and qualitative efforts can be diluted in the muddy waters of the communal bath. Here's the fascinating story of what one Languedoc co-operative resolved to do about these challenges.

It decided to hire an ethnologist.

The co-operative in question was formerly known as the Cave de Montpeyroux; now it's known as 'CastelBarry, Co-opérative Artisanale à Montpeyroux'. 'I'm convinced of the value of co-operation,' says director Bernard Pallisé. 'But I noticed that no one was proud of being in a co-operative. The members didn't want the word appearing on labels, for example. I worried that in a decade, we'd no longer be relevant because we wouldn't be able to make the most of what we've got.' A local retired policeman had begun a history study on the village, and it gave Pallisé the idea of creating a project based around the 'societal memory' of the co-operative. So, in 2011, he contacted ethnologist Marie-Ange Lasmènes.

She recorded lengthy interviews with present and former members of the co-operative and, working with photographer Alain Tendero, turned

206   WINE IN A LIFE

her work both into an exhibition and a short book publication. 'When I presented the book to the members just before Christmas 2014,' remembers Pallisé, 'three-quarters of them were in tears.' The project not only had a motivating and galvanizing effect on members, but it also inspired Marie-Ange Lasmènes herself to become 'an independent ethnologist'. She has since worked with the co-operative at Puisseguin-St Emilion and with Plaimont Producteurs, too.

Montpeyroux (the name comes from Mont Pierreux – 'Stony Mountain') not only has a historical appellation of its own within the Languedoc AOC, but it also lies in the newer quality appellation of Terrasses du Larzac. The origins of the village (a collection of five hamlets) are three Roman villas, dominated by a huge 12th-century walled enclosure on the hillside up above known as the Castellas de Montpeyroux. The co-operative's name is a contraction of Castellas and St Martin du Barry, a celebrated chapel in one of the hamlets. The summits of Mont Saint-Baudille and the Montagne de la Seranne lie above, and the Cévennes beyond. It's rugged upland country.

Phylloxera heralded a chapter of disasters in Languedoc: over-production, fraud, World War I, competition from Algeria. The resulting crisis brought half a million demonstrators onto the streets of Montpellier in 1907. Inspired by the leadership of socialist pioneer Jean Jaurès, many Languedoc villages began to form co-operatives from 1905 onwards – but not Montpeyroux, which was a village divided into 'red' left-wing republicans and 'white' monarchist conservatives.

The village had two schools, two cafés, two hairdressers, two bakers... to serve each section of the community. 'You also had social divisions,' added Lasmènes, 'between the small producers and those who owned a lot of land, and there were further divisions between the believers (whether Catholic or Protestant) and the non-believers, the secularists.' An initiative to form a co-operative in the 1930s collapsed because this river of divisions proved unbridgeable.

'After World War II,' continued Lasmènes, 'the vineyard was in a poor state. But agriculture here is monoculture: if the vineyards sank, the whole village was going to sink with them.' Winemaking conditions were atrocious – tiny cellars where old casks shared space with donkeys and mules and their droppings. Casks leaked or gave way; wines oxidized or turned acetic. The purchasers were local négociants who exploited the weakness of the producers.

The smaller-scale producers realized that they had to form a co-operative to survive; it came into being in 1949. At first, the village's larger producers wanted to spurn it – but thanks to a visionary village mayor (Michel Teisserenc) and a retired general called Alfred Guyomar who agreed to bring all his harvest to the co-op cellar and act as its first president, they were gradually won over. What Lasmènes shows is that the co-operative not only kept wine-production alive in this hilly vineyard area where bulk production was never an option, but it also gradually healed the fractures in the village itself. It taught the villagers not only that they could work successfully together, but that modest prosperity could even beckon via communal action.

Nowadays the village is a very different place – but it's still surviving and prospering, and the co-operative is still a lynchpin of village life. There are outstanding independent producers today, notably Sylvain Fadat, but the multiple challenges of viticulture, winemaking and wine-selling are not for everyone; more and more growers are part-timers in any case, with other jobs. The co-operative still has 110 members and 500 hectares; unusually for the Languedoc, it produces more AOC wine than IGP wine, with 50 percent exports.

I'll leave the last word to grower and co-operative member Yvon Carceller, who inherited 10 hectares from his father and now has 26 hectares. 'The co-operative was the treasure of the village and for me, it still is. Of course, like everyone, there are times when you want to chuck it all in. But somehow you recognize that it's not too bad, and that it brings you a bit of freedom. You're your own boss; you don't have fixed hours. Afterwards, when you have to treat the vines, it doesn't matter if it's Sunday or not: you've got to go. That's part of the deal. I could have an easier life, but there you are, it's in my mentality, I've always wanted to grow the domaine. We'll leave it to our children. They'll do what they want with it, but at least they'll have a patrimony. Good vineyards will always have value.'

Up the Steep Hill

On the afternoon of June 25th 2013, I stood with a Wachau winegrower called Peter Veyder-Malberg. We looked across to a terraced vineyard on a slope a couple of hillsides away called Brandstatt.

Veyder-Malberg is an incomer, a former Vienna advertising executive who quit, learned winemaking at Pine Ridge, Villa Maria, Esk Valley and Franz Keller, then, after working as general manager for Graf Hardegg in the Weinviertel, bought a few morsels of terraced vineyard for himself.

Why terraces? 'My idea was to farm land where tractors have never driven. We're in the north. It rains. Tractors do a huge amount of damage when driven on wet soil. This work is more like gardening, and that was fascinating to me.' He concentrated his purchases on the Spitzer Valley at the Wachau's western end. 'People on the banks of the Danube say that these vineyards never get ripe, but I thought that would be interesting with climate change. And most growers here take their fruit to a co-operative, so I could just afford the land prices.' He's acquired 20 tiny parcels up and down the Wachau, making a total of about four hectares.

He pointed across to Brandstatt: a steep hill whose terraces were half-abandoned. 'I bought that vineyard in 2009 from an old lady in her 80s. She was called Margarete Siebenhandl – a tiny lady, very slender, with a very precise voice. She was unmarried. She'd tended those vineyards all her life. She used to come up here every day. You see that hut?' A little black shack crouched at the bottom of the vineyard. The slope meant it was sited at a crazy angle; it looked as if it would slide away at any moment. 'That was where she used to shelter from the storms. She used oak stakes for the vines. She used to remove them every winter, so no one would steal them, and put them back in spring. But one day she couldn't come up the hill any more. So she asked the firemen to cut all the vines off, and the vineyard fell into ruin.

She went to live with her sister. I talked to the sister, who told her: "This man wants to buy your vineyard." The old lady didn't believe it. No one thought that vineyard would ever come back to life. Many growers in this part of the valley are old. Their backs go, and then they have to give up, because the children are all happy with their jobs in Vienna.'

Veyder-Malberg reclaims four terraces of Brandstatt every second year: he hasn't got the funds or the time for more than that, but he does a thorough job, restoring the walling as well as clearing and replanting. In six years' time, he should have finished his restoration of this beautifully exposed mica-schist vineyard; he's planted Riesling ('it's too free-draining for Grüner'), and he has high hopes for it. What, I asked him, did Margarete think of his work?

'I felt very sorry for her when I heard her story. Later, I called back and talked to her sister. I asked if I could show Margarete what I was doing. "No," she said; "she's in bed and doesn't get up any more now. But anyway I told her," the sister went on. "When she heard that her Brandstatt was going to be replanted, she cried."'

For some reason, I haven't been able to forget tiny, aged Margarete Siebenhandl, who walked herself up the steep hill every day of her working life to look after her vines, who lived on the modest sums her grapes brought her at the co-op each year, and who felt, when her strength failed, that she had to ask firemen to destroy her life's work because no one would now want it. It's a more typical story than the good fortune of the ultra-wealthy and the self-satisfied, those ceaselessly profiled in the wine press. A common tale in all the difficult parts of Europe; common, too, in all the have-a-go places outside Europe where high hopes grind to a halt before crumbling. Every time you drink a co-operative-produced wine, it will brim, silently enough, with stories like Margarete's. At least this one ended happily. And Margarete knew.

Mille Fois Morte, Mille Fois Revécue:

2008 Chateau Musar Blanc

I don't like this wine. That was my first thought on tasting it. It didn't smell interesting. Slightly funky; I'm not funky enough to like funk. Then nothing much beyond. Wide yet dry on the palate; softly sharp. Hardly allusive. I can't do much with this. Let's try something else.

Serge Hochar, dead these five years, is smiling. He isn't fully dead yet because the wines he made, like this one, live on; and because I who remember him am not dead yet. You don't die until the last person who remembers you dies; only then do you slip beyond claim of life. Not only do I remember Serge, but I can see him sitting at the table behind me, next to the open bottle, and watching me type these words, and smiling. 'It is very important that you don't like this wine,' he murmurs in his soft voice, having seen me type, 'because the wine doesn't want you to like it yet. The wine is wanting to teach you something, but first it has to see if you can be taught.' What do you mean, Serge? 'It has to see if you walk away, or if you walk back. If your mind is still open. If it knows your mind is still open, it can teach you something.' And then Serge vanishes quite slowly, beginning with his legs and ending with his smile, which remains for some time after the rest of him is gone.

The wine is made from old-vine, ungrafted Obaideh and Merweh varieties, grown not on the Beka'a Valley floor but on the western, seaward slopes of Mount Lebanon, and on the foothills of the Anti-Lebanon mountain range. Serge used to suggest a relationship between Chardonnay and Obaideh, and between Sémillon and Merwah, the Crusaders having furnished the line of transmission. *Wine Grapes** is sceptical, but offers no

* *Wine Grapes – A complete guide to 1,368 vine varieties, including their origins and flavours* by Jancis Robinson MW, Julia Harding MW and José Vouillamoz, Allen Lane (London) 2012.

alternative theory. Even given seven centuries of adaptation, and even planted around 1,200 metres, could any vine with Chardonnay and Sémillon genes support a summer below 34°N, rainless from February's end, and still have produced a vividly acidic wine of 12% abv when harvested on the 4th and the 11th of October? A tall order, a tall tale – or not; one day we'll know. Anyway, part barrel-fermented and part-steel.

'My whites,' Serge said to me, while his heart was still beating back in May 2003, 'are my first reds. Serve them at room temperature, they will go with foods more than any of my reds, and the dimension of my whites is way bigger than the dimension of my reds. Although my whites are much more difficult than my reds. Just talking about this would take us one hour. If I put in front of you any red and any white, by the end of the day, if I say which one will you drink now, 99 percent of the people will say, OK, I will drink the white. After one hour, two hours of comparison. They are difficult, but whenever somebody gets there, they are hooked.'

So I have come back. Or rather I didn't go away; I poured a glass for dinner, an hour or two later, and noted that the wine worked effectively, it did its job, it drank well, it was shapely and energetic, it slipped down. Then after dinner I went back to hunt about some more. I still wasn't sure I liked the scents much: bandages and green beans. They seem to want to push the drinker away. But the flavours intrigue. It's just 12%, yet it's a wine of substance. Acidity is a significant element of its structure, yet there is no greenness, no sharpness, just fullness and wealth. Preserved lemons and umami wealth; Japanese mushrooms, maybe Japanese citrus fruits, maybe soy. It's very fermentative; in fermentation lies complexity. I keep coming back: day two, day three. There are walnuts now, and rotting hazelnuts, and green sap. Maybe the lemons are pickled, not preserved. Or bitter: Cyprus, Alexandria, the library going up in flames. I remember how Serge used to taste: it was a process more akin to psychoanalysis than the MW practical paper, more Bachelard than Peynaud. He'd try this, try that, to see if the wine would respond, and often it would; thus he'd drag his fellow tasters round to new knowledge. But the wine would answer like Serge: by telling you something else, and then asking: 'Is it an answer?' Now it's telling me about pine trees in sunlight, and resin. Beirut, Rhodes, Athens: a straight line, a Phoenician highway. 'Lebanon is not the New World,' Serge used to say. *Mille fois morte, mille fois revécue*: the words of the Lebanese francophone poet Nadia Tuéni on the tattered poster of Beirut in the Lebanese consular office in London, when I first queued up for a visa in 1993. That phoenix identity ('a country that commits suicide every day while it is being assassinated' – Tuéni again) fascinated Serge, and he saw it in his wines, too. 'The power of life is something strange. I have seen wines dying, and then getting back to survival. I have made the decision myself: this wine is dead, throw it away. And then it has come back.' And now I come back again, four days later, to talk to the dregs, and at last I like the smell of it, fresher than ever now, as if dusk has come round to dawn, and bakers are baking, and sprinkling olive oil on their bread, and squeezing lemons. Serge, you were right.

All Quiet:

2016 Bouzeron, Domaine de Villaine

The Great Lockdown fell on us like snow in the small hours. When we woke, the conditional right of free movement had been snuffed out. A new quietness blanketed the land. Every city, I remember thinking, must now be Venice: a place of voices and footsteps. With an added frisson of disquiet. Every voice, every footstep needs justification. Every breath could kill.

In France, with its grand bureaucratic traditions, we were obliged to wave a piece of paper at unsmiling enquiry – an *attestation*. (This, by the way, is one of the two most French words in existence, along with *inadmissible*.) And so we stole about our localities 'on brief journeys, close to the place of residence, linked to the individual physical activity of persons, to the exclusion of all collective sporting practices'.

It was my good fortune that I heard, on April 8th 2020, after a walk through silently unfolding vines, the three quiet 'hoo' calls of the hoopoe, freshly come from the Sahel; eight days later, falling like flakes through the novel silence of the afternoon, the first vocal press-ups of a nightingale, landed perhaps from Senegal. We humans were stilled, but others were on the move. The sap was on the move. The year was on the move.

Wine, along with birdsong, is our chief consolation now. Turn on the radio and out tumbles tragedy: lives concluded too soon, and in perplexing solitude; businesses sent sprawling; the active rendered idle, lonely, poor and anxious. We mark time, live on our reserves, while those whose business is health exhaust their own, working on the edge, risking all. Wine has never seemed more superfluous as an edifice, a vast palace of fussiness; yet its essence, as not just a physical but a psychological or spiritual restorative, has never been more useful. Much and sometimes all of the customary texture of life has been stripped away, so we treasure that which fortifies resolve – like a glass of wine at day's end. Wine, for the time being, has gone elemental.

And this was the elemental wine I sought out as the quietness fell. I had one bottle, bought last year in crowded Beaune, shortly after I'd helped some Hong Kongers disburse thousands of euros on lordly Grands Crus and debonair Premiers Crus. Bouzeron is a little appellation, a paradigm of modesty – just 60 hectares of vines in a hidden valley. It's for Aligoté; the valley is so deeply hidden they forgot to tear out the Aligoté after phylloxera had cut its swathe through the Chalonnais, after all the village men had gone off to work on the railway. Or at least they did up at the top of the hills, above 270 metres or so, where the old stumps of Aligoté Doré linger; down at the bottom there is Chardonnay and Pinot for Bourgogne. Aligoté upslope seems to like its cool, stony marl. It's altogether less articulate than Chardonnay, less rich and less giving. Snowier. More hushed.

I've visited Domaine de Villaine with students over the last few innocent summers. Aubert de Villaine's nephew Pierre de Benoist explains, with a poetical metaphysics all his own, his 'celestial definition of terroir'. It's a kind of monastery fresco. 'In the wine, the fruit is dead. What is alive is the water – which links alcohol, tannins, dry extract and acidity. The water is a liaison of mineral energy, vegetal energy, astral energy from the sun. It keeps the memory of water from the sea that was here 200 million years ago. And the last energy is the human energy: my energy, Eric's energy [Eric Devaux, who works with Pierre], the energy of all animals which cross the vineyard at night, which live and die in the vineyard; we are all linked by the living water that is in the wine.' Pierre has usually come, in summer shorts, straight from the vines, with the dirt of the hillside on his hands and the sun on his brow. The soft, textured limpidity of the wine does its own explaining, too.

So here it is, in all its quietness and understatement, all its locked-down glory. It's a green-gold in colour, though more gold than green. It smells like a cousin of Sancerre: the smell of cold, juiced. There might be a little apple seepage, and maybe green plum, too, a week or two before it is ready to eat, freshly fallen under the cartwheels, squashed into the stones and the clay. Not much scent, actually. Hunt about, and you might find some memory of yeast, of clumped woodland moss, even of dried rose. All quiet, though. Like our streets.

How about a taste? Acids; rain on stone. Maybe even acid rain on stone, melting the lime into the muddy marl. It's not hard acid, though; it's rounded, chaptered, rich, even a little salty. There's something in the taste that takes me back to moss and barrows, too; to dripping days. It's a burgundy that reminds you that the Jura isn't far away, that reminds you that we are not, after all, in a dreamland or a Cockaigne but somewhere rather northerly, when any day picked at random out of the year might well be uncomfortably cold and penetratingly damp. You might catch a chill, or worse. As a wine, it is very pure, vinous, comforting, complete, wholesome, refreshing. Thank you, thank you; we'll swallow, it will help. Quiet above all; a living water. Doesn't want to please; just is.

Lessons from the Laureate

A stuffy seminar room; a warm afternoon; a discussion of Henry James. Which novel? *Portrait of a Lady*? That I can't quite remember: it was over 40 years ago. Some of the students had lost interest; one or two may have been dozing. A single student, though, had buried his teeth in a typically long and convoluted Henry James sentence and, like a terrier with a teddy bear, he wasn't letting go. He was trying to disentangle the relevant and subordinate clauses, reconcile pronouns with antecedents, and thereby expose exactly what it was that James was trying to say. The knotty thickets of the sentence, though, defeated him. 'What does he mean?' he kept asking.

I thought back to that moment at around midday on October 5th 2017, when my brother sent me a text message to say that the fellow student in question, Kazuo Ishiguro, had just won the Nobel Prize in Literature. Bear with me for a paragraph or two, and I'll explain what this tale might have to do with wine.

The Ish I knew back then (so we all called him) was a former housing charity resettlement officer whose plan to become the British Bob Dylan hadn't worked out, but whose rejected radio play had landed him on the recently created Creative Writing MA course at the University of East Anglia. (I was a student of the taught MA course from which the Creative Writers took two modules.) Ish's stories were quiet, strange, oddly uneventful – but they had internal coherence; they compelled. He emerged as the most talented student of that year, and Faber & Faber signed him up; his first novel, *A Pale View of Hills*, followed two years later. More have followed, including the Booker Prize-winning *The Remains of the Day*.

If you've read any of them, and compared them to other contemporary novels, you'll be aware of their distinctive differences. The language, to begin with, is simple, apparently artless. They are literary novels so devoid of

216   WINE IN A LIFE

literary flamboyance as to seem barely 'literary' at all – an enormous plus for many readers. You never need scurry for the dictionary. Translators love his work (he's said that he writes with translators in mind).

The novels are indeed artful; structure and 'technical problems', I remember, were an early Ish concern. The words may be simple, but they are thoughtfully chosen. His greatest accomplishment lies in narrative itself, in storytelling, since he contrives to implicate the reader in the unfolding of the tale to a much greater extent than novelists of a more evidently 'masterful' kind. The effect of the unintimidating, highly accessible surfaces of his stories is that reader swiftly slips beneath the waters and becomes the discoverer of what lies beneath; it's the reader who does the realizing, who lives in the story, rather than being a seated and passive spectator at the novelist's great show.

Added to that stylistic modesty and collaborative technique is a curiosity and an empathy for those whom the tale describes, even when (as is the case for Stevens, the butler who is the central character in *The Remains of the Day*) they are unlikeable, and the architects of their own distress. The Ish I remember was an asker of questions, an enquirer into people's lives; it was, indeed, hard to out-manoeuvre him into revealing a little more about his life than he had just managed to get you to reveal about yours. The imagined other, not the writerly self, lies at the centre of his work; and that cast of others is deeply realized and nourishing, as readers soon grasp.

A work of art, of course, is wholly a creation of the human mind, whereas the winemaker simply stewards the transformation of one product into another. Winemaking is craft, not art.

The two processes are, though, similar to the extent that both artist and craftsman have to make an endless suite of significant choices whose results will be reflected in the final work, the finished object. There is an aesthetic element to the appreciation of wine; and a great wine is much more than a felicity of nature. It is indeed a crafted object. Might Ish's narrative art tell us anything about the crafting of wine?

A lack of flamboyance would be a good starting point. It's very easy in winemaking to turn up the volume, to introduce intrusive elements or to heighten contrasts for a showy result. Such wines will often stand out in tastings, just as a dazzlingly written novel draws critical attention to itself. This is not it itself a culpable strategy: great novels have been written in this way (think of the focused incandescence of *Moby-Dick* or the fecund chaos of *Ulysses*) and wines of this sort can be enjoyable to taste and add to the brightness of life.

Drinkability, though, is another matter, and the profounder satisfactions of wine emerge most clearly in those where the surfaces are not too distracting, and the contrasts not too brightly drawn. Having the courage to do nothing is often the most taxing skill of the winemaker – supposing, that is, that she or he has first gone to infinite pains to ensure that the raw materials, the grapes themselves, are as perfect as season and place permit. That would be the equivalent of choosing simple words – but assaying them for every ounce of meaning.

A second lesson from Ish's work would be the primacy of narrative – and I'd suggest that the equivalent of narrative in a novel is the expression of place and of origin in a wine. What matters most about a novel is its story – what it tells us; and what matters most about a wine is also a sort of narrative, a narrative of place. Place, in the end, is what distinguishes all serious wines (the equivalent of literary novels) from one another; that is the origin of their diagnostic uniqueness, for which in certain cases we are prepared to pay so much. Any strategy that takes you off the story, or effaces the sense of place in a wine, is a setting aside of high vocation.

The difference is that novelists choose their narratives, whereas winemakers in the main don't choose their places – but fidelity to that narrative, that sense of place, is primordial. The ideal here is one of limpidity, of transparency, of honesty and of truth to origin; that is what, as winemaker, you are giving the world, just as a novelist gives his or her written narrative to the world. It is up to the world to make of both what it will.

The final lesson? The Nobel citation referred to the 'emotional force' of Ish's work, though the Swedish committee then went on rather gloomily to point out that this 'uncovered the abyss beneath our illusory sense of connection with the world'. I would put it in a simpler and perhaps more positive light: Ish is a deeply though subtly compassionate writer. In his acceptance speech, he said that 'for me the essential thing [about stories] is that they communicate feelings. That they appeal to what we share as human beings across our borders and divides … stories are about one person saying to another: This is the way it feels to me. Can you understand what I'm saying? Does it also feel this way to you?'

There is a kinship here with what winemakers give to their drinkers. Thanks to its alcohol content, wine has an emotional force, and works on our feelings; but there is something more. The alcohol inside great wine is not raw and uncovered, as it is in cheap vodka or superstrength beer; it is clothed in much else. Through its allusive force, it constantly evokes the natural world, and our sensual memories and recollections of that world. By grace of alcohol, it does this emotionally – thus it's barely an exaggeration to say that a great wine can rouse in us a compassion and a loving engagement with the natural world itself, akin to the compassion that novelists evoke in us for their characters. Skilled winemaking is that which brings beauty and subtlety of allusion to the foreground, awakening that engagement with our sensual environment. We are richer for the experience, as we are when we close the final page on a great novel.

Meanings that Nourish:

2003 Château Meyney, Saint-Estèphe, half-bottle

What turns the wine world? Is it wine, or the meaning that wine can bring to our lives? Of course it's wine, my younger self would have said: why else do tastings happen? Why else do certain wines sell at 10 or 50 times the price of others? Why else do we dig into the earth to hack out cellars in which to stack more bottles of disparate origin than we could ever hope to drink, or travel half-way around the world to visit a hallowed domaine address and taste its wines while gazing out over the vines from which they came?

Now, I'm not so sure. The wine itself is bait, fuse, decoy; but the main event – the catch, the explosion, the prize – is the layering of meaning into our lives. This is meaning as resource, as nourishment, as sustenance – though our lives are filled with other meanings, too: meanings more bitter; meanings that hobble, or leave scars, or frame failure. We cling to the meanings that nourish. Thus some of us cling to wine.

It helps that it's a heart-gladdening beverage, that it's sensually alluring, that it turns meals into feasts, that it lies in the private realm, that it's a gateway to rest and recreation, that it comes from distant and exotic places, and that its culture is rich and complex. The fact that every bottle is a historical fact locked to a time and a place offers further purchase on meaning. It helps that wine can hold time at bay for a while, and at best engage in a joint project with time that results in an intensification of its own beauty. This forest of scaffolding makes it easy for us to build meaning around wine. We can shelter in the edifice we frame there long after the wine has drained away. To the point at which we may realize that it was the shelter and the edifice we loved so, and loved more than the liquid in the bottle.

I bought these half-bottles 17 years ago; they cost me £7.15 each. They come from a place that I have never visited, but which the buttresses and stanchions of wine knowledge help me to know: an early-planted, water-fronted stone mound dating back to the time when the Médoc was a kind of archipelago, thus a place bathed in light, reflected light and ceaseless marine breezes; a neighbour of the great Montrose; a place where buried blue clays might help moisten the roots of vines through a hot summer. That was why I bought this wine, for no summer (I knew back then) was hotter than 2003, though we have had hotter since. Clay, roots and light might have made a wine, I fancied, to see out time as wines from this place can do, and to furnish a drink that might contrive to be both generous, textured and austere in youth and later mellow and burnished and intelligently languid. So I hoped – and hope brings meaning, too.

It's delivering. I've always been fond of this wine, though it carries blemishes. It's not exquisite to smell, but earthy, sturdy, like Madiran (another clay-grown wine I love), with just a little too much oak – and incense spice from the hot summer. But it's still dark (no bricking, even in the half) and dense, squat, firm, energetic and concentrated on the palate. Not sublime, not meriting a high 90s score, not remotely languid (perhaps

Saint-Estèphe never is)... but so satisfying with its retained youth, its energy, its darkness of fruit, its thrust: the textured richness is matched by stormy-weather acidity. Meyney '03 is bobbing about like a well-trimmed galleon on waves of time.

Maybe I like it so much because it only cost £7.15; maybe because it's survived dislocation (delivered to the house with a cellar when I had a house with a cellar, then it went to my brother Steve's house – endowed with a beautiful cellar – then some of it went to my friend Stuart's house, from which I salvaged a few halves and suitcased them to successive cellar-less houses in hot-summered France, the final bottle of that stock being the one I have opened for this text – though I think there are still a few remaining halves back at Steve's house, too). Maybe it's because I bought a case of magnums for my nephew Luke, born in 2003. He's not remotely interested in wine, and may not even realize or remember that he has, since his 18th birthday, owned this case – since it, too, is stored at his Uncle Steve's house. But as my stocky little halves are going strong, his broad-shouldered magnums should manage to dawdle around long enough for a time to come in which wine from his birth year may seem of interest.

Apologies for this superfluity of personal information. It's testament, though, to the web of meaning within the arc of a lifetime that wine can give to us. Every time I've opened a half of the Meyney '03, it not only diverts and delights me with its flawed, gutty, wabi-sabi loveliness, with its fantasy of light and breeze and clay, and with its status as a gorgeous bargain; but unleashes a chain of recollection of lived experience, of family bonds and of friendship. What else other than these mounds of meaning can arm us for the darkness that awaits?

222   WINE IN A LIFE

CHAPTER NINE

AGAINST WINE WORLDLINESS

Wine and Astonishment

Wine is quietly unique: 'A pure biological expression of environment interpreted by rational and creative thought,' in the words of Australian winemaker Brian Croser. Human actors and the natural world play equal roles in its coming into being. This creation is experienced sensually, intellectually and emotionally; at times, it even seems to have a spiritual force, too.

Can wine take us closer to being itself, to the principle of existence? Perhaps. One mechanism by which it might do this is astonishment.

Astonishment

'Why is there something rather than nothing?' The formulation is that of Gottfried Leibniz in 1718, but many philosophers before and since have posed it.

Religion, obviously, has an answer to the question: the 'something' is the intended work of a divine creator. Scientists search for answers to this question as they probe the origin and scope of the universe, the tiniest of unseen particles and all the matter between, together with the forces that govern all interactions.

Philosophy has no answer to the question – but the asking of the question has always been significant and fruitful. One 20th-century philosopher, Martin Heidegger, made this question the centre of his philosophical enquiry. He did so via a book called *Being and Time* (*Sein und Zeit*), published in 1927, and via a series of subsequent essays and lectures.

Heidegger maintained that, in the torrent of existence, being itself ('*Sein*', a word that he capitalized) has been forgotten. What is the difference between existence and being? Existence is the extant; it is what exists. You bump into it, trip over it, look at it, touch it, smell it and eat it. You could call it 'stuff'.

Being, by contrast, is the 'isness' inside everything that exists. The fact that this seems such a strange concept indicates how complete our forgetting of being is. We're so obsessed with 'stuff', with appearances and externalities, that we forget 'isness'. Or, to go back to the original phraseology, we're so distracted with existence that we forget being.

Heidegger's project was to 'uncover' being, to 'think' being and to 'say' being, though he recognized that this was difficult – given the inauthenticity, distraction, ambiguity and hunger for novelty in which most of our lives pass.

Being for Heidegger was not the metaphysical matter or question of ideals that had been associated by previous philosophers with notions of 'essence'; still less did it equate to God. It is, rather, something earthly and worldly, embedded (though at the same time hidden) in the density of things. All of existence, in other words, is secretly saturated in being. Being streams – like photons and other elementary particles – through that which is, through existence. The challenge is to break through the crust or carapace of existence to find being again.

Heidegger's own technique for doing this is a set of new words, often forged clumsily out of clusters of existing words. He uses these to shock and dislocate the reader into the re-thinking that might reveal forgotten or lost being within the familiar, mechanical thrum of existence.

Language is key. 'Language is the house of Being,' Heidegger wrote in his 'Letter on Humanism'. 'In its home man dwells.' For you and I, it is through words and language that things come into being. Customary philosophical thinking, he maintains, is unable to take us back to being. That can only be achieved, says Heidegger, by what he calls 'poeticizing thought' or 'thinking poetry'.

There are kinships between Heidegger's work and Buddhist (and Hindu) tradition. Heidegger's 'existence', the aggregated and inauthentic externalities that hide being from us, might bear some kinship to *samsara*, the ceaseless flow or drift of transitory desires, emotions and experiences that every Buddhist is urged to repudiate, and the directionless 'wandering' cycle of death and rebirth from which Hindus struggle to liberate themselves.

Heidegger's 'Being' and its locus, by contrast, spoken of as a 'clearing', or *Lichtung*, shares much with the positive Buddhist notion of emptiness, better seen as a space capable of being filled by light. The koans of the Zen Buddhist tradition perform a similar jolting task to Heidegger's 'poeticizing thought'. The posture of 'care' is not dissimilar to the attentiveness and compassion of Buddhist practice.

Being, Heidegger stresses, is also temporal: it can only exist in time. It is therefore fully accomplished only as it ends, in death, or rather in ceasing-to-be. It is care and attention to being itself that makes human existence meaningful.

Because being is projected in time and completed by death, it must necessarily involve anxiety. This positive, end-focused anxiety stands in opposition to the negative, formless fear that the daily run of inauthentic existence provokes. Out of that positive, directed anxiety comes care, concern, apprehension and attention.

To be authentically in the world, says Heidegger, is to care for, or be answerable to, being itself. Astonishment is essential: it is astonishment that reveals the presence of being inside existence.

The process of questioning, the questioning of everything that surrounds us, is a translation of astonishment into action; care or carefulness is how that action might be maintained. There is no particular answer to this questioning. Both it, and care itself, are a kind of practice.

Wine

Now let's return to wine. Those who love wine enough to read books about it can often trace their enthusiasm back to a single moment of astonishment. In some cases, this would be strong enough to be called an epiphany, variously defined as 'any moment of great or sudden revelation' or a 'sudden manifestation of the essence or meaning of something'. These moments are regularly written about or discussed in wine circles; some like to cite the particular bottle that led to the revelation or epiphany.

Assigning the impact of such moments to a particular wine in a particular vintage is what wine minds (often obsessed with the granular) tend to do – but it misses the point. The wine involved on such occasions may not be great. It certainly wasn't in my case – an encounter with a bottle of anonymous Beaujolais in the mid-'70s. Good wine is good enough.

What happens, I'd suggest, is that for a moment we see or sense the being of wine inside the existence of wine. This has a physical dimension, of course: we suddenly relish the wine we are tasting in a more comprehensive manner than we have ever been able to do before. We suddenly 'get it', often with overwhelming force. We suddenly grasp, through a single glass, the radical principle of beauty common to all good and great wine, and gasp for a moment at the extent of its appeal. We understand how wine creation might mesh with other cultural activities. At the same time, we come to realize just how intimate its relationship with the natural world is. It has a maker, but who is that maker? The wine grower, or the place from which the wine came? The question is resonant. We become one with all of those who have understood this beauty and this uniqueness in the past, and we become one of those by whom it will be transmitted in the future. All this is often wordless and instantaneous, a kind of explosion of insight.

Might the mechanisms at work in that moment of epiphany not stand behind all of our interactions with wine? We should try not to forget, in other words, the first astonishment we felt as we looked, tasted, and tumbled into the being of wine. Being is always there, inside existence; it just requires the torch of astonishment to shine a light on it.

Alcohol

The first of these mechanisms is alcohol. Yes, the epiphany that I am alluding to and that you experienced is an alcohol-lifted one, though not alcohol-induced. (Many alcoholic drinks are incapable of triggering astonishment.)

Alcohol, strangely enough, has become problematic, even for those who love wine. Some commentators and wine creators would prefer wine to be alcohol-free if only it could retain its sensual personality intact in that form – and if not alcohol-free, then 12.5% abv and no more. Others might discount the initial experience entirely on the basis that alcohol has a role in it, and suggest that the glimpse of being contained in that moment is consequently inauthentic or 'drug-induced'.

Yet it is alcohol that lends wine an emotional dimension or force, which enables us not just to perceive wine's beauty, but to feel it, to be moved by it. Alcohol humanizes wine. Nothing is more human than seeking the means in nature to access emotion in this ritualized or formalized way. If ever and whenever we are able to perceive being inside existence, there will be an emotional aspect to that perception – because we are human. No epiphany is ever purely intellectual or purely rational. There may be other drivers of emotion in moments of epiphany – like religious rapture, or long-sought spiritual insight, or the physical forms of human longing. There's no reason, though, why alcohol should be considered secondary to these merely because its trigger is chemical. It seems likely, indeed, that chemical triggers of all sorts play a larger part in the life of the mind than most of us realize.

Whenever yeast begins to work on sweet fruit, alcohol comes into being. Alcohol belongs in wine; alcohol helps define wine; without alcohol, wine does not exist. Alcohol is central to the appeal of wine. A little wine brings spiritual music to secular or material life. Alcohol plays a role in that. What would wine be without the solace it imparts? Alcohol plays a role in that, too. Alcohol itself is never easier to assimilate or more nourishing than in wine. A large part of our astonishment at wine's being is connected with its diversity or difference. Everything in wine sings difference, undulating alcohol levels included.

Naturalness

Nature dwells in wine. I remember my own sense of wonder, during the winter of 1974 and spring of 1975, as I realized that in drinking wines from different countries, continents and hemispheres I was ingesting a liquid whose physical form and sensorial outline had been brought into existence by a plant or plants anchored in those places. Agreed, the liquid had been through a transformation; grape juice had become wine thanks to the agency of yeast (and winemakers). The substance itself, though, had come into existence through physical pathways in root and leaf, and through a suite of interactions with soil, rain and sunlight, in vineyards in Tuscany, in Portugal, in Burgundy. The birth both of that substance and of its personality had taken place inside grapes hanging in clusters on vines… there, there and there. Cold, drizzle, mud, stones, a misty dawn, bright noon, storms at dusk: the liquid I was rolling on my tongue had synthesized all of those, snug inside its grapeskin. They in turn were a part of its being. There was a direct line of transmission from the distant vine's vascular tissue to my waiting tongue. With nothing added and nothing subtracted, or so I believed.

This made wine special, a contrast to beer or to spirits made in a brewery or distillery by assembling ingredients, adding water and yeast, and following a kind of recipe. A glass of grapefruit juice may follow a similar line of transmission to a glass of wine, but it is silent concerning its place of origin, and the absence of alcohol robs it of an emotional dimension, of the same capacity for solace, and thus of cultural significance.

This still astonishes me today. I'm still shocked by the naturalness and wholeness and strangeness of wine. I think this is a common experience among new wine drinkers. It is one reason among many why I would urge anyone who has a hand in making wines to seek to respect the integrity of the raw materials, the harvested grapes, in so far as this is commensurate with purity and stability. Drinkers want to hear nature's heartbeat in wine. They want to sip distant places, to taste geographical difference rendered with astonishing articulacy; this shock or jolt of place is part of the being of wine.

Our species has come into being on earth. It will cease to be on earth. Wine enables us to drink a little of the diversity of our planet's life forms, topographies and geological phenomena. Through wine, the earth becomes more precious to us. If wine, all wine, even inexpensive wine, is served and regarded with a kind of respect that eludes beer and other alcoholic drinks, that's a reason. We erode or discard that respect at our peril. It's care; it's attention; it brings meaning.

The human hand

In the epiphany or moment of astonishment that first seals our bond with wine, of course, there is the implication of craftsmanship. Meeting a wine is not like meeting a wind, or gazing at the Aegean. We know that wine is made. Yet what sort of making is this?

Man, Heidegger wrote in his 'Letter on Humanism', 'is not the lord of beings. Man is the shepherd of Being'. Men and women are the shepherds of wine. There may be a direct line of transmission from vascular tissue in a Rhône Valley vineyard to a palate in Stockholm or Baltimore, but it is not uncomplicated, and it requires close supervision. It is an uncovering: the finding of potential inside a crop. At another level, it is the revelation of the sensual personality of place. You might almost call it a transhumance – the leading of the object from a settled lowland circuit, where it exists as fruit, to a nourishing summer upland altogether elsewhere, in which it has become wine. The process of transformation itself will happen anyway, in some way or another, given the right conditions; it is not alchemy, but one of nature's metamorphoses. Nature, though, is bent on making vinegar; the human shepherd leads wine away from that destiny and towards a place where wine can endure. For longer than nature intended, at least.

The notion of the winemaker or the wine grower fascinates many drinkers, who imagine a magician of pleasure, half-chemist and half-alchemist, conjuring perfume and flavour from the hillsides via mysterious cellar arts.

They're not wrong, though the truth is both more banal and more complicated. On the one hand, there is the technocratic or industrial ideal of the winemaker as master or mistress of his or her variable and inconsistent raw materials, engineering a desired wine outcome that will be consistent and reliable and deliver value for money at the target price for what is often called a 'product'. This indeed is the winemaker as 'lord of wines'. We are familiar with such figures. Those possessing a reassuring if incomprehensible expertise invite us to trust them – with our money, with our journeys across the face of the earth, with our health. Thus the hazards of life can be mitigated. In most cases, the trust is well-placed, though when it isn't, the ensuing failures can be catastrophic. The measure of success, note, is generally satisfaction, but no more than that.

This technocratic ideal (winemaking, for example, as mastery or lordship over raw materials) is what Heidegger later called *Gestell* in an essay entitled 'The Question Concerning Technology'. *Gestell* means 'frame' or 'rack' – an imposed system that does not bring Being to light or make it radiant, but rather denatures it and falsifies it. Such systems are of course useful, but they come at a price. Heidegger contrasts this kind of technique with the technique of the farmer who does not provoke and master the earth but works with it in a process of custodianship and renewal, via rhythms of donation and acceptance.

Behind the winemaker stands the 'wine grower'. Fruit is grown, but wine is made. The word elides two separate actions.

When you talk to those who have crafted wine the longest, or to those creating wines that inspire, most prefer the term 'wine grower' to that of 'winemaker'. The critical decisions affecting the personality and quality of the wine, they feel, are those taken in the vineyard, and they will make every effort not to betray the vineyard in their work. Custodianship and renewal are indeed ideals cherished by wine growers.

Choice of variety, the way in which the plant looks at the sun, the way in which it is sculpted each winter, and the way the soil is maintained and nourished: all matter. Crop size is another key factor, together with fruit positioning and attention to the growing vine. The moment at which harvest takes place, and the way in which it takes place, are significant too. Every season makes a conditional offer of perfection. The vinifying gestures that follow are immensely important too, but they cannot do more than respect and make manifest that offer. It's not uncommon to hear experienced wine growers in long-established regions say that they can do nothing further in the cellar to improve quality. The only way they can improve on past performance is by growing better grapes, and then doing the same things to them. The expressive melody that 30 years' work then proceeds to trace in sensual form is that of nature: the play of the seasons. It is a gift that the winemaker has done his or her best to honour. This accords with Heidegger's gloss on the Greek word *technē* as a coming into radiant being of that which was already inherent, or 'the bringing-forth of the true into the beautiful'.

What happens in the winery, in other words, is the use of craft to realize potential: a secondary intimacy with nature. Wine growers read skies and soils and seasons. They parent the vines in their charge, give them as much care as economic circumstances permit, and then realize the potential inscribed in the vine's fruit over that season with maximum sensitivity: shepherd and not lord.

Where else in agriculture do you find stewardship and craftsmanship so conjoined? Astonishingly, nowhere. No other farmers work with a crop capable of giving sensual voice to the nuances of place in this way, nor do they customarily craft that crop themselves. Chefs, perfumers and jewellers may practice their craft on nature's gifts, but have no role in shaping and shepherding those gifts. The rare intimacy of stewardship and craftsmanship is part of the being of wine. Every wine grower, I think, will have moments when the being of wine will be evident to them despite the existential drudgery; when they will be bringing not just *their* wine into being, but wine itself.

Poetry, science and wine

The initial moment of joy at our own consuming realization of wine's being may be wordless; perhaps it's always wordless. Words, though, will flock like birds around it when we do anything with it, such as tell others about it or attempt to understand its intimacies. Words become part of the mechanism of that moment as it takes shape in time.

Yet words and significances settle quickly in place; they become part of the familiar fabric of existence, and thus come to hide being rather than reveal it. Hence Heidegger's emphasis, mentioned a little earlier, on 'poeticizing thought' or 'thinking poetry'. He moves towards the articulation of being only by chiselling words anaesthetized by familiarity into a strange, re-made language. The taste of wine, inside which the being of wine lurks, is famously unsayable; we must chisel with metaphor, yet those metaphors, unless constantly challenged and renewed, can quickly take on anaesthetic force themselves.

The moment when we first experience wine's being will be an exciting one, and perhaps a dislocating one; we may well have the sense that it has rearranged our world. This, of course, is what poetry does. It treats of what we know, but makes it new. At that moment of epiphany, wine is indeed, as Robert Louis Stevenson called it, 'bottled poetry' [*see* pages 34–36].

By 'poetry', though, we don't simply mean written literary texts. There is a poetry of doing and of being; a making new, even of the most familiar acts. Science and scientific insights need not stand in opposition to poetry;

232 AGAINST WINE WORLDLINESS

they use a different set of tools to arrive at truth. The scientific journey must proceed by objective means, via experiment; the poetic one proceeds by subjective means, through insight. There need not be war between the objective and the subjective; the two can walk hand in hand. There is a common end – in the thing itself. The scientist wishes to understand what that thing is, stripped of its veils of incomprehension; the poet wants to feel, show and tell what that thing is, underneath the rust of familiarity. Arriving at the being of the thing – raw, pure, fresh, true – is the aim of both.

How does this relate to our moment of drinking astonishment? If we are to preserve astonishment, and remain as close as we can to the being of wine, then we need to sift our experiences of wine for the poetry that inhered to the initial moment itself. The newness, or the remade-ness, which implies astonishment and which helps define poetry is an essential quality of the best thinking (talking, writing) about wine. Science, in the end, confirms or refines the insights made by the attentive, many of which were first couched in poetic terms. You might know that malolactic fermentation is the conversion of malic acid to lactic acid by bacteria; or you might, a thousand years earlier, have known it was mischievous springtime sprites at work in the wine, disturbing it and troubling it for effects that are finally beneficial. The process, though, is the same; attentiveness and astonishment led us to understand it.

What is less satisfactory is the use to which scientific insight is put as wine is taken away from agriculture and made industrial. Industrial ideals are founded on the requirements of existence as opposed to being: that there should, in other words, be a sameness and a consistency to goods, and that functionality is paramount. Agricultural ideals, by contrast, are consonant with being, in that the inconsistency and primacy of nature is accepted, along with a spectrum of natural difference that will both fail and exceed the standards of functionality.

Perhaps it is naïve to expect wine to remain entirely agricultural when even agriculture itself can be industrialized. Industry has its virtues, too: access and plenty for all. Remember the initial moment of astonishment, though – that sudden incandescent glimpse of the being of wine. This had little to do with the return of the same, with the consistent satisfaction of demand, with the exclusion of surprise that lies somewhere at the heart of the successful industrial object. Those things are not astonishing; they are a large part, in fact, of the unseen familiar fabric we need to penetrate in order to reach being itself. Those who love to drink wine are not in search of an industrial object, like a liquid brake pad or an internet connection. We are prepared to find inconsistency, just as we are prepared to live through and relish four seasons. We value truth to place in wine's sensual personality, even if this personality seems strange at first, as places inevitably do in our own wanderings across the earth. We want to re-experience the astonishment that might lead us to the being of wine.

Difference

The final mechanism at work in our initial moment of epiphany, the moment at which we glimpse the being of wine, is an apprehension of difference. That moment is rarely if ever our first glass of wine; we're seasoned drinkers by then. We've moved from simple consumption of wine to a state of attentiveness to wine's sensual discourse. What we realize in that pivotal moment is that there is something irreducibly different about the wine we are drinking, something that is both aesthetically overwhelming yet also rooted in a truth to place. The sensual pleasure may well be perceived as deriving from that sense of place. It is not just the taste of wine that is sensually appealing, but there is also physical joy in taking our world-home into our mouths, into our nostrils, into our bodies, in making it something that is no longer external and 'out there' but inside us. This is not true of other drinks and foods, because they cannot reflect place in the same way, nor do they carry the same emotional charge. We may well feel a kind of vertigo of difference at that point, since we realize on the instant that there is no limit to the differences of place that wines might beautifully encapsulate, and with which we could become sensually and emotionally intimate.

This, I think, is the heart of wine's being; indeed, wine's ability both to embody difference and to take difference into our bodies may be the main reason why it has the cultural significance and importance it does for us. An attentiveness to the being of wine is an allegiance to difference, played out indefinitely, since nature itself generates nothing but difference and, inspired by nature, those who craft wines most skilfully weave further layers of difference into wine. Wine's being in time creates yet more levels of difference. The role of those who speak to or for wine would be to tell or to call those differences in a manner that honours the being of wine rather than busies itself exclusively with the existence of wine. In practical terms, that means never losing touch or breaking faith with the moment of epiphany in which the being of wine first becomes apparent.

Against wine-worldliness

Received language, received opinions, personal dogma, the seductions of fashion, critical disengagement: these play a role in wine-worldliness, which is a taking-for-granted of the givens of wine, and the assumption of a kind of assurance or familiarity over the subject that precludes astonishment. Naturally, this mastery pays lip-service to difference, because difference is the grain of wine, but the differences are told demeaningly, as if they exist in a settled world incapable of expansion, thereby perhaps to aggrandize the teller, who is the master of all.

The scoring of wines is a form of wine-worldliness. It does, of course, acknowledge difference: numbers exist to call difference. Yet it also freezes difference by rendering it numerically immutable. The wine is thereafter pinioned to its score, and the teller of that score then becomes in some sense the master of the wine, under whose heel the wine might squirm but cannot escape. The consumer of the wine, meanwhile, loses his or her own primary and unfettered relationship with the wine in favour of a relationship with the scoring intermediary. Scores are a technocratic innovation – another example of what Heidegger called a 'frame' or a 'rack'. In the shuttling to and fro of settled existence, they prove useful; the price we pay for this mundane usefulness, though, is that the being of the wine is diminished or hidden, and our own unfettered relationship with it is snatched away from us.

Another aspect of wine-worldliness is proprietorial familiarity. Wine is never more astonishing than when viewed innocently, though the eyes of the unknowing; and never less astonishing than when viewed through the eyes of one who cannot even remember what it was *not* to know wine, or who has long 'known it all'. Part of the struggle to find our way back to the being of wine is the challenge of seeing wine unknowingly or innocently once again. The solution may lie in exploring the relationship between the expression of wine difference and the expression of other forms of difference. Wine is sensual, but also cultural, geographical, historical – and sometimes literary and political. Its being becomes most apparent when we care for wine under those broad eaves.

Let's return to Heidegger, and to a consideration of wine and time. Being, Heidegger asserted, was inseparable from temporality; 'outside time' is a meaningless phrase, though the geologist's or astrophysicist's time frame is of course different from that of the historian. All being is therefore a being-towards-death, and being is only completed by death – hence the generative anxiety felt by human beings as they contemplate non-being.

Part of the affection we feel for wine is that it mimics our own trajectory towards non-being. In wine, we can taste the different stages of being. We can taste what it is to be youthful, to be mature, to be elderly. We can even taste what it is to be dead, to have lost the being that once existed. We have the pleasure of tracing an infinity of differences in life trajectories in wine; we can see both the beauty and the ugliness wrought by time, and we can see how decisions taken early in life can lead to beauty or ugliness later in life. Wine, in this way, can reconcile us to time; it gives us the chance to practise the journey towards non-being, to share it and understand it. It does this while taking us closer, in the most intimate manner, to the infinity of differences with which we are surrounded in our world, our home; and it gives the lucky few who chose to 'grow wine' the chance to use craft to embody, reflect and echo nature itself.

CHAPTER TEN

THREE LAST WINES

The Startled Hind:

2012 Pouilly-Fumé, Haute Densité, Château de Tracy

I visited Château de Tracy on a chill November day. Moisture clings to the air here; winter in the Central Loire is a dismal succession of penetrating mists and fogs. The wide, indolent, isle-scattered river marks a rheumatic pause between two vineyard zones: the assertive hills of Sancerre on the left bank; the gentler rises of Pouilly on the right. Tracy-sur-Loire must be Pouilly's most thickly wooded commune. The hamlet of Boisgibault lies nearby; most vineyards finish in forests whose rummaged earth margins betray the boar within. One of the *lieux-dits*, stranded between the woods, is called Les Froids – the colds.

My fingers were numb as I walked the vineyards around the château with Juliette d'Assay, who directs Château de Tracy. I clamped them to my neck to restore a little digital flexibility, but the warmth never lasted. The mists, though, were clearing; the hilltop town of Sancerre loomed suddenly across the river, sunlit above a silvered fillet of mist, like an apparition.

A short while later we stood underneath Château de Tracy's cedars, planted by Juliette's grandmother in 1926, and gazed across the vineyards of green sod and black clay at the château. It doesn't have the colossal Renaissance grandeur of Château du Nozet nearby, but it's hardly a sketch in snug domesticity, either; I could count five turrets from where I stood. A gang of rooks loped about the sky. How many dozen rooms lay inside those walls, I wondered? Were I sitting in one of them, would the plumes of my breath spiral in the air? Thirty-three hectares of vines won't pay for log-laden servants to bustle from fireplace to fireplace all winter; keeping the roof watertight must be challenge enough. The vineyards here, though, have been in cultivation since 1396, or so a de Tracy parchment (referring to the Champs de Cri site) attests, and the property has been a possession of what is now the d'Estutt d'Assay family since the 15th century. Things, somehow, endure.

Pouilly-Fumé is the only appellation name in France that doubles as a tasting note. *Fumé* means 'smoked' – alluding, at least in part, to the scent of struck gunflint (which most must imagine: flintlock weapons were superseded by the mid-19th century), and in part to the smoky bloom common on Sauvignon Blanc grapes at maturity. The reason is straightforward: the appellation Pouilly-sur-Loire, the natural counterpart of Sancerre, is for Chasselas-based wines, so 'Fumé' distinguishes the Sauvignon-based version. (After the railway reached Pouilly in 1861, it prospered as a supplier of Chasselas eating grapes to Paris – up to 3,000 tonnes a year, with a special train leaving Pouilly at 4pm every day for Les Halles during the harvest season. Phylloxera killed the trade, but a little Chasselas lingers on.) The memorable name has undoubtedly helped the zone greatly, especially after Robert Mondavi named his dry Sauvignon 'Fumé Blanc' in 1968 (this term is now legally accepted as a synonym for Sauvignon Blanc in the US). But it's regrettable.

Regrettable since it weaves a bundle of expectations and assumptions about this wine that prevent us from seeing it clearly. Flint is a form of chert that occurs in limestone; it's tough, insoluble and composed of inert silicon dioxide. In itself, it smells of nothing and tastes of nothing: it has no sensual presence. Zero.

In a flintlock, soft iron strikes hard flint. This produces a spark of burning iron, which ignites gunpowder. The distinctive smell of 'flint' is, in fact, that of burning iron. Any 'smokiness' in these wines is probably a varietal trait unrelated to flints in the soil. Pouilly's soils aren't all flint-scattered in any case; there are many parcels (like Champs de Cri, where this wine is grown) whose clays are punctuated by limestone pebbles. Clays – cold clays – are what all the soils of Pouilly have in common.

When Juliette d'Assay's now-retired brother Henry d'Assay was running the domaine, he planted some parcels at up to 17,000 plants per hectare (5,000 to 6,000 is typical here) in an attempt to encourage the vines to root deeply and intensify the sense of terroir: each vine is limited to three bunches, or one bottle of wine. The overall yield is 30 hectolitres per hectare.

Mysteriously, the INAO (the controlling body for France's AOC) decided in 2009 that the planting limit for Pouilly should be 10,000 plants per hectare, so the high-density vineyards from which this wine is made have a special derogation. It's large-wood fermented – and sold in aged form, both to show consumers that Pouilly-Fumé can age, and to maximize its gastronomic appeal.

Forget smoke; this wine smells and tastes of cold itself. Cold is a sensation rather than an object with a palpable scent or flavour, I know, but it comes clustered with suggestions of its own – of immobile reeds in iced lake fringes, of woodland on the northern side of hills where the night's frost never melts, of moss peeping from snow, of the clay of ploughed fields hardened into ridges that boots barely break. Shy smells: brooding, forbidding. That's what's here: uninsistent, ungossipy, taut, aquiline, nearly austere. There is a welcome greenness to it, but even that is a wintry greenness, a greenness that you'd have to tease out of the undergrowth in the silence of leafless woods; the wine runs like a startled hind from every obvious analogy. Even its alcohol would not qualify as warmth; rather sap and sinew, quickened by the arrow of acidity. This wine is coolness rendered liquid, imprisoned in a heart of glass.

Unsettled:

2014 Cannonau di Sardegna Mamuthone, Giuseppe Sedilesu

I've a bottle of this wine on my desk in front of me. Vintage, wine name and producer's name are picked out on the black label in red lettering, and the DOC designation of origin in silver. The only other mark on the label is an image: an unsmiling, almost despairing mask, its lines lifted from the paper darkness in silver, too. A huge nose, fierce eye-sockets, the mouth grimly set. It's the most unsettling image I've ever seen on a bottle of wine. This bleak, horror-struck face fixes me as I drink the dark, unbridled wine the bottle contains.

The wine comes from a village called Mamoiada, in the mountainous heart of Sardinia, and it's made from Cannonau – a synonym of the Grenache or Garnacha grape. Sardinia was ruled by the Aragonese for almost 400 years (1324–1713; a form of Catalan is still spoken in the northwestern port city of Alghero). Perhaps the Garnacha arrived with the Aragonese ships. On ancient Sardinia, though, they believe that the genetic traffic went in the other direction, and that Cannonau is indigenous to their island. This slow, scholarly tug-of-war remains unresolved.

What's certain is that the variety is happy here, and flourishes. This inexpensive wine is dark, earthy, rooty-juicy, firmly tannic, exuberantly allusive. It has two elder siblings: the 2010 Giuseppe Sedilesu Riserva Cannonau (produced from older vines in the best years only) and the 2010 Ballu Tundu Riserva Cannonau (produced from a small parcel of 100-year-old vines and aged in large barrels). Both are strong, sweet, primeval, impolite, detaining. The eerie mask looks out from all three, but especially from the Riserva, the most mouth-scouring of the trio. Why? What's 'Mamuthone'?

If you ever go to Sardinia, go in mid-January; try to be in Mamoiada on the 17th. There will be tree-stump fires in the street; look out for processions of masked figures. The first figures you'll see will wear the familiar white masks of Italian carnival, elegant and expressionless. They wear black boots, white trousers and red tunics with bell-studded straps; they toss light ropes at girls and others in the crowds as they leap, dance and shimmy their way forward. These recognizably human gallants are called *issohadores*, and they lead the *mamuthones* who follow: dark, heavy, sinister figures, terrifying to children, clad in ragged black sheepskin, glaring out from their awful black pear-wood masks, each one carved into a different disposition of despair, all held in place by dark brown shawls over black berets. On their backs, each beast-man carries perhaps 30 or 40 cowbells of various sizes, bunched like a giant metal wasp's nest. They stamp and buck rhythmically, in unison, and the bells clang as they do so. The effect is like an army of perfectly drilled cattle, marching on the village. Other villages in Barbagia (the mountain zone of inner Sardinia) have similar rituals but different figures and masks. All express, somehow or other, the bond between men and animals; and a sense of elemental forces, not necessarily benign, at work.

Catholicism has attempted to claim this festival and ritual (it takes place on Saint Anthony the Abbot's day), but its roots seem obviously older and pagan: a propitiatory ritual for a pastoral economy. Sardinia still needs its shepherds: the island has four million sheep – half of Italy's national flock. The granite-sand soils of the Sedilesu hillside vineyards, all of them biodynamically cultivated, are still ploughed by oxen. Ox bells and sheep bells season the hours here.

The despair of the Mamuthone mask on the label may be unjustified. We are, here, in one of the world's 'Blue Zones' (areas of the world where people live measurably longer lives than elsewhere); indeed this concept sprang out of research into male centenarians in Nuoro province, where Mamoiada lies. There are 21 centenarians per 10,000 here, compared to (for example) a US average of just four per 10,000. Genes? Eleven years of research suggest that genetic factors are not the principal driver of Sardinian mountain longevity. Instead, researchers credit a mixture of diet (little meat; lots of vegetables, beans and bread); constant moderate physical exercise (a shepherd's life is ideal, but everyone walks the village, and men hoe their vines by hand); social engagement, especially close family links – and Cannonau, which in contrast to much Grenache elsewhere has high polyphenol levels here. I drove with Francesco Sedilesu through the village. In one narrow street we slowed to a standstill as an elderly woman on a Zimmer frame made her way up the hill, with a young woman walking behind her, holding her elder's black dress to stop it dragging on the ground. It was Francesco's mother Grazia – and his daughter held her train. Three generations met in the village street, in the light of March.

Until 2000, the family simply produced bulk wine from their vines, and sold it in the other mountain villages. Then they began to wonder if the scents and flavours they had known since their childhood could be appreciated more widely. Francesco is the winemaker, but he says he brings little to the wine 'compared to the rich life-force already present in it'. And that's what you taste: blood, fire, the way that plants rise up from stones, the juicy sweetness that explodes from their fruit at summer's end, the bitter mask of tannins, and the comfort that wine can bring to those who live hard lives unflinchingly, and survive.

242   THREE LAST WINES

Restoration:

2018 Saint-Mont, La Madeleine de Saint-Mont, Producteurs Plaimont

Black wine, filling the glass: restorative.

I've never walked the long roads to Santiago de Compostela, and perhaps I never will. Were time to jolt, though; were I to tumble back six centuries through a crack in the floor and find myself hauled up before a buzzard-eyed bishop; were he to order me to follow the tracks from Saint-Guilhem-le-Désert to Santiago as a penance for my sins... well, then I might find myself tramping into Saint-Mont one evening. Several of the routes to Santiago funnel through here before the high passes to Jaca or Roncevalles beckon.

My legs would ache; appetite would be sharp. I'd tug off my sweat-soaked hat, and give the tonsured hosteller a few coins in return for food and shelter in Saint-Mont's high-chambered monastery. There would be bread and beans, some scraps of meat, bitter herbs – and wine. And this is just what I would want the wine to be: black, sturdy, restorative. Wine that fulfils just a little of the function of blood, so that drinking it seems a kind of transfusion. (No heresy intended.)

It smells of plums, prunes, sloes, of clustered half-wild fruits from the edge of the forest; and tastes of those same fruits... but not fruits alone. It also seems to taste of the hot sunlit stones, the thick hedges, the warm woods, the trodden dust – of the way itself. I'd drain every drop, and any other drops I might be allowed, then step slowly up to some dormitory bed whose hardness would not keep sleep at bay for long. The black wine would work in me all night so that, come dawn, the next day's rigours would not daunt but (as the bishop in part intended) salve. I would walk out a better person.

A kind of fantasy, of course: six centuries ago, all dry wines were thin and most pale. (Cahors' 'black wine' was black by dint of the boiling of its must.) In other respects, though, the threads of past and present gathered together by this wine and its fellow bottles are not fantasy at all.

If you ever see a wine from Saint-Mont, it has been made by Plaimont (it produces 98 percent of the appellation's wines). This remarkable co-operative was led for many years with great vision and distinction by André Dubosc; since his retirement, Olivier Bourdet-Pees has grasped the vine-wood baton. This is a co-operative for growers who truly need a co-operative: many of them also grow maize or kiwis, feed ducks, milk cows; grapes are just a part of their farming picture. It's fuelled by IGP Côtes de Gascogne: soft, fresh, pretty and highly commercial white wine grown in former Armagnac vineyards. The colossal success of Côtes de Gascogne permits the rescue of forgotten grape varieties: the Pyrenean foothills are stuffed with genetic treasure. It also permits the restoration of ancient vineyards.

The only French vineyard to be classified as a 'Monument Historique' lies in Saint-Mont (at Sarragachies: mixed vines, some unknown, dating back to 1830 and ungrafted, thanks to sandy soils); La Madeleine, too, is antique. It's a little clay-soiled parcel (4,000 bottles a year or less) planted straight after phylloxera in the 1880s with the hybrid Noah – onto which Tannat (plus a little Cabernet Sauvignon and Pinenc, or Fer Servadou) was later grafted. The grapes are hand-harvested and, after a month on skins (with gentle pump-overs and punch-downs), it undergoes malo and ages for up to 14 months in 400-litre casks, most of them second fill. The label shows a 14th-century walled arch through which the vineyard is accessed.

Plaimont has other wines of remark, too – notably the white Le Faite, with its dangling clackety wooden label, and the oaked white Cirque Nord. These are blends of Gros Manseng with Petit Manseng and Courbu: taut, pristine balances and innate complexity and length. Drinking them is like washing in a stream: an experience familiar to all pilgrims. And Plaimont's variety researches have given us Manseng Noir, salvaged from a single vine: an iron-and-raspberry red that, even harvested in October, only deigns to give 12%. A global warming gift.

Plaimont members, when on public duties, always wear black berets; Olivier Bourdet-Pees even wears his beret to Zoom. And in unpandemical times, members are bidden by rote to leave home and travel long roads of their own to meet the as-yet unenlightened, as Mormons and Witnesses do; failure to do this does not involve the penance of pilgrimage, but it does see the imposition of a token fine as a smack on the wrist. The co-operative, needless to say, owns Saint-Mont's Monastery; another of the red wines is called Monastère, from monastery vineyards, shown on the label beneath a medievally star-clustered sky. You can stay, now; the beds are a little softer.

I once mentioned to a friend that I would like to walk the long roads to Santiago de Compostela. 'I take it,' she wrote back, 'that all of life is the road to Santiago.' A road, she intimated, often dreary, through dull landscapes under mournful stratus; a road truffled with wrong turnings, and errors to be re-traced; a road to blister skin and scourge joints; a road along which hope and belief are abraded daily. Just so – but there is a salve. Restorative black wine.

Ein voller Becher Weins zur rechten Zeit
Ist mehr wert als alle Reiche dieser Erde!
Dunkel ist das Leben, ist der Tod!

(A full cup of wine at the right moment
Is worth more than all the riches of earth!
Dark is life, is death!)

'*Das Trinklied vom Jammer der Erde*'

(Drinking Song of Earth's Misery)

Gustav Mahler: *Das Lied von der Erde*

Text by Hans Bethge, loosely adapted from the original of Li Bai
(called Li-Tai-Po)

Glossary

anion *See* ion.

AOC Abbreviation for 'Appellation d'Origine Contrôlée', or 'name of controlled origin' – the base designation for French quality wines, and a model for systems of controlled geographical origin in other wine cultures. The French term for the pan-European equivalent is AOP ('Appellation d'Origine Protégée'): the two are synonymous. Note that it is origin that is being controlled or protected, not quality.

brett A short form of the word *Brettanomyces*, a yeast genus desired by brewers for certain beer styles but often regarded as a wine fault. Wines bottled with detectable aromatic levels of brett may remind the drinker of farmyards, stables, adhesive bandages or hospital corridors, and during bottle maturation this character may come to dominate the wine to monotonous effect. Below sensory thresholds, by contrast, brett may add to the aromatic complexity of wines and bring them a wider range of allusions. *Also known as* Dekkera.

Brix A scale used for measuring the dissolved compounds (chiefly sugar) in grape juice, and therefore of the potential alcohol level of a wine. It is not the only such scale: others are Baumé, Oechsle and Balling.

bush vine Small, free-standing vines with no trellising: a pruning system suitable for certain cultivars (notably Grenache) in warm climates. Many vineyards were planted this way in the past, so old-vine vineyards are often composed of bush vines.

canteiro The traditional, high-quality though slow method for ageing Madeira – in pipes (wooden casks) in above-ground warehouses with several floors, exposed to the balmy, year-round heat of this Atlantic island. The finest categories of Madeira (notably vintage Madeira) are aged in this way. *Compare estufagem.*

cation *See* Ion.

climat The traditional Burgundian name for a long-established vineyard site – and part of Burgundy's registration on UNESCO's World Heritage listing (number 1425, added in 2015: 'The Climats, terroirs of Burgundy'), where it is defined as 'a vine plot, with its own microclimate and specific geological conditions, which has been carefully marked out and named over the centuries'. *Compare lieu-dit.*

côte A French word that means 'slope', and is often used in AOC (*qv*) formulae – since propitiously orientated hill-slope sites are ideal for quality viticulture in temperate latitudes.

cru A French word that means 'growth'. It is used of distinguished vineyard sites or well-known properties in fine-wine regions, as well as of high-quality areas within larger appellations or within aspiring, up-and-coming regions. Classification systems often distinguish between different tiers in formulae such as Grand Cru ('great growth'), Premier Cru ('first growth') or Cru Classé ('classified growth'). There is, however, no ready equivalence between these terms. A Grand Cru in Saint-Emilion is a near-meaningless term, whereas Grand Cru in Burgundy is used of what were, at the time of classification, considered to be the 33 finest single sites or *climats* (*qv*): a mere two percent of the planted vineyard zone.

chaptalization The addition of sugar or rectified grape juice to must (*qv*) or fermenting wine in order to increase final alcohol levels. Global warming has made this intervention a rare one. Named after the inventor of the technique, the gifted Jean-Antoine Chaptal, an applied chemist and Minister of the Interior under Napoleon.

Colheita The name for a port of a single vintage that has been aged in cask rather than in bottle (as Vintage port is). Colheita port is only bottled when considered ready for sale and consumption.

coulure   A French word signifying poor fruit set, hence a reduced crop. It varies with vintage (and is often closely related to weather conditions during flowering) and variety. *See also millerandage.*

cuvée   A French word meaning 'lot' or 'blend', derived from the word for 'tank' (*cuve*).

diacetyl   A product of the malolactic conversion process (*see* malo) with distinctively 'buttery' or 'nutty' aromas.

dimethyl sulphide (DMS)   An important chemical compound produced in the world's oceans by phytoplankton (and thus sometimes described as 'the smell of the sea', though it is only one part of this complex of odours). DMS is the major source of cloud condensation nuclei (CCN) over remote, unpolluted areas of ocean. More CCN means 'whiter' clouds with a higher albedo effect, helping cool our planet (two-thirds of which is ocean), so this climate feedback is regarded as an important one in earth system science. In wine, by contrast, elevated levels of DMS are regarded as problematic. Its characteristic aroma (resembling tinned sweetcorn, asparagus or cooked vegetables more generally) will see affected wines, often made from Chardonnay or Sauvignon Blanc grapes, rejected from Australian wine shows, whose judges are trained to spot and react to such flaws. DMS is also common in lager-style beers: the malts for these are kilned more gently than are the malts for ales, and DMS is formed from its precursor S-methylmethionine, or SMM, during the kilning process. In contrast to wine judges, drinkers of the British lager brand Carling Black Label regard DMS as a desirable element of its aroma and flavour, so malts for this beer are deliberately kilned to create higher-than-usual DMS presences.

en primeur   A French phrase that, in the wine context, signifies pre-arrival purchase, urged by producers and their intermediaries on customers as a means of securing sought-after wines at the earliest opportunity and (in theory though not always in practice) at the lowest price.

estufagem Method used to age inexpensive Madeira. After fermentation, the wines are heated in tanks at up to 50°C for at least 90 days. *Compare canteiro.*

extraction The textural component of red wines is derived from grape skins (and stems, where used), and the process by which these substances are transferred to the wine during fermentation and maceration is known as 'extraction'.

hectolitres per hectare (hl/ha) A coarse measurement of yield in European wine-producing nations. When yields are expressed in weight of grapes (as is common in English-speaking zones: tons per acre, for example), the measurement is coarser still, since it's necessary to know how much liquid is subsequently pressed from that weight of grapes to arrive at a comparable figure. Even where hl/ha is cited, the planting density needs to be taken into account in order to arrive at a liquid yield per vine: the most significant figure. Remember, too, that great vintages are often higher yielding than poor vintages, and that too much concentration from ultra-low yields may vitiate drinkability. All wine questions are complex and yield is no exception.

hybrid A variety resulting from a crossing of *Vitis vinifera* with a non-vinifera variety.

IGP Abbreviation for 'Indication Geographique Protégée', a designation used in France and elsewhere in Europe to designate any agricultural product, wine included, whose quality or reputation is related to its geographical origin. In wine, this term is the successor to Vin de Pays, designating wines of simpler aspiration than AOC (*qv*), and often sold under a variety name (*see* varietal wines).

ion An atom, or a molecule consisting of several atoms, with a net electrical charge. Cations are positively charged; anions negatively charged. Cation exchange capacity (CEC) affects the manner in which soil nutrients are available to the vine, and varies according to the soil's origin, texture and percentage of organic matter. CEC therefore plays a significant role in soil performance and terroir profile, though it is little discussed in wine literature. Vine roots do not absorb 'minerals'; they absorb ions in solution.

lees (contact) The word 'lees' means the sediment left after a fermentation process has terminated. Lees are chiefly composed of dead yeast supplemented by other deposits resulting from winemaking. Wines that remain on lees for an extended period ('lees contact') tend to be richer, softer and more texturally ample than those that are removed swiftly from yeast lees. Bottling directly off the lees (in Muscadet, labelled *sur lie*) is thought to maximize freshness.

lieu-dit Literally 'spoken ('named' or 'recognized') place': a French term for a small geographical zone which may or may not be inhabited (a *hameau,* or 'hamlet', by contrast, must be inhabited). This term is often used in Burgundy to indicate a vineyard site that does not enjoy Premier Cru or Grand Cru classification but which is nonetheless well-known enough to be named on a label. We are in France, though, so there is a further complication. You might imagine in Burgundy that a *lieu-dit* is synonymous with the local term *climat* (*qv*). Not so. Some *climats* include a number of different *lieux-dits* (Echezeaux includes 10, in whole or in part). *Climat* is the older, traditional term for a Burgundian vineyard site, and was first used in 1584; a *lieu-dit* was a post-Revolutionary classification made for tax purposes, and refers to entries in the French *cadastre*, or land register.

malo Short for 'malolactic', referring to the bacteriological conversion of malic ('appley') acid to lactic ('milky') acid, undergone by all red wines and some white, rosé and sparkling wines. The effect of malo is to soften the overall acid profile of the wine and in some cases bring the wine added structure, sinew and vinosity (*see* pages 89–91).

mercaptans Unpleasant aromatic compounds formed of carbon, hydrogen and sulphur, often found in newly fermented wines. These compounds can be removed by aeration – though some members of the mercaptan family constitute desired 'varietal traits' in white wines made from Sauvignon Blanc and other varieties. Mercaptans are also known as thiols. *See also* reduction.

millerandage   A condition in which a large percentage of the grapes in a bunch remain as live green ovaries (LGOs) or small seedless berries; neither develop. The condition is also known as 'hen and chickens', the hens being the berries that develop normally and the chickens being those that don't. *See also coulure.*

must   Unfermented grape juice.

oxidation   Chemically, oxidation means the loss of electrons and is the complement to reduction (*qv*), the gain of electrons. More generally, oxidation means the combining of a substance (such as wine) with oxygen. Some exposure to air is necessary and beneficial and undergone by all wines; different wine styles require different degrees of exposure, and 'controlled oxidation' is a technique used to bring complexity to certain sorts of wine. A wine that is said to be oxidized, by contrast, has been flattened, dulled and tarnished by excessive exposure to air.

passito   An Italian term for a sweet wine made from dried grapes.

phylloxera   Near-microscopic insect with a complicated life cycle that feeds on the roots of *Vitis vinifera*, causing deformations and fungal infections that eventually kill the vine. This insect was originally called *Phylloxera vastatrix* but is now known as *Dactylasphaera vitifoliae*. Phylloxera brought about the collapse of much European wine cultivation in the late 19th century; the solution was to graft *Vitis vinifera* onto the roots of American vine varieties, which have natural defences against this pest.

primary fruit   Fruit flavours in wine are at their most prolific in youth – regarded as being the 'primary' stage of a wine's life. The 'secondary' stage sees the fruit settle down and mesh with the wine's other components in early maturity; the 'tertiary' stage is that of full maturity, with attendant harmony of the wine's flavour components. By the tertiary stage, fruit flavours are much less obvious than in early youth.

pump-over   Winemaking technique in which fermenting wine is pumped over the cap of grape skins and other solids (*remontage* in French).

punch-down   Winemaking technique in which the cap of grape skins and other solids is broken up and pushed down into the fermenting wine (*pigeage* in French).

racking   The movement of a wine from one recipient vessel to another to freshen it with air and remove it from sediment or lees (*qv*).

reduction   With respect to oxygen transfer, reduction means the loss of oxygen and is the complement to oxidation (*qv*): the two processes cannot occur in isolation (oxidation signifies the loss of electrons and reduction the gain of electrons). In the wine context, however, reduction loosely refers to the volatile sulphur compounds often found in wines that have been protected from oxidation (*see* mercaptans). Wines that have been bottled in a 'reduced' state and exhibit these unpleasant smells (reminiscent of rotten eggs, drains or intestinal gas) sometimes clear with exposure to air.

saignée   A French term that literally means 'bleeding'. In red winemaking, this refers to the practice of running off an amount of juice from a vat of fermenting red wine in order to increase the ratio of skins to the juice that remains, thereby making a darker or more concentrated wine. In rosé winemaking, this refers to running off the wine relatively early in fermentation, once a sufficient (usually pale or very pale) tint has been obtained from a red-grape ferment.

stems   The stems and pedicels holding grapes on a bunch are sometimes included (in whole or in part) in what are called 'whole bunch' or 'whole cluster' ferments for both red and white/amber wines.

TCA   The short form of 2,4,6-trichloroanisole, the substance responsible for cork taint or 'corkiness' in wine. TCA smells 'chemical' and musty, like damp or rotting cardboard.

terroir   A French term now widely adopted in English-language wine discourse. It references the notion that the sensual personality of a wine or other processed agricultural product might derive in some way from inherent singularities in the physical milieu in which that product came into being (especially climate, the seasonal weather pattern of a particular vintage, topography and soil). French wine-world definitions stress that local viticultural and winemaking practices, too, contribute to terroir; this is often overlooked in English usage. (The term is also casually but wrongly used in both French and English to refer to soil alone.)

ungrafted   After phylloxera (*qv*), almost all *Vitis vinifera* vines require grafting onto phylloxera-resistant American-vine rootstocks. Ungrafted *Vitis vinifera* vines, by contrast, may be planted in soil media where phylloxera cannot survive (such as deep sands), or in zones where phylloxera has never become established (such as parts of Chile and Australia).

varietal wines   Wines preponderantly or exclusively made from a single cultivar or grape variety.

VDQS   Acronym for 'Vin Délimité de Qualité Supérieure', formerly an intermediate quality designation between Vin de Pays (or 'country wine') and AOC (*qv*). This category of wine was abandoned in 2010.

Chronology

All the original texts have been revised by the author for publication in this book.

2022
Scored Rigid (page 183) – *Decanter* magazine (March)

Meanings that Nourish: 2003 Château Meyney, Saint-Estèphe, half bottle (page 219) – *The World of Fine Wine* (issue 73)

Jewelled Absence: 2016 Petit Chablis, Les Crioux, William Fèvre (page 98) – *The World of Fine Wine* (issue 74)

A Honeycomb of Light: 2010 Masd del Serral, Pepe Raventós (page 59) – *The World of Fine Wine* (issue 75)

2021
Call in the Plumbers (page 160) – *Decanter* magazine (September)

Bathing Without Washing: 2005 Châteauneuf du Pape Blanc, Réservé, Château Rayas (page 102) – *The World of Fine Wine* (issue 70)

Wine's Transactional Flaw (page 176) – *The World of Fine Wine* (issue 72)

Restoration: 2018 Saint-Mont, La Madeleine de Saint-Mont, Producteurs Plaimont (page 243) – *The World of Fine Wine* (issue 72)

2020
Burning Vines (page 174) – *Decanter* magazine (April)

The School of Hard Wines (page 87) – *Decanter* magazine (November)

Mille Fois Morte, Mille Fois Revécue: 2008 Chateau Musar Blanc (p 211) – *The World of Fine Wine* (issue 67)

All Quiet: 2016 Bouzeron (page 213) – *The World of Fine Wine* (issue 68)

2019
Wine's Drab Roses (page 147) – *Decanter* magazine (May)

Nuance from Disdain (page 36) – *Decanter* magazine (July)

In Praise of Young Wine (page 162) – *Noble Rot* (issue 19)

Washed Up on the Shores of Illyria: 2015 Teran, Santa Elisabetta, Benvenuti (page 52) – *The World of Fine Wine* (issue 65)

2018

Downhill All the Way (page 38) – www.decanter.com (February)

Nature in All Her Glory (page 153) – *Decanter* magazine (May)

Tonic Bitterness (page 73) – *Decanter* magazine (August)

The Curse of the Vertical (page 180) – www.decanter.com (August)

Wine Versus Food (page 91) – *Decanter* magazine (November)

Drinking with the Valkyries (page 143) – www.decanter.com (December)

The Illuminati of the Bottle (page 136) – *Noble Rot* (issue 17)

The Startled Hind: 2012 Pouilly-Fumé, Haute Densité, Château de Tracy (page 238) – *The World of Fine Wine* (issue 59)

Homo Imbibens: The Work of Patrick McGovern (page 18) – *The World of Fine Wine* (issue 60)

Forest Whispers: 2011 Château-Chalon, Vin Jaune, André and Mireille Tissot (page 107) – *The World of Fine Wine* (issue 60)

2017

Freshness Young and Old (page 83) – *Decanter* magazine (March)

The Ethnologist in the Cellar (page 206) – www.decanter.com (September)

Terroir, Tasting and Tonewood (page 42) – *Decanter* magazine (October)

Taste First, Then Look (page 71) – www.decanter.com (December)

Lessons from the Laureate (page 216) – www.decanter.com (December)

A Sea Interlude: 2015 Picpoul de Pinet, Cuvée Anniversaire, Beauvignac (page 47) – *The World of Fine Wine* (issue 57)

Liquid Rags in Your Mouth: 2013 Barbaresco, Produttori del Barbaresco (page 57) – *The World of Fine Wine* (issue 58)

2016

Beyond Best (page 149) – www.decanter.com (August)

Only Endure (page 172) – *Decanter* magazine (October)

The Antidote: 2010 Madiran, Cuvée du Couvent, Domaine Capmartin (page 110) – *The World of Fine Wine* (issue 52)

Unsettled: 2014 Cannonau di Sardegna, Mamuthone, Giuseppe Sedilesu (page 240) – *The World of Fine Wine* (issue 53)

2015

Some Useless Notes (page 112) – www.decanter.com (February)

Angela's Lemon (page 49) – www.decanter.com (March)

Disarming the Mafia (page 139) – *Decanter* magazine (May)

Dr Mistral (page 54) – www.decanter.com (May)

Palate Fitness (page 93) – www.decanter.com (May)

Why Wine? (page 15) – *Decanter* magazine (October)

Journey into Forbidden Territory (page 79) – www.decanter.com (October)

Wine Is Also a Dream (page 164) – www.decanter.com (December)

Tears and Threats: 2003 Tokaji Aszú, 6 Puttonyos, Disznókő (page 201) – *The World of Fine Wine* (issue 47)

2014

Auction Fever (page 155) – www.decanter.com (March)

The Two-Pin Dinner (page 115) – *Decanter* magazine (April)

Yeast: Call Me Dad (page 77) – www.decanter.com (June)

Happy Birthday, Breaky Bottom (page 45) www.decanter.com (September)

Behind Vinous Eyes (page 89) www.decanter.com (September)

Lucky Us (page 190) – www.decanter.com (December)

2013

Touchdown in Wine Central (page 62) – www.decanter.com (April)

Hill Sages (page 196) – www.decanter.com (May)

The Party's Over (page 157) – www.decanter.com (June)

The Crazed Giant (page 170) – www.decanter.com (July)

Up the Steep Hill (page 209) – www.decanter.com (August)

Of Jellyfish and Guardsmen (page 145) – www.decanter.com (November)

Hot and Bothered (page 141) – www.decanter.com (November)

2012

Tannin and the University of the Vat (page 75) – *Decanter* magazine (March)

The Blue Corruptor (page 32) – www.decanter.com (April)

Earth's Cream, Skimmed (page 34) – *Decanter* magazine (August)

Old, Big and Quiet (page 85) – www.decanter.com (August)

Time's Engine Room: 2010 Langhorne Creek, Reserve Shiraz, Noon (page 40) – *The World of Fine Wine* (issue 36)

Wine and Astonishment (page 224) – *The World of Fine Wine* (issue 36)

A Rosary of Reasons: 1882 Colheita Port, Ne Oublie, Graham's (page 117) – *The World of Fine Wine* (issue 37)

2011

Through the Mangrove Swamp (page 69) – www.decanter.com (November)

An Evening With the Lilac-Berried Mutant: 2008 Gewurztraminer, Herrenweg de Turckheim Vieilles Vignes, Zind-Humbrecht (page 198) – *The World of Fine Wine* (issue 32)

Very Like the Cuckoo's Call: 2005 Rioja, Gran Riserva, La Granja Remelluri (page 105) – *The World of Fine Wine* (issue 33)

2010

Not Quite the White Queen: 1999 Corton-Charlemagne, Bonneau du Martray (page 100) – *The World of Fine Wine* (issue 30)

2008

Knowing and Loving (page 203) – *Waitrose Food Illustrated* (March)

The Cup that Consoles (page 122) – *The World of Fine Wine* (issue 19)

2007

Bags, Butter and Biscuits (page 66) – *Waitrose Food Illustrated* (September)

It's a Tough Job (page 192) – *Waitrose Food Illustrated* (December)

Acknowledgements

The texts in this book were written between 2007 and 2022, and revised in 2021–22. Many hundreds of people have helped me during that time. I cannot name them all but I thank them all. The wine world is welcoming and generous, made so by its participants.

There are, though, some friends, colleagues and collaborators I would particularly like to mention. Most of these texts were commissioned by Sarah Kemp and her colleagues at *Decanter* magazine, notably John Stimpfig, Amy Wislocki, Chris Mercer and Sylvia Wu; and by my friend Dr Neil Beckett at *The World of Fine Wine*, with whom I have worked since issue 1 of that quarterly. Fellow writers Jancis Robinson MW, Hugh Johnson and Oz Clarke have been both encouraging and inspiring down the years. I have often travelled professionally with Anthony Rose, and enjoyed every minute of his company. Some of these texts allude to the matchless hospitality of Michael and Monika Schuster, and I have greatly relished travelling and working with Michael in Riga, Latvia; the generosity and hospitality of Frank and Lisbet Ward is also alluded to in these pages, and has meant much to me. I am deeply grateful for the hospitality, friendship, good cooking and frank conversation about wine and many other matters of my friends Stuart Tunstall and Zo Pacuła. The period my family and I spent in Adelaide, Australia was inspiring and educational, and was possible thanks to the kindness and generosity of Brian and Ann Croser and Javier Molle, and the indulgent welcome I received from the staff of the Economics Department of Adelaide University. I have learned much from Kym Anderson, George Gollin Professor Emeritus, School of Economics, University of Adelaide; Alex Maltman, Professor Emeritus of Earth Sciences, Department of Geography and Earth Sciences, University of Aberystwyth; and Mike Summerfield, Professor Emeritus of Geomorphology, School of GeoSciences, University of Edinburgh. Professor Barry C Smith of the Institute of Philosophy, School of Advanced Study, University of London was kind enough to read and to make comments on an earlier draft of the essay that constitutes Chapter Nine.

I would also like to thank Lisa Airey, Paul Balke, David Berry Green, Julien Boulard MW and Jade and Margot Boulard, Stephen and Sophie Browett, Fred and Elise Brugues, Julien and Céline Camus, Robert and Marianne Clark-Majerus, Li Demei, Natalie Earl, Anastasia Edwards and family, Ed Eisler and his colleagues at Jing Tea, Harry Eyres, Rosemary George and Christopher Galleymore, Christelle Guibert, Peter and Christina Hall and the Hall family, Sarah Hargreaves, Julia Harding MW, Rosamund Hitchcock and Rupert Ponsonby, Justin Howard-Sneyd MW and Amanda Howard-Sneyd, Chris Howell, Louise Hurren, Cédric Jenin, Robert Joseph, Magdalena Kaiser, Dan Keeling, Tina Kezeli and her colleagues in Tbilisi, Mary Kirk and the students of the Wine Scholar Guild, Natalie Leggett, Lin Liu MW and Philippe Lejeune, David Longfield, Wink Lorch, Chris Maillard, Carole Meredith and Steve Lagier, Nico Manessis, Caro Maurer MW, Christian and Cherise Moueix, Dorli Muhr and colleagues, Jean Natoli, Dirk Niepoort, Aigars and Marite Nords and their generous friends and colleagues in Riga, Françoise Peretti, Michèle Piron and her colleagues, Pepe and Susana Raventós, Stephan Reinhardt, David Schildknecht, Christian Seely, William Sitwell, Robert Slotover, Saša Špiranec and his colleague Ana Hozjan, Matthew Stubbs MW, Kazumi Suzuki, Paul Symington, Fiona Morrison MW and Jacques Thienpont, Ch'ng Poh Tiong, J C Viens, Monty Waldin, Simon Woolf, Jon Wyand and Catherine Yen. Gerard Basset, Denis Durantou and Steven Spurrier are much missed. Heartfelt thanks to Susan Keevil, Hermione Ireland, Simon McMurtrie and Tim Foster of Académie du Vin Library for their enthusiasm, and for making our collaboration so enjoyable.

Finally, I would like to thank my brothers Michael and Stephen Jefford and their families; and above all Paula, John and Joe, without whose love, affection, teasing, interrogation and support none of this work would have been possible.

Index

'20 Rows' vineyard 42

A

Abydos 27
Abymes 39–40
acidity 83–4, 87, 98, 163
acids, organic 20, 25
Adelaide Hills 41, 174, 175, 181
Africa 29
Ajara 25
Alaverdi Monastery, Kakheti 62
Alba 58
Albariño grape 37
Albarola grape 51
alcohol 122, 227–8
  abstention 30
  clouds in Universe 20
  effects on brain 165–6
  first production of 28–30
  and flavour 91–3
  hard wines 87
  Homo imbibens 18, 27, 30
  as medicine 28, 30
  as necessity for human mental health 27–8
  pottery vessel residues 19–27
  tasting wines 71–2
  and vinosity 89–91
  'wild' alcohol 21
  wine labels 71
Aligoté grape 161, 214

Alsace 145, 152, 153, 184, 200
Alta Mesa AVA 146
Altesse grape 39, 40
Amgoorie tea estate 125–6
Amontillado sherry 66
Ampuis 164
Amsterdam 124
Anatolia 21, 23, 24, 25, 26
Anjou 160–1
Anti-Lebanon mountains 211
Anyang 23
AOC (Appellation d'Origine Contrôlée) 160–1, 240, 247
appellations 160–1
Apremont 39–40
Arbois 108–9, 145
archaeology, pottery vessel residues 19–27
Argentina 77, 171, 175, 193
Armagnac 244
Armenier, Catherine 55–6
art 177–8
Asia Minor 26–7
Assam 125–6, 130
Assay, Henry d' 239
Assay, Juliette d' 238–9
astonishment, wine and 224–6
Atlas Peak 196
auctions 155–7
Austin, David 147–8
Australia 79, 174–5
  see also individual regions and wines
Australian Wine Research Institute 76
Austria 153, 171
Aÿ 141

B

balance 72–3
Baltimore-Washington Wine Advocate 183–4
Bandol 32–3, 74, 141–2
Banyuls 49
Barbagia 241
Barbaresco 57–9, 74, 181
Barbera grape 57
Barolo 57–8, 59, 74, 76, 151, 181, 202
barrels, oak 85–6, 87, 88
Bartoshuk, Linda 73
Bâtard-Montrachet 150
Bault de la Morinière, Jean-Charles le 101–2
BBC Radio Three 44
Beare, Charles 44
Beaujolais 83, 227
Beaujolais-Villages 140
Beaune 156, 194, 214
Beaune, Château de 117
Beauvignac 49
beer 20, 22, 26, 27, 28, 80–1, 229
Beka'a Valley 74
Belgian beer 80
Benoist, Pierre de 214–15
Benvenuti, Nikola 52, 53–4
Berry Bros & Rudd 190
best wines 149–53
Bethge, Hans 246
Bettane, Michel 183
Bevan, Russell 157
Bevan Cellars 157
Biomolecular Archaeology Laboratory for Cuisine, Fermented Beverages and Health 18

261

Bird in Hand 174
bitterness 73–4
black tea 128, 130
'black wine' 243–5
Blanquette de Limoux
  Méthode Ancestrale 140
Blass, Wolf 41
blind tastings 44, 69–70,
  82, 165
'Blue Zones' 242
Boal, Madeiran 190–1
Boisgibault 238
Bonanini, Matteo 50, 51
Bonneau du Martray 100–2
Bordeaux 116, 163, 167, 181
  climate 37
  geology 158
  mature wines 88
  oak 86
  scoring systems 183–4, 185
  tannins 74, 76
  tasting wine 153
  see also individual Châteaux
Bordoni, Sauro 51
Borrett, George 42
Bosco grape 51
bottles 167
Bourdet-Pees, Olivier 244, 245
Boursiquot, Jean-Michel 197
Bouzeron 214–15
Bowers, John 197
brain, effects of alcohol
  165–6
Brand 200
Brandstatt 209–10
Breaky Bottom 45–7
Bremer river 41
Brettanomyces yeasts 78–9,
  80, 247

Briones 105
Brix scale 247
Broadbent, Michael 183
  Vintage Wine 183
Brunello di Montalcino 76
Buddhism 122, 123, 132,
  225
Burgenland 171
burgundy
  2012 vintage 113
  appellations 161
  geology 158
  hail storms 170, 171
  red burgundy 100
  tannins 76
  vinosity 90–1
  white burgundy 100–2
Burton-upon-Trent 80–1
bush vines 247
bushfires 174–5
buying wine 155–7

C
Cabalié 192
Cabernet Franc grape 161
Cabernet Gernischt grape
  146
Cabernet Sauvignon grape
  67, 74, 79, 146, 167,
  173–4, 181, 185, 244
caffeine 122, 131
Cahors 146, 186, 244
Cain Five 79–82
California 104, 153, 173,
  175, 193
  see also individual regions
  and wines
Camargue 41
Cambie, Philippe 55, 56

Camellia sinensis 123, 125,
  126
Canaanites 18
Cannonau di Sardegna
  Mamuthone 240–2
Cannonau grape 241, 242
canteiro 247
Canterbury, New Zealand
  173
Cantina Sociale de
  Barbaresco 58
Capellini, Angelo 51
Capmartin, Domaine 110
Caravaggio 177–8
Carceller, Yvon 208
Carignan grape 33, 87
Carmenère grape 146
Carneros 196
Carter, Howard 26
Casanova di Neri Brunello di
  Montalcino 185
CastelBarry 206–8
Catalonia 175
Catholic Church 242
Caucasus 23, 24, 25, 123
centenarians 242
cereals, beer 28
Chablis 83, 86, 88, 98–100,
  101, 140, 146, 158, 194
Chalonnais 214
Chambertin 166
Chambolle 202
Champagne 66, 141, 148,
  158
Changzikou 23
chaptalization 37, 248
Chardonnay grape 126, 146,
  148, 211–12, 214
  burgundy 100, 101, 161

262   INDEX

indigenous fermentation 79
in southern hemisphere 181
vinosity 91
white burgundy 100–1
wine tasting language 66, 67, 98
Chartreuse 106
Charybdis 18
Chasselas grape 239
Château *see individual Châteaux*
Château-Chalon 107–9
Chateau Musar Blanc 211–13
Châteauneuf-du-Pape 49, 54–7, 80, 86, 89, 102–4, 161, 166
Chaucer, Geoffrey 166
Chenin Blanc grape 161
Cheval Blanc, Château 151, 163
Chianti 143
chickens 176
Chidaine, François 170
children 201–2
Chile 146, 173, 175, 185, 193
chimpanzees 29
China 21–3, 24, 30, 123–5, 126–30, 132, 138, 146, 182, 191
Chinon 170
Christchurch 173
Christianity 62, 122, 131, 132, 166
Christmas truce (1914) 191
Cinque Terre 49–51
Cinsault grape 33
Circe 18

citric acid 20, 25
Clairette grape 48, 103
Climat, definition 248
climate
    climate change 15, 141, 160–1, 175, 209
    Japan 37
    Maunder Minimum 43
    Mistral 55
Clos des Lambrays 80
Clos Saint Jacques 146
Clos Saint Urban Rangen de Thann 146
Clos Vougeot 117–18
cloud seeding 170–1
co-operatives 206–8
Coates, Clive 183
coffee 122
Colheita port 119, 248
colour of wine 98
Condrieu 84, 98, 152, 163
Conti, Prince de 166
cooking 92
copper 148
Cordillera Cantábrica 105
Corison 157
corked wines 85
corks 167
Corney & Barrow 47, 112–13
Coronica 54
Corton-Charlemagne 100–2, 113
cost of wine 149–51, 165, 178–9
Côte, definition 248
Côte de Beaune 170
Côte d'Or 100–1
Côte Rôtie 164

Côtes Catalanes 192
Côtes de Gascogne 244
Côtes du Jura 145
coulure 56, 113, 148, 249
Counoise grape 161
Courbu grape 244
Crimea 138
Crioux 99
Croatia 52–4, 197
Croser, Brian 79, 154, 175, 224
Cru, definition 248
culture, wine and 166–7
cuvée, definition 249
Cyclops 166

D
Danube, River 209
Darjeeling 126, 130
Davit, Metropolitan of Alaverdi 62, 63–4
de Vogüé 115
Decanter magazine 89, 183, 184
Decanter World Wine Awards 69, 173, 186
Delille, Reynald 33
dental health, palate fitness 94
Devaux, Eric 214–15
diacetyl 80, 249
Diel, Armin 116
dimethyl sulphide (DMS) 81, 249
dinner parties 115–17, 201–2, 203–6
Dionysus 137
DNA 145, 146
Dolcetto grape 57

263

Domaine *see individual Domaines*
Domizio Cavazza 58
Douglas, Lord Alfred 198
Douro 49, 144, 158
DRC *see* Romanée-Conti, Domaine de la
Dream, wine as a 164–8
droughts 175
dry wines 139
Dubosc, André 244
Dureza grape 197

E
earthquakes 172–4
East India Company 125
Echezeaux 113–14
Egypt 27, 30
Eisenberg 171
emotions, wine and 166
en primeur 249
enzymes 30
Esk Valley 209
Estienne, Freddy 32
estufagem 250
Etang de Thau 48–9
ethanol 20, 21, 165–6
Ethiopia 29
ethnologists 206–8
Euripides, *The Bacchae* 137
The European 115
European Union 148
existence 224–6
extraction 76, 87, 144, 250

F
Faber & Faber 216
Fadat, Sylvain 208
Fantini, Lorenzo, *Monografia* 58

Farr Vintners 155, 185
Fer Servadou grape 244
fermentable sugars 28–9
fermentation
    malolactic fermentation 86, 233, 251
    yeasts 78–9
Ferrero, Patricia 33
Fertile Crescent 23
Fèvre, William 99
Fiano 83
fine wines 48, 137, 185, 190
fires 174–5
flavours, food versus wine 91–3
flint 239
flower teas 129–30
flutes, Jiahu 22
Folgosa do Douro 118
food
    flavours 91–3
    and wine 139–41
fortified wines 118–19
France 138, 153
    appellations 160–1
    port market 143
    see also individual regions and wines
freshness 83–4, 98
Friedrich, Caspar David 196
fruit, 'wild' alcohol 21
Fujian Province 127, 129

G
Gadachrili Gora 25, 123
Gaja 58
Galicia 83
Garnacha grape *see* Grenache grape

Garway, Thomas 124
Gaza 27
geekdom, wine 136–8
genetics 21, 145, 146, 147–8
geology 157–9
Georgia 24–5, 62–4, 123, 148, 153
Germany 83
    see also individual regions and wines
Gewurztraminer grape 98, 145, 152, 198–200
Giacosa 58
Gigondas 178
Givry Rouge 100
glass bottles 167
Goddard, Matthew 78
Godin Tepe 25–6
Goldert 200
Goldthorp, Anthony 116
Goñi, Amaya 105
Gordion 25, 26–7
Graciano grape 106
Graf Hardegg 209
Graham's 119
Grands Echezeaux 113–14
Grange 167
Granier 39
La Granja Remelluri 105–7
grapes
    archaeology 20
    fermentable sugars 28
    flavours 92–3
    hard wines 87
    tannins 74, 75–7, 87, 131, 163
    varieties 28, 145–7
    see also individual grapes

264   INDEX

Graves 158
Great Rift Valley 29
Greece 30, 124, 140
green tea 127, 130
Gregorio, Miguel Angel de 105
Grenache grape 33, 56, 86, 103, 106, 161, 192, 241, 242
Gros Manseng grape 244
Grüner Veltliner grape 210
Guangdong 129
Guigal, Philippe 164, 168
Guria 25
Guyomar, Alfred 208

H
hail 170–2
Hajji Firuz Tepe 23–4, 25
Hall, Peter 45–7
hard wines 87–8
Hatton, Fritz 156–7
Haut-Brion, Château 117, 125, 166, 185
health
  medicinal uses of wine 28, 30
  tea and 130–1
hectolitres per hectare (hl/ha) 250
Heidegger, Martin 133
  Being and Time 224–6, 236
  'Letter on Humanism' 230, 232
  'The Question Concerning Technology' 230–1, 235
Hemingway, Ernest 60–1
Henan Province 21–3
Henriot, Joseph 117

Henschke 174
Hermacinski, Ursula 156
Hermitage 158
Hinduism 225
Hirsch, Paul 204, 206
history, wine and 166–7
Hitler, Adolf 191
Hochar, Serge 211–13
holiday wines 140
Homer 18, 124
  Iliad 26
  Odyssey 124, 166
hominids 20–1
Homo erectus 20–1
Homo imbibens 18, 27, 30
Homo neanderthalensis 21
Homo sapiens sapiens 21, 27
honey 29
horizontal tastings 151, 180–2
Hospices de Beaune 156
Howell, Chris 79–81
Howell Mountain 196
Hughes, Ted 176–7
Huizong, Emperor, *Treatise on Tea* 124
Humbrecht, Olivier 200
Hume, David 186
Hungary 138, 195
hybrids 250

I
ice 170–2
IGP (Indication Geographique Protégée) 208, 244, 250
Illustrated London News 191
Illyria 52–4
INAO 240

India 30, 125–6, 130
indigenous yeasts 78–9
insurance, hail storms 171–2
International Violin Competition (2010) 44
ion, definition 250–1
Ioseb, Father 62
Iran 23–4, 25–6
Irancy 100
Iron Age 26
Ishiguro, Kazuo 216–19
Islam 63, 122
Issan, Château d' 170
Istria 52–4
Italy 148, 153, 173
  see also individual regions and wines

J
Jacquère grape 39–40
James, Henry 216
Janin, Eric 140
Japan 29, 36–8, 124, 132–3
Jaurès, Jean 207
Jefford, Andrew, *The New France* 153–4
Jehovah's Witnesses 122
Jiahu 21–3, 27, 28–9
Johnson, F G 125–6
Johnson, Hugh 181
  Pocket Wine Guide 183
Jordan Valley 27
Journal of Wine Research 158
Joyce, James, *Ulysses* 218
'JS Wine Ratings' 185
Judaism 62
'Judgement of Paris' (1976) 44, 167
Jura 108–9, 215

K

Kakheti 62
Kant, Immanuel 186
Karis, Harry,
  *The Châteauneuf du Pape
  Wine Book* 55, 56
Keller, Franz 209
Kenya 125, 126, 130
Korea 124
Koshu grape 36–8
Kroenke, Stan 101
Krug 185

L

La Cadière d'Azur 33
La Fleur Pétrus, Château 150
La Madeleine de Saint-Mont
  244
La Mouline 164
La Tâche 114, 129, 178–9
labels 71, 167
Labranche Laffont 110
lactic acid 20, 233
Lafarge, Domaine 170
Lafite, Château 185
Lagier, Steve 196–8
Laidière, Domaine de la 32
Laithwaites 192
landslides, Savoie 38–9
Langhe 57–9
Langhorne Creek 40–2
language 66–8, 137, 225
Languedoc 48, 74, 81, 86,
  110, 142, 175, 206–8
Laos 123, 129
Larcis-Ducasse, Château 185
Larkin, Philip 136
Lasmènes, Marie-Ange
  206–8

Latour, Château 117, 129
Le Castellet 33
Le Pen, Marine 138
Le Pin 116–17
Lebanon 74, 211–13
lees 40, 49, 86, 251
Leibniz, Gottfried 224
Lenswood 174
Léoville-Las Cases, Ch 167
Les Vergelesses 101
Li Bai (Li-Tai-Po) 18, 246
Lichine, Alexis 89
lieu-dit 99, 251
Liguria 49–51
limestone 38–9
literature 34–5, 176–7,
  216–19, 232–3
Loeb, O W 116
Loire 161, 194, 238–40
London 124–5, 156
Lower Kartli 25, 123
Lu Yu, *Chá Jing* (*Tea Classic*)
  124
Lynch-Bages, Château 150

M

McGovern, Patrick 18–30
  Ancient Wine 18
  Uncorking the Past 18,
  27–30
McKercher, Sir William
  125–6
McLaren Vale 42
Mâcon 100, 101
Macron, Emmanuel 138
Madeira 118, 119, 129,
  190–1, 202, 247, 250
Madiran 74, 110–12, 220
Mahler, Gustav 246

maize 30
Malbec grape 146, 197
malic acid 25, 233
Malmsey 203, 205
malolactic fermentation 86,
  233, 251
Maltman, Alex 157–9
  Vineyards, Rocks, & Soils 158
Malvazija 52
Mamoiada 241–2
Marcoux, Domaine du 55
Marengo, Fiorino 58
Margaret River 146, 181
Margaux 42, 146, 170,
  183–4
Margaux, Château 150, 185
Marlborough 146
Marsannay 100
Marseilles 32
Mas del Serral 59–61
Massif de Chartreuse 38–9
Master Sommeliers 165
Masters of Wine 165, 205
Matopo hills 29
Matthews, David 115
Matthews, Jenifer 115
Maunder Minimum 43
mead 20, 22, 27, 29
medicine, alcohol as 28, 30
Mediterranean 32–3, 48–9
Médoc 42, 158, 167, 182,
  185, 220
Melville, Herman, *Moby-Dick*
  218
Mendoza 77, 146, 171
Menzel, Jiří 202
mercaptans 80, 251
Mercurey 100
Meredith, Carole 196–8

266 INDEX

Meredith, George 89
Merlot grape 116, 149, 181
Merweh grape 211
Mesoamerica 30
Mesopotamia 26
Mexico 138
Meyney, Château 219–21
'Midas mound', Gordion 26–7
Milky Way 20
millerandage 113, 148, 252
mineral flavours 84, 88, 152, 158–9
Ming Dynasty 124
Minho 83
Miró, Joan, *La masía* 60–1
Mirror (film) 106
Mistral 54–7
Mondavi, Robert 197, 239
Mondeuse grape 197
Mont Granier 38–9
Mont Ventoux 54
Montlouis 170
Montpellier 58, 207
Montpeyroux 206–7
Montrachet 100–1, 102, 117
Montrose, Château 117, 220
Montus, Château 111–12
Mormons 122
Moscato grape 57
Mosel 49, 158, 166
Motovun 52
Moueix, Christian 81
Mount Lebanon 211
Mount Lofty 41
Mount Veeder 196–8
mountain wine regions 39
Mourvèdre grape 32–3, 86
Mouton Rothschild, Château 185

Muscadet 37, 83
Muscardin grape 161
music 22, 43–4, 46, 178, 204
Musigny 151
Mussolini, Benito 58
must 93, 153, 154, 244, 252
Mutter, Anne-Sophie 43
Myanmar 123

N
Nagyvary, Joseph 43–4
Napa Valley 34–6, 74, 77, 79, 146, 152, 172–4, 196–8
Napa Valley Vintners Barrel Auction for the Wine Trade 156
Napanook 81
Napoleon I, Emperor 166
National Academy of Sciences of the United States of America 24–5
National Gallery, London 177–8
National Gallery of Art, Washington 61
natural wines 154–5, 180
Nature 43–4
Ne Oublie 119
Near East 23, 25
Nebbiolo grape 34, 57–9, 86
Neolithic 21–5
New Zealand 78, 86, 146, 173, 181, 193
Nile Valley 27
Nino, St 63
Noah 123
Noah grape 244
Noilly Prat 49
non-interventionism 153–5

Noon, Drew 42
Norfolk 142
novels 216–19
Nozet, Château du 238

O
oak 85–6, 87, 88
Obaideh grape 211
Oberpfalzer, Dr Stephan 171
Odysseus 18, 166
Okakura, Kakuzo, *The Book of Tea* 133
old wines 162–3, 190–1
Oloroso Dulce 202
oolong tea 128
Oregon 173, 181
organic acids 20, 25
Oxford English Dictionary 89
oxidation 83, 85–6, 87, 128, 252

P
paintings 174, 175, 177–8
Palaeolithic 29, 30
palate fitness 93–5
Pallisé, Bernard 206–7
Palmer, Château 185
Pape-Clément, Château 156
Paris 37, 239
Parker, Robert 183–4, 186
passito 51, 252
Pauillac 42
Penfolds 185
Penn Museum *see* University of Pennsylvania Museum of Archaeology and Anthropology
Penning-Rowsell, Edmund, *The Wines of Bordeaux* 183

267

Pepys, Samuel 124–5, 166
Petaluma 174
Petit Chablis 98–100
Petit Manseng grape 244
Petra 27
Petrus 184
pH values 98
philosophy 131–3, 224–6
Phoenicians 18
phylloxera 35, 58, 207, 214, 239, 252, 254
Phrygians 26–7
physical fitness, palate fitness 94
Picardin grape 161
Pichon-Baron, Château 150
Pichon-Lalande, Château 150
Picpoul de Pinet 47–9, 83, 162
pictograms 22
Piedmont 86
Pine Ridge 209
Pinenc grape 244
Pingus 86
Pinot Grigio/Gris grape 140, 145–6, 149
Pinot Meunier grape 148
Pinot Noir grape 91, 141, 145, 148, 181, 186, 214
Plaimont Producteurs 146, 207, 244–5
Planchon, Jules Emile 58
poetry 34–5, 176–7, 232–3
Pogba, Paul 151
Pomerol 116, 152
Pommard 170
Pompadour, Madame de 166
Pontac, Arnaud de 125
Pontac, François-Auguste 125

port 88, 118–19, 143–4, 163
Portugal 117–19, 148, 173, 175
Potensac, Château 167
pottery
  archaeology 26
  vessel residues 21–7
Potts, Frank 41
Pouilly 238–40
Pouilly-Fuissé 100
Pouilly-Fumé 146, 167, 239, 240
Pouilly-sur-Loire 239
prehistoric man 20–1, 29
prices of wine 149–51, 165, 178–9
primary fruit 252
primates 21, 29
Priorat 158
Pritchard Hill 196
PROP (propylthiouracil) 73
Provence 32, 84, 140, 172
pu-erh tea 128, 129
Puisseguin-St Emilion 207
pump-over 244, 253
punch-down 244, 253
Pyrenees 244

Q
Quandt, Richard 165
Quarts de Chaume 161
quiet wines 48

R
racking, definition 253
Ramusio, Giovanni Battista, *Navigationi et Viaggi* 124
Raventós, Pepe 61

Rayas, Château 102–4
red wines
  bitterness 74
  tannins 75–7
  vinosity 90
  see also individual wines and grapes
reduction, definition 253
Reims cathedral 60
religions 28, 62–4, 166, 224
Remelluri 105–7
retsina 27, 140
revisionism 47–9
Revue du Vin de France 184
Rhine Valley 49
Rhône Valley 54–5, 76, 153, 172, 194, 197, 230
Ribera del Duero 181
rice beer 22
rice wine 23, 28–9
Richebourg 114
Riesling grape 40, 109, 199
  Alsace 184
  Australia 79, 83
  Mosel 158
  vinosity 88, 89
  Wachau 210
Riga 103
Rioja 76, 85, 105–7, 181
Rodríguez, Jaíme 105
Rodríguez, Telmo 105
Romanèche 140
Romanée-Conti, Domaine de la (DRC) 47, 110, 112–14, 115, 166
Romanée-St-Vivant 114
Romania 186
Romans 30
Roquefort, Château de 170

268   INDEX

rosé wines 33, 84

roses 147–8

Roussanne grape 39, 40

Rousseau 115, 146

Roussillon 153

Ruel, Jon 173

Russia 138, 191

Rutherford 146

Ruwer 83

S

Saar 83

Saccharomyces cerevisiae 78–9

saignée 157, 253

Saint Amour 100

Saint Chinian 167

Saint Chinian-Roquebrun 158

Saint-Estèphe 219–21

Saint Julien 42

Saint-Mont 146, 243–5

Saintsbury, George, *Notes on a Cellar Book* 183

Salon 47

Samegrelo 25

San Andreas Fault System 172

San Francisco Bay 196

San Gimigniano 57

Sancerre 83, 146, 167, 215, 238, 239

Sandeman 143

Sangiovese grape 86

Santa Elisabetta vineyard 52–4

Santenay 100

Santiago de Compostela 243, 245

Santo Domingo de Silos 60

Santorini Assyrtico 158

Sardinia 240–2

Saumur 167

Sauternes 141, 202

Sauvignon Blanc grape 67, 79, 83, 88, 146, 149, 185, 239

Sauvignon de Touraine 167

Sauzet 150

Savagnin grape 87, 108–9, 145–6

Savennières 167

Savoie 38–40, 197

Schlossberg 200

Schuster, Michael 89–90, 203–6

  Essential Winetasting 205

Schuster, Monika 203–6

Sciacchetrà grape 51

science 232–3

scoring systems 183–7, 235

Scorpion I, King of Egypt 27

screwcaps 167

Scylla 18

Sedilescu, Francesco 242

Sedilescu, Giuseppe 240

Seguier, Didier 99

Sémillon grape 211–12

Serbia 193

serving temperatures 142

Seyval Blanc grape 46–7

Shafer Sunspot Vineyard 156

Shakespeare, William 18, 52, 166–7, 177–8

Shang dynasty 23

Shennong, Emperor 123

sherry 66

Shi Jing (Book of Odes) 123–4

Shine Muscat grape 37

Shiraz grape 40–2, 140, 146

  see also Syrah grape

Shulaveris Gora 25, 123

Siebenhandl, Margarete 209–10

Sisseck, Peter 86

Slovenia 52, 193

Smith, Dr Paul 76

soil 38, 157–9

Song Dynasty 124

South Africa 138, 175, 185, 193

South Australia 40–2, 86

Southern Rhône 54–5, 76, 153, 172

Spain 194

  see also individual regions and wines

Spätlese 202

Spitzer Valley 209–10

Sporen 200

Spring Mountain Vineyards 157

spruce tonewood 43–4

Spurrier, Steven 44

Sri Lanka 125, 126, 130

Stag's Leap Wine Cellars 167

Stags Leap 196

stems 253

Stern, Isaac 44

Stevenson, Robert Louis 34, 232

  The Silverado Squatters 34–6

Stone, Reynolds 46

Stradivarius 43–4

Straka, Thomas 171

succinic acid 20, 25

269

Suckling, James 185
sugars, fermentable 28–9
Sullivan, Thomas 125
Sunday Times Wine Club 158
supertasters 73
Sussex 45–7
Sweden 115
Switzerland 34, 164
Symington, Andrew James 119
Symington, Paul and Jane 118–19
Syrah grape 33, 126, 146, 161, 181, 197
    see also Shiraz grape

T
Taiwan 29
Tannat grape 146, 244
tannins 74, 75–7, 87, 131, 163
Taoism 132
Tapanappa 79
Tarkovsky, Andrei 106, 107
tartaric acid 20, 22, 25
tastebuds, palate fitness 95
tasting wine
    alcohol levels 71–2
    bitterness 73–4
    blind tastings 44, 69–70, 82, 165
    food versus wine 91–3
    freshness and acidity 83–4
    hard wines 87–8
    horizontal tastings 151, 180–2
    language of 66–8
    palate fitness 93–5
    sighted tastings 69–70

tannins 74, 75–7
vertical tastings 151, 180–2
vinosity 89–91
wine as an acquired taste 167–8
'wine flaws' 80
and yeast 77–9
Tate Modern, London 61
Tbilisi 62–3
TCA 80, 85, 253
tea 122–33
tea ceremony 132–3
Teisserenc, Michel 208
tej (mead) 29
temperature, serving 142
Tempranillo grape 106–7
Tendero, Alain 206–7
Teran grape 52–4
terraces 209–10
Terrasses du Larzac 207
Terrebrune, Domaine de 33
Terret grape 48
terroir 35, 42–4, 153, 167, 254
Tesco 140
Thackeray, William Makepeace 89
Thar, Richard and Theresia 204
Thienpont, Jacques 116
Tigris-Euphrates Valley 26
Tilbrook, James 174, 175
Tissot, Bénédicte 107
Tissot, Stéphane 107–9
Tokaji 138
Tokaji Aszú 202–3
Tokyo 36, 37
Tollot-Beaut 115
tongue scrapers 95

tonic water 74
Toulon 32
Touraine 170
Tourdot-Maréchal, Raphaëlle 78
Tracy, Château de 238–40
Tracy-sur-Loire 238
transactional flaw of wine 176–80
Transcaucasia 123
trees
    vines trained in 25
    wood for violins 43–4
Trefethen 172–4
Trefethen, Janet 172–4
Tribidrag grape 197
Trotanoy, Château 185
Tuéni, Madia 213
Tumbarumba 181
Tunstall, Stuart and Pacuła, Zo 81–2
Turkey 122, 138
Tuscany 86, 142–3, 146
Txakoli 37

U
Ukraine 138, 191
ungrafted vines 254
United States of America 138 (*See also individual regions and wines*
Universe, alcohol clouds 20
University of East Anglia 216
University of Pennsylvania Museum of Archaeology and Anthropology (Penn Museum) 18, 23, 26
Usseglio, Jean-Pierre 55, 56

V

Vaccarèse grape 161
Vakhtang VI, King of Georgia 63
Valais 49, 164
Valtellina 34
varietal wines 254
VDQS (Vin Délimité de Qualité Supérieure) 160, 254
Veneto 74
Vengerov, Maxim 43
Verdicchio 83
Vermeer, Johannes 177–8
Vermentino grape 51
vermouth 48–9
vertical tastings 151, 180–2
Veyder-Malberg, Peter 209–10
Viala, Pierre 58
Victoria 86
Viella, Château 110
Vietnam 129
Villa Maria 209
Villaine, Aubert de 112, 214
Villaine, Domaine de 214–15
Villeneuve, Raimond de 170, 172
vin jaune 107–8, 145
vines
    archaeology 23, 24–5
    breeding 147–9
    trained in trees 25
vineyards 196
    bushfires 174–5
    geology 157–9
    hail storms 170–2
    soil 38, 157–9

terroir 35, 42–4, 153, 167, 254
    see also individual vineyards
Vinho Verde 37
vinosity 89–91
vins de voile 108
vintage wines 162–3, 190–1
Viognier grape 164
violins 43–4
Vitis vinifera 24, 28, 74, 123, 125
Voiteur 108
Volnay 170
Vosne 100
Vosne Suchots 186
Vouvray 170

W

Wachau 209–10
Wałěsa, Lech 71
Ward, Frank 89–90, 115–17
Ward, Lisbet 115
Washington 173
water 122
weather
    hail 170–2
    see also climate
Weaver, Geoff 174, 175
Weinviertel 209
white tea 127
white wines
    hardness 88
    vinosity 90
    see also individual wines and grapes
'wild' yeasts 78
Wilde, Oscar 198
wind, Mistral 54–7
Wine Advocate 183–4, 186

Wine Grapes 211–12
wine growers 231–2
wine labels 71, 167
wine merchants 192–5
wine-worldliness 235–6
winemaking 217–19, 230–2
Winewise 205
Wittgenstein, Ludwig 67
wood
    oak barrels 85–6
    violins 43–4
The World of Fine Wine 158
World War I 58, 190–1
Wu, Sylvia 89
Wu Lu 132

Y

Yamanashi Prefecture 36–7
yeasts 77–9, 80, 92–3
yellow tea 127–8
Yinxu 23
young wines 162–4
Yunnan Province 123, 125, 126, 128–9

Z

Zagros Mountains 23–4, 25–6
Zimbabwe 29
Zind-Humbrecht 146
Zinfandel grape 197
Zoroastrianism 62
Zukerman, Pinchas 44

Other books from Académie du Vin Library we think you'll enjoy:

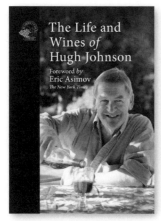

THE LIFE AND WINES OF HUGH JOHNSON
The world's best-loved wine author weaves the story of his own epic wine journey.

OZ CLARKE ON WINE
Your Global Wine Companion
A fast-paced tour of the world's most delicious wine styles with Oz.

ON BORDEAUX
Tales of the Unexpected from the World's Greatest Wine Region
Susan Keevil
Why these wines are the most talked-about.

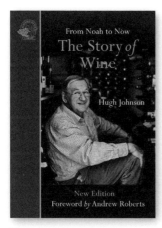
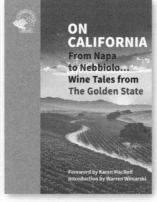
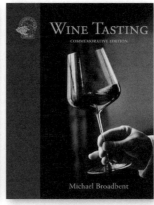

THE STORY OF WINE
From Noah to Now
Hugh Johnson
The new edition of Hugh Johnson's captivating journey through wine history.

ON CALIFORNIA
From Napa to Nebbiolo…
Wine Tales from the Golden State
Susan Keevil
California's great wine adventure as told by our A-list team of experts and enthusiasts.

WINE TASTING
Commemorative Edition
Michael Broadbent
The definitive guide that began it all.

www.academieduvinlibrary.com